FLASHPOINT

FLASHPOINT

How a Little-Known Sporting Event Fueled America's Anti-Apartheid Movement

Derek Charles Catsam

ROWMAN & LITTLEFIELD
Lanham • Boulder • New York • London

Published by Rowman & Littlefield
An imprint of The Rowman & Littlefield Publishing Group, Inc.
4501 Forbes Boulevard, Suite 200, Lanham, Maryland 20706
www.rowman.com

6 Tinworth Street, London SE11 5AL

British Library Cataloguing in Publication Information Available

Library of Congress Cataloging-in-Publication Data Available

Names: Catsam, Derek, author.
Title: Flashpoint : how a little-known sporting event fueled America's anti-apartheid movement / Derek Charles Catsam.
Description: Lanham : Rowman & Littlefield, [2021] | Includes index. | Summary: "This book provides a unique perspective on the anti-apartheid movement in the United States through its examination of a little-remembered rugby tour across the country by South Africa's national team. The tour became a flashpoint for the nation's burgeoning protests against apartheid and a test of national values and American foreign policy"—Provided by publisher.
Identifiers: LCCN 2021009851 (print) | LCCN 2021009852 (ebook) | ISBN 9781538144695 (board) | ISBN 9781538144701 (ebook)
Subjects: LCSH: Springboks (Rugby team) | Rugby football—South Africa—History. | Discrimination in sports—South Africa—History. | Anti-apartheid movements—United States—History. | Sports—Political aspects—United States. | Sports—Political aspects—South Africa. | United States—Relations—South Africa. | South Africa—Relations—United States.
Classification: LCC GV945.6.S6 C37 2021 (print) | LCC GV945.6.S6 (ebook) | DDC 796.3330968—dc23
LC record available at https://lccn.loc.gov/2021009851
LC ebook record available at https://lccn.loc.gov/2021009852

To George:
See? It only SEEMS like I just sit on the couch.
I love you more than you can possibly understand
and everything I do is for your future.

CONTENTS

Acknowledgments   ix

Preface: Rise Up, Zwide!   xv

Introduction   xix

1 The Accidental Tourists: Planning for the United States Tour   1

2 Starting to Play: The Irish in South Africa   17

3 Apart Hate: Planning to Resist the Springboks   39

4 The 1981 Springbok Tour to New Zealand: A Country Divided   51

5 Cloaks, Daggers, and Rugby: The Springboks in the Midwest   79

6 Albany I: Facing Off in the Courts and Against the Colonials   107

7 Albany II: The Test Match   129

Conclusion: The Long Tail of Post-1981 South African Rugby   147

Notes   169

Works Cited/Bibliography   189

Index   205

About the Author   215

ACKNOWLEDGMENTS

This project was a labor of love. It turns out, labors of love require more than love. They require the labor of lots and lots of people.

This book would not have happened had it not been for the persistence (and ruthlessly firm editorial hand) of my agent, Amaryah Orenstein. This has been a partnership with her because she believed in it when I started to think I did not. At every turn, from proposal through proofs, she made it better. Similarly Christen Karniski, my editor at Rowman & Littlefield, had a clearer vision than I did at times about what this book could (and should) look like. On top of that, the Rowman & Littlefield folks in marketing and publicity and everything else have been amazing.

The University of Texas of the Permian Basin (UTPB) has been my academic home for the last seventeen years. My colleagues (past and present) have been fantastic. I owe Jeffrey Washburn, Jenny Paxton, Diana Hinton, Jay Tillapaugh, Steve Andes, and Roland Spickermann my gratitude. Our 2017 loss of Chad Vanderford at a tragically young age still hurts. To my itinerant friend, and former UTPB colleague, Jaime Aguila, who made me think more broadly about race (and also always knows the best new places to eat), a thank you (and Holly, Ben, and Ellie) for both academic and gustatory reasons. UTPB provost, Dan Heimmermann; two deans of the College of Arts & Sciences, Mike Zavada and Scott McKay; and UTPB's presidents, David Watts and Sandra Woodley, have supported this project. I cannot possibly thank the Dunagan family enough for their support of my endowed professorship. In addition to supporting my research, the endowment allows me to help promote the humanities to the Permian Basin, and more important, to expand opportunities for our students.

My most enduring professional academic relationship is with Rhodes University; I arrived there in 1997 as a postgraduate student just learning about South African history. Had I not done that, this book would not have happened. Rhodes hosted me as the Hugh LeMay Fellow in the Humanities in 2016, and has allowed me to be a senior research associate and occasional visiting professor since. Paul Maylam, Gary Baines, and Alan Kirkaldy have been wonderful department heads who have gone overboard in making me feel like a full-fledged member of the Rhodes history department over the years. Jaco Bezuidenhout and Craig Paterson have been good friends. Enocent Msindo, Helena Pohlandt-McCormick, Janeke Thumbran, Nicole Ulrich, and Julia Wells have been fantastic colleagues.

Indeed, my experience with South African rugby is not an abstraction. In 1997, I was a postgraduate fellow at Rhodes thanks to the Rotary Foundation. After enough nights at the pub, I was convinced to try out for the rugby team. Playing an entirely different sport in another country (with a former Springbok, the late Frans Erasmus, as the Rhodes head coach) changed my life. I also want to thank Qondakele Sompondo, who was coach of the rugby club at Rhodes when I was there for the year in 2016, and who continues to meet with and communicate with me about some of the subtleties of race and South African rugby, especially in the Eastern Cape.

A book like this one does not happen without considerable support from various institutions that provided me with funding, a short-term academic home, resources, encouragement, and intellectual succor. These include the John Hope Franklin Research Center of African and African American History and Culture Travel Grant at Duke University in 2010–2011. The Hoover Institution Library & Archives at Stanford University, which provided me with a US Scholar Research Support Grant/Fellowship in 2015. University College Dublin's Clinton Institute for American Studies provided me with a short-term visiting fellowship in July 2017. Similarly. innumerable archivists at a wide range of archives from the United States to the United Kingdom, Ireland to South Africa, and Australia and New Zealand helped me in ways impossible to enumerate. These archives are listed first in my bibliography for a reason, and every single one of them made this book (and a number of future projects) far richer.

Robert "Buck" Buchanan of the Wisconsin Rugby Community provided a wide range of support, including opening the doors of his expansive rugby library, giving me access to several members of his club, sharing photos (some of which appear in this book), and answering every possible question I could have about Midwestern rugby in the early 1980s.

Speaking of photos, I made good-faith efforts to contact and obtain permission for images used in this book. Should the rights owner come forth for any images without appropriate permissions, I shall obtain such permission and include appropriate acknowledgment in future printings of this book.

Lacy Molina was my research assistant during the bulk of my work on this project. We went from you creating files of my research under the just incredibly useful heading of "Race Relations" to you becoming someone who could consistently understand all of this transnational stuff. You read the earliest chapters of this book and made it clear that it should be more readable. You wouldn't have played Sun City. Abbey Whigham helped me to pull together my bibliography from a cacophony of notes.

Several people saw this project in its early stages. Peter Alegi, one of the key figures in African sports history in the United States, saw the earliest version of this when it was a very long paper at a NEWSA meeting. His feedback over the years on so much of my work has been vital, and he's a good friend to boot. Chris Bolsmann has been a good friend and advocate of this work. He made a couple of chapters significantly stronger and saved me from at least one dumb mistake. John Nauright has been a friend, ally, and collaborator. Gerard Akindes and the Sports Africa community have provided a consistent forum for my work. Among the many fellow scholars, I wish I could say more about individually are Tarminder Kaur, Rob Skinner, Malcolm Maclean, Tyler Fleming, Philani Nongogo, Todd Cleveland, Sandra Swart, Michelle Sikes, Mark Dyreson, Zack Bigalke, David Pottie, John Aerni-Flessner, Mark Fredericks, and Dean Allen. Others who provided various forms of academic support include Ken Wilburn, Aran MacKinnon, Simon Lewis, Jack Parson, Jill Kelly, Meghan Healy-Clancy, Harry Edwards, Richard Lapchick, and Andre Odendaal. Gerald Gems and Steve Riess graciously invited me to give a Newberry Library Seminar on the earliest stages of this project. I also gave talks at the Palmerston North Public Library, at a departmental seminar series at the University of Auckland, and at the Wits History Worksop at the University of the Witwatersrand. Ray Haberski invited me to talk about these issues at Marian University and Ray, Andrew Hartman, and Daniel Rinn had me on their podcast about US intellectual history, *Trotsky & The Wild Orchids*, to discuss rugby politics. Lon Hamby continues to be an inspiration and a model for me. Charlie Alexander set the bar for me for what it meant to be a historian who writes about sports. Charles Dew is my gold standard for what it means to be a teacher-scholar. Sean Jacobs of *Africa is a Country* has provided me with a consistent outlet for my rugby and other South Africa–related writing over the years, as have the *Mail & Guardian*, *Eastern Province Herald*, *Weekend Post*, *Sunday Independent*, and *Sunday Times*. Additionally, my work on the journal *Safundi* has consistently provided me with a solid transnational grounding. I thank my colleagues Andrew Offenberger, Andrew van der Vlies, Shane Graham, Rita Barnard, Karin Shapiro, Annel Pieterse, Monica Popescu, Tiffany Willoughby-Herard, and Alex Lichtenstein.

I owe an enormous debt of gratitude to Albert Grundlingh, one of the vital historians of South African sport who provided a sounding board over the years. Albert gave me access to an as-of-yet unprocessed South African Rugby Board collection that really turned this from an abstraction into a book project. He also hosted me for a wonderful seminar that I did with his graduate student Sebastien Potgieter at Stellenbosch University. Before the seminar started, into the room walked 1981 Springboks Div Visser and former Bok captain Theuns Stofberg. Given the nature of my project, they could have given me the cold shoulder or worse. Instead, they could not have been more gracious and appreciative, and Visser, in particular, became a warm correspondent whose insights enhanced this book significantly.

Indeed, rugby people in South Africa have been almost universally supportive. Andy Colquhuon of the South African Rugby Union has given me countless leads, provided me with contacts for individuals, is my go-to for media-related matters, press credentials, and just about anything else that I have needed not just for this book, but really for my work writing about rugby for the last decade. I spent several hours with former Springbok head coach Peter de Villiers at his home in the Western Cape talking about rugby and he was a gracious host who provided great insight into the racial politics of South African rugby past and present. Wessell Oosthuizen is one of the finest photographers in the history of sports journalism. He graciously allowed me to use his work, including on the cover of the book. Longtime South African sports journalist Dan Retief, who accompanied the Springboks throughout the 1981 tours, answered some questions that I had lingering and led me to some fruitful sources.

Heindrich Wyngaard is a triple-threat print, radio, and television journalist. After we covered a Springbok match side-by-side at Ellis Park, he asked me to be on his SABC radio program and to contribute a preface to his fine book on Errol Tobias, *Bursting Through the Half-Gap* he read a version of this manuscript and saved me from a series of embarrassing errors. Hendrik Snyders, too, has been an source of insight and resources. David McLennan, the owner and proprietor of Select Books, has been a great supporter and friend who has bent over backwards to provide me with material on Springbok rugby. Phil Matheson provided me with a wealth of New Zealand rugby materials.

Shannon Phibbs saw much of the sausage being made from a distance. She served as a charming ad hoc research assistant and an audience and sounding board outside of academia.

My dear friend and wonderful historian, Poppy Fry, reminded me that the world existed before 1900. Don and Melissa Graves, Rob "Thunderstick" Simler, Minerva Gonzales, Diana Ruiz, Chris Frantz, Josh Pepin, Larry Claassen, Doug Sanyahumbi, Tony Palmer, Pete Mendoza, Mark and Lucy Nyandoro, and Roger Johnson all warrant more than this shout out. No, I'm not sharing royalties with you.

Bill Harlow, Zero Eldridge, Mike Frawley, and John Wilks continue to be people with whom I am willing to make bad decisions. You guys (almost) make all the bullshit worthwhile. Ben Farmer did more than any single person to delay the progress of this book and to contribute to my dissolution. Thanks! Oh, he also did the index for the book.

As always, the courteous thing for me to write is that all faults that exist in this book are my own. Unfortunately, that is not true. All of the wisdom, insight, and cleverness is obviously mine. Every flaw, factual error, and interpretive problem is the fault of Tom Bruscino and Steve Tootle. I suffer for their flaws.

In the process of finishing this book, my mother-in-law, Yolanda Martinez, passed away. I grew up with all of the cultural clichés about mothers-in-law. I never saw any of that from her, and in fact, Ana and her sisters, Lupe and Ariana, who have also always supported me, probably always resented the fact that their mom regularly took my side in any family debates. She was wise and wonderful and always right. To Mom, Dad, and Marcus, as always.

I owe everything to Ana, a wonderful historian and fantastic teacher who is also my boss, my light, my love.

Finally, this book is devoted to George.

I am the most selfish person I know. Yet for you, I became selfless.

I love you more than you know. It is to you that I devote this book. It is to you that I devote everything that I do.

PREFACE
Rise Up, Zwide!

"Rugby is the story of the world we live in and how it was made."
—Historian Tony Collins [1]

On June 9, 2018, in their first match of a three match Test series against England in the legendary Ellis Park stadium in Johannesburg, Siyamthamba "Siya" Kolisi made his debut as captain of South Africa's national rugby team, the Springboks. This was, by any measure, a big deal. Before and during the apartheid era in South Africa, rugby was a sport that embodied the ideals of white, especially Afrikaner—South Africans—ideals that in a society forged by white supremacy did not include "non-whites." And nothing captured these ideals more than the Springboks. The men in green and gold were larger-than-life heroes, and, of course, they were all white. And for the majority of the history of the Springboks, their all-white nature was a central pillar of their identity.

Siya Kolisi's debut as Springbok captain was a historic moment, one that broadcaster Kaunda Ntunja, himself a fine rugby player and the first black captain of the South African (SA) Schools team, captured perfectly. "On the sixteenth of June in the year 1991 was born a child of the Kolisi in Zwide, Port Elizabeth,"[2] Ntunja boomed in Xhosa, one of South Africa's eleven official languages. Xhosa is also Kolisi's native tongue, one spoken by so many who fought so hard against apartheid, including Nelson Mandela. It is also the African language most prevalent in the Eastern Cape of South Africa, one of the country's black rugby heartlands. Thus, Njunja's Xhosa commentary was especially apt. "This child, he was not raised by his father or his mother. This child was raised by his grandmother. He was given the name Siyamthanda—'We Love Him.'"

As Kolisi made his way from the changing room up the tunnel leading to the pitch, he held hands with a young white boy who had the honor of both accompanying the Springbok captain and carrying the game ball. Fireworks exploded and fire shot into the air, the crowd screamed and whistled and rejoiced. The rest of the Springboks, each also accompanied by a child, followed in a line behind the newly anointed captain and the lucky child.

"Even though he grew up in struggle and poverty, they loved him very much," Ntunja continued. "In his upbringing he met a man named Father Eric Songwiqi. That man, Father Songwiqi, told him, 'Boy, you'll play rugby one day and you'll become a Springbok.' And his mentor led him to play rugby, and as the English say, 'The rest is history.'"

At this point, Kolisi received a bear hug from Tendai "The Beast" Mtawarira, the legendary Zimbabwe-born Springbok prop, who has played the most games at forward in Springbok history, and who inspires cries of "Beeeaaaassst" every time he carries the ball or makes a crushing tackle.

"Now has come the day which we have been waiting for. Siya is the first black captain in the Springbok team to come through the trials in the new South Africa."

Recognizing the importance of this day for millions of black South Africans, but especially those in the townships near Port Elizabeth, Ntunja, who was thirty-eight at the time of his tragic death from COVID-19 in 2020, celebrated them by name as Kolisi received hugs and handshakes from his teammates, black and white, in what they all well knew was a profound historical moment:

Rise up, Zwide!
Rise up, Motherwell!
Rise up, Walmer!
Rise up, Kwazakhele, Kwamagxaki, and New Brighton!
Because this boy of yours who represents the black nation, represents all of us!
Siya is our grandson, our son, our nephew and our younger brother!

He is father of Nicholas, husband of Rachel.
He is Gwayi, Gqwashu, Gxiya—our leader!
A cement truck with no reverse gear!
Rooster! Rooster! Gnashing—Let them battle each other!

That day the Springboks won 42–39 in a thriller but the story was the man whose name means "We love him." It would once have been an unimaginable story.

A note on racial terminology: Racial terminology in contemporary South Africa is tricky. This book will generally use the word "black" in the way that Steve Biko used it—to refer to all South Africans who would have fallen under the unfortunate blanket apartheid category of "nonwhite." But at times I will also use common designations—especially "coloured," a term applied to mixed-race South Africans who also were vitally important to the development of South African rugby, including the eventual integration of the Springboks. At other times, as appropriate, I will use the historical language appropriate for the time, especially when quoting or in context.

INTRODUCTION

1981

In September of 1981, late summer and early autumn in the United States, rugby, which sat well on the fringe of the American sporting consciousness, made headlines. South Africa's Springboks, the national rugby team that so embodied their home country's white supremacist apartheid policies, traveled to the United States to play a series of matches against what would inevitably be hopelessly outgunned American sides. A heated debate, familiar to Americans who had seen their country and a host of its allies boycott the 1980 Summer Olympics in Moscow over the Soviet Union's invasion of Afghanistan, broke out over the intertwining of sport and politics. But because of the specific contentions that the presence of the Springboks raised, the events of 1981 also served to prime the pump of an American anti-Apartheid movement that lagged behind many other parts of the world. In no small part, that lag was the result of sporting protests, which had been visible in many countries in the face of tours from South African soccer, cricket, and rugby teams or of tours of their teams to South Africa. It is perhaps not a coincidence that Americans in the decades leading up to 1981 had virtually no cricket culture, a negligible rugby culture, and an execrable soccer culture (especially at the national team level).

US POLICIES TOWARD APARTHEID SOUTH AFRICA AND THE AMERICAN ANTI-APARTHEID MOVEMENT

American policies toward apartheid in the period after 1948 ranged from tacit support to stated loathing of apartheid with reluctant support. The United States enabled apartheid. It sometimes actively supported apartheid. Sometimes it would cluck its tongue but maintain connections with Pretoria out of perceived self-interest. The American connection to apartheid South Africa is a good example of the sometimes deleterious effect that the Cold War had on American relations with much of the world, and especially with sub-Saharan Africa where the United States, whether led by Democrats or Republicans, liberals or conservatives, was a consistent source of support for leadership, however authoritarian, however corrupt, however draconian, however ruthless, as long as that leadership took the side of the United States and turned its back on the Soviet Union in the struggle for Cold War mastery.

In South Africa, this meant support for the National Party government and its apartheid policies, because however authoritarian, corrupt, draconian, or ruthless the apartheid government was—and it was all of those things and more from 1948 to 1994, and certainly was all of those things in 1981—the National Party and the apartheid government were allies in the Cold War. They were ardently anti-communist. They preached free markets though the market was only free in South Africa for a tiny slice of the population. They preached rule of law because they had made every aspect of the loathsome system of apartheid completely legal. Furthermore, they managed to depict the African National Congress (ANC) and other liberation groups as in thrall to communism (and, of course, some within the liberation struggle were, and indeed some were actual communists), in part because, unlike the United States, communist countries, including the Soviet Union and Cuba, fully supported the liberation struggle and denounced apartheid in word and opposed it in deed. In an existential struggle, the communists embraced the existence of the ANC and of black South Africans.

Thus, the burgeoning American anti-apartheid movement found that much of its ire was aimed at its own accommodationist government, which, by the Reagan administration's ascension, embraced "constructive engagement" with South Africa, a policy articulated (and describing already existing realities to some degree) by Chester Crocker, a thirty-nine-year old wunderkind academic who, as one of the few conservative Africanists in his era, was appointed assistant secretary of state for Africa when Ronald Reagan took office. In that capacity, Crocker could erect the full edifice of constructive engagement, especially because Africa was, then as now, an afterthought in American foreign policy circles.

The American anti-apartheid movement thus as often found itself protesting its country's policies as South Africa's, per se. As the 1970s progressed, there was an increasing (and increasingly effective) anti-apartheid movement on American college and university campuses calling for these institutions to divest their investment portfolios of all connections with South African corporations. Larger protest movements called on corporations to eliminate their engagement with South Africa and South African companies and for local governments to similarly withdraw. The American anti-apartheid movement called for the cultural boycott of South Africa and condemned those musicians and other artists who engaged Sun City or otherwise broke that boycott.[1] And they called for a sporting boycott. This most obviously would manifest itself in the demands to exclude South Africa from the Olympic movement and from individual Olympic sports. But, until 1981, a comparable American was largely invisible in South Africa's major team sports because in the United States cricket was a bug; rugby a type of shirt; and soccer, more often than not, a punch line, though that was beginning to change by the 1970s.

Not surprisingly, some of the most vocal anti-apartheid activists were African American, many coming from the civil rights movement, from Black Power and organizations such as the Black Panthers, and with spokespeople and supporters in the Congressional Black Caucus. For many, these demands to divest and disengage, for boycotts and pressure, were not abstract because white supremacy was not abstract, and their demands drew sympathetic white allies, many of whom had themselves been veterans of civil rights and peace struggles. They found sympathetic ears and voices in college students who in many cases were clamoring for the protest environments and political activism they had heard about from the still-recent 1960s.

ISOLATING SOUTH AFRICAN SPORT

South African prime minister and apartheid architect Hendrick Verwoerd once gave an explanation as to why the South African government could not allow New Zealand to include a Maori player onto a touring team. "You see, if we allow this black man into the country, we will have to let him play on sports fields meant for whites only. We will have to let him stay in white hotels, go with his teammates to white bars and restaurants." But it would not end there. "And how will we be able to say to our black people that you can't play in our national sports teams? It will be the end of apartheid, and it will be the end of the white man in South Africa."[2]

Thus, apartheid's architects did not overlook sport. The National Party restricted the participation of blacks with whites on the same teams, but they also prohibited them from playing against one another. In sport, as with most aspects of South African life, the government preached "separate development." And as always there was more separation than development. In the first decade or so of apartheid, these policies went largely unnoticed outside of South Africa's borders. It was not until the 1960s that global anti-apartheid activists recognized the leverage they had in pressing for removing sport-mad South Africa from global competition.

The pressure these activists applied, coupled with the predictable South African government intransigent resistance to it, led to the banning of South Africa's sporting teams from most international competitions. By 1970, South Africa had been excluded from the Olympic Games, and almost every individual Olympic sport excluded them as well. They were isolated from world test cricket. In 1964, FIFA suspended the white Football Association of South Africa (FASA) and expelled it in 1976.

Anti-apartheid activists, politicians, and others recognized sport as a potential pressure point to apply against sports-mad South Africa. Increasingly, South African teams and athletes found themselves isolated. Rugby, however, refused to go along, and the International Rugby Board never did exclude South Africa, leading to increasingly tense protests against visiting South African rugby teams in England, Wales, Scotland, and Ireland in 1969–1970, Australia in 1971, and most intensely in 1981 in New Zealand in arguably the most controversial, politicized sporting event or series of sporting events in history. It is here that the context of the 1981 Springbok tours becomes clear, for these events begin the culmination of trends that had been accelerating for decades and that would reach their fullest fruition in the 1980s.

The Basil D'Oliviera affair captured South Africa's abnormal approach to sport in its abnormal society. D'Oliviera was a native of South Africa classified as "coloured" under apartheid, and he was a talented all-rounder who, when it became clear that he would never play first-class cricket in South Africa, and that he would never represent the national team, moved to England, where he slowly climbed the ranks and eventually earned selection to the England national cricket team. By 1966, he earned selection to the England team.

South Africa's status in world cricket was not as clear as in other sports. By 1964, the country was excluded from FIFA, the international governing body for world football, as well as from the Olympic movement. But D'Oliviera's exclusion from the 1968–1969 England tour of South Africa, over the initial objections (and then with the acquiescence) of the Merylbone Cricket Club, which oversaw the game in England and served as a de facto international governing body, proved a decisive moment in stigmatizing South African sport, and not just cricket, globally. D'Oliviera was initially excluded from the South Africa tour, based on allegations of his form faltering, but that probably did not hold much muster. But an injury to another player ironically made room for D'Oliviera, forcing the hand of Prime Minister John Vorster's South African government, which effectively called for the banning of an England team with D'Oliviera on it. The MCC then voted to cancel the tour after a rigorous debate and close vote. All of this created a massive controversy in a pastime that more than any represented the genteel ideals of British and colonial sport.

The stage was thus set for the events of 1969–1970 that culminated in the "Stop the Seventy Tour Campaign." South Africa's national cricket team was due to tour the United Kingdom in 1970, and the antitour campaign was to be a massive protest movement against apartheid and as importantly against apartheid collaborators. The campaign was headed by, among others, Peter Hain, who would rise to prominence as an anti-apartheid activist, with the sports boycott central to his approach. Although the campaign was aimed at the cricket tour, they used the Springbok rugby tour that began at the beginning of November

1969 and ended on the last day of January 1970 as their backdrop, thus in effect protesting both the real rugby tour and the proposed cricket tour. During those three months the Springboks toured the United Kingdom on a rugby tour that included twenty-five matches, including one test each against the home nations, Scotland, England, Ireland, and Wales. The South Africans lost to Scotland and England in close matches and drew with Ireland and Wales. It was the least successful tour in terms of rugby performance in Springbok history up to that point. Off the pitch things were even worse for them. Everywhere they went they met protesters, sometimes in the thousands, inside and outside the stadiums, and things got heated, occasionally violent, and required more than 20,000 police in total to control the protests.

The Stop the Seventy Tour campaign, by-and-large, used a rugby tour they were unable to prevent to successfully get a cricket tour canceled. They did so by adhering to nonviolent mass protests, drawing attention to apartheid sport in a way that had not happened before. In the end, opponents of the tour estimated that they had 100,000 participants in various aspects of the protests, and they claimed two victories—the South African cricket team would not travel to the United Kingdom in May 1970. No more South African national team cricket or rugby tours would land on those shores until after the fall of apartheid, though teams from the Home Nations of England, Scotland, Wales, and Ireland would visit South Africa on occasion, as would the British and Irish Lions, a select team drawn from the national sides of the four Home Nations, in 1974 and 1980.

Australia saw similar protests in June and July 1971 when the Springboks visited. This was influenced by the anti-apartheid sport activist, Dennis Brutus, a South African who was banned and eventually, exiled. He would go on to found the South African Non-Racial Olympic Committee (SAN-ROC) in 1962. These protests were also influenced by British anti-tour campaigners such as Hain, the Australian protests, and like those in the United Kingdom that divided communities and families, young and old. It resulted in vibrant protests and regular clashes between protesters and rugby supporters, protesters and police. The end result was similar: after 1971, apartheid teams would no longer be welcome in Australia. Indeed, part of the reason why the American tour took place in 1981 was that the Australians even denied landing rights or their airspace for traveling Springbok teams, thus forcing solutions like flying to New Zealand from South Africa via the circuitous route of the United States. Were it not for Australia's complete disengagement from hosting South Africa's national rugby team, the 1981 American leg of the tour may well never have gotten off the ground.

By 1977, the Commonwealth Nations had signed the Gleaneagles Agreement, strongly discouraging sporting contacts with South Africa among member nations. This would prove to be a largely toothless agreement that relied on moral suasion, though many Commonwealth nations did adhere to it.

Apartheid South Africa found itself more and more isolated, especially in the high-visibility team sports of cricket and rugby that were so central to white identity. The answer increasingly became "rebel tours," a term coined to describe seven cricket tours between 1982 and 1990 but adopted to describe tours by players from nonnational teams as well. These tours would usually consist of players from any given national team or from multiple national teams from nations whose rugby and cricket unions had not been willing to allow or whose governments had not granted their national teams the right to tour. The seven rebel tours included an English XI in 1982–1983, a Sri Lankan side in 1983–1984, West Indian tours in 1982–1983 and 1983–1984, Australian tours in 1985–1986 and 1986–1987, and another England XI in 1989–1990. In some ways, the most vexing were the West Indies tours. This is because several of the players, who had been members of the great West Indies teams of that generation (teams that were likely the most dominant sports teams on earth, but that also represented black nationalism to many of their supporters, especially after they had defeated previously bullying English and Australian national teams in the 1970s), were seen to have sold out for a lucrative pay packet. In the West Indies, this was seen as a betrayal, and several players became pariahs in their Caribbean home nations. The Australians similarly faced a great deal of criticism for their high-profile rebel tours.

GLACIAL CHANGE

Perhaps paradoxically, throughout the 1970s and into the 1980s, actions on the part of politicians in Pretoria and Cape Town revealed that the years of sporting isolation had done little to soften their approach to apartheid sport. In April 1975, the minister of sport and recreation, in preaching the maintenance of separate development in sport as in all other aspects of South African life, said, "Each nation has for 300 years administered its sports by itself in SA and has had its own sport body and bodies to do so." In responding to media reports that the Transvaal cricket union and perhaps other sporting bodies were considering pursuing "mixed club competitions," Minister Hansard left no room for interpretation. "I now want to state by repetition clearly and frankly that such action will not be in accordance with Government policy and that violation and disregard of the policy of the Government will force us to regard it in a serious light, because it will not promote sport in SA."[3] So much for sport and politics not mixing.

In 1976, the government had engaged in reform in large part to try to counter the increasing isolation South African teams faced across the globe. The realities on the ground changed little, and in the words of the South African Institute of Race Relations' 1977 edition of its influential *A Survey of Race Relations in South Africa*, "The Republic's standing in international sport did not improve" as a result of these reforms that had little concrete effect. "Attempts during the year to form single controlling bodies in individual sports failed because non-racial bodies refused to join anything which they felt was tainted with 'multi-nationalism,'" the policy of separate development that, among other things, created the apartheid "Bantustans," "and because they argued that the white-dominated bodies were not prepared to face up to the full consequences of open sport."[4] Opponents of apartheid sport were not prepared to accept tokenism or gradualism, which ultimately was all that the National Party intended with their paternalistic and self-serving reforms. As an example of the local realities that prevailed even in the midst of so-called reforms, the white Western Province Rugby Union had "discussed removing a 'Whites Only' clause from its constitution but had not done so" by early 1978.[5]

Throughout 1978, the revised government policy had led to a substantial increase in inter-racial sport at all levels, But the conditions of a year earlier prevailed. Heading into the 1980s, changes in the structure and organization of sport in South Africa continued to be largely cosmetic. Consequently, opposition to South African teams competing internationally was never just about apartheid sport, but rather was an expression of opposition to apartheid in all of its guises, with sport providing a useful and visible outlet to oppose apartheid comprehensively, and not just South Africa's slowly evolving sports policy. An irony in the National Party's reforms is that they led to rising opposition and protest from a growing and disenchanted base of right-wing whites.[6] This trend was hardly limited to the sporting arena, and the rise of these conservative challenges to the already-right-wing National Party would prove deeply problematic for the governing party. Indeed, even if the situation in sport seemed to be improving, largely because of the desire of South African officials to return to international competition, the political situation throughout the 1980s deteriorated dramatically.

RACE AND AMERICAN SPORT

The United States was hardly immune from racism permeating sport. Indeed, the long history of organized sport in the United States can be seen as a microcosm of the country's racial problems, where stated ideals of opportunity and meritocracy crashed on the shores of the country's racial realities. When Jackie Robinson desegregated the Brooklyn Dodgers in 1947, he rewrote baseball's unwritten rule. Across "America's pastime," owners, management, and coaches had kept black players from playing in the major and minor leagues for nearly six decades, since Moses Walker had last played in the International League in 1889. In the decades after Robinson took the field for the minor league Montreal Royals in 1946 and the Dodgers in 1947, African American players were some of the most prominent, most dominant, and best in the history of a game from which they would have been excluded before April 1947.

But baseball was hardly alone. The National Football League excluded black players from 1933 to 1946 and, in the college game, teams across the South excluded black athletes, as they oftentimes did black students, well into the 1960s. The National Basketball Association (NBA), the most culturally black sports league in the United States, only desegregated in 1950. Yes, the NBA itself was only two years old at the time, but at best professional basketball's history on racial matters was of a piece with other leagues. Similarly, the first black player in the National Hockey League, Willie O'Ree of the Boston Bruins, did not don that black and gold sweater in a game until 1958.

Furthermore, desegregation hardly implied full integration, and full integration hardly meant that racial problems disappeared. By the late 1960s, the "Revolt of the Black Athlete," embodied in John Carlos and Tommie Smith's famous raised fists gesture on the medal stand during the National Anthem at the 1968 Olympics, proved that black sportsmen and women in the United States had not only found their voice but found that their sport provided a platform to speak out against injustices. Black college athletes protested their treatment by refusing to practice or play. Black professionals used their access to the media to criticize American racial policies, many of which they confronted despite being famous and well-compensated.[7]

Many Americans could thus look at South African racial policies and not see a completely alien world but rather one that differed in degree but not in kind. By 1981, much had changed in the United States, but white supremacy was not merely a thing of the past or something that allowed Americans, especially white Americans, to point their fingers in judgment at apartheid South Africa.

THE ACCIDENTAL TOURISTS

Planning for the United States Tour

FALSE STARTS: WHISPERS OF ENGAGEMENT

The phone call came into the offices of the South African Rugby Board (SARB) on July 15, 1980, at 12:35 p.m. It came from an American named Douglas Reid, and the message that was left read, "Please phone back—urgent. Wants to organize international tour, which will be very profitable for our country." After these words, which were written in English, someone left a biting parenthetical note in Afrikaans, which read, "As if we do not have enough."[1] In fact, South African rugby and the Springboks, arguably the most powerful rugby union on earth, were not underresourced, and the prospect of interaction with the lowly Americans as a path to enrichment held little or no appeal for a national rugby side that considered itself the best in the world. South African rugby did not need riches.

But as South African rugby found itself increasingly isolated, it did need allies. The Americans may have been rugby nonentities, but they offered the possibility of a safe harbor in hostile, stormy waters. Thus, SARB secretary Alex Kellermann and J. P. "Hannes" Pretorius, SARB executive committee member, chairman of the board's finance committee, and president of the Western Province Rugby Football Union, nevertheless met with Reid, a San Diego native who had spent some time in South Africa and had grand plans for how American–South

African relations should operate. They congregated at Cape Town's D. F. Malan Airport on July 22, 1980. Throughout the course of the "lengthy discussions," they considered two possibilities. One was to organize "reciprocal tours between South Africa and the United States of America, assuming the South African and American governing rugby bodies could sort out all financial arrangements and logistics." Failing that, the men also talked about the potential for an October or November 1980 tour of the United States "by a Junior Springbok or S. A. Country Districts team for say a three/four week tour of six/seven matches (not on Sundays), provided the official invitation is issued to this office by the United States of America Rugby Football Union."[2]

The only problem with Douglas Reid's rugby diplomacy outreach plan? He had absolutely no standing to pursue it, a fact that became clear when Kellermann wrote Edmund Lee, international fixture secretary for the United States of America Rugby Football Union (USARFU) to pursue further the possibilities of US–South African rugby engagement.

"I do not know [Reid] and cannot recall that I ever heard of him," Lee responded in a letter dated August 3. "I have examined my address lists for the Pacific Coast RFU, Southern California RFU . . . and Northern California RFU as well as USARFU and can find no record of him. I know of my own knowledge that he is not an officer, director or committee chairman of USARFU."[3] Nor did Reid's efforts at name-dropping—he threw around the name Robert Watkins in his meeting with the South Africans—help to establish his insider credentials. Watkins had been involved in American rugby circles as "a most active and competent administrator and on several USARFU committees," and even though he had interacted with South African rugby officials in planning for an aborted American Cougars tour to South Africa, he had never served as an officer or director of USARFU. "I have a very high regard for Bob," Lee continued, "but if Mr. Reid was trying to impress you and Hannes with name dropping he could at least have mentioned some of the officers and directors of USARFU." And, in any case, Lee explained, USARFU president Dick Moneymaker "last year issued a memo to all USARFU officers and directors announcing my appointment as International Fixtures Secretary and directing everyone not to communicate with other unions on international matches except through me." Lee went on to dismiss the logistics of Reid's proposal as absurd, insisting, "Anyone familiar with tours of the caliber of teams you and Reid discussed knows it takes nearly a year or more rather than 2 or 3 months to organize a tour, especially for the length of the tour mentioned." He minced no words in rendering his judgment: "I conclude that Douglas W. Reid must be an intruder-promoter."[4]

Kellermann seems to have drawn the same conclusions about Reid. Those suspicions were confirmed after a December 5 letter from the ambitious Californian. Apparently, after meeting with Reid and sharing a memorandum with the SARB executive board, Kellermann sent Reid a letter in which he expressed either reservations or skepticism about Reid's grandiose plans. It took some time for Reid to respond, but when he did, he confirmed any suspicions Kellermann and anyone else had about this strange, bombastic interloper.

Nevertheless, Reid continued to maintain his legitimacy. "I have just re-read your letter to me dated July 22, 1980 and I must say sir, that your total lack of commitment and honour are in question," Reid wrote to Kellermann in December of 1980. He recalled three main topics of conversation at the airport meeting, including "to promote S. A. rugby on a high professional level"; "To assist the growth of U.S. rugby through an exchange with the recognized world leader in rugby—South Africa"; "But more important——to help put two powerful nations together through your rugby organization—where the men in power politically have failed to be successful you had the power to get the ball rolling."[5] To that end, Reid, who lamented the state of relations between the United States and South Africa, promised: "You and your nation will have support from the Free World like never in the history of time and the U.S.A. under Ronald Reagan and with many of my friends at his side." A litany of other promises that Reid was in no position to make followed: "We will not make South Africa look small"; "We will not have a holier than thou attitude"; and "We will not put sanctions on you. As you saw on November 4, 1980," the date of Reagan's defeat of Jimmy Carter, a "noise was heard from the bottom to the top—it was a noise so loud that the Free World stood up together and said 'America is back[.]' [W]e took the Liberal left and sent them running, our nation is now looking to a real leader with a real congress with God at his side, we will turn it around and from very good authority sir, we want to walk side by side with South Africa."[6] Douglas Reid, it appeared, was ready to make both America and South Africa great again.

Though Reid had failed to reach out to American rugby officials, he did seek to establish relations with political officials who could legitimize him. On the same day that he met with the South Africans at the airport in Cape Town, he wrote to Richard Nixon at the former president's New York City law offices, where Nixon was in the early stages of recovering from the ignominy of his resignation and rehabilitating his image as a wise man, especially in matters of foreign policy. Reid wanted to express his "concern and total agreement with you regarding the Soviet position in Southern Africa," a stand firmly ensconced in the rhetoric of the Cold War, whereby the struggles for liberation from white supremacy in southern Africa fell under suspicion for their ties, both real and imagined, to Soviet Communism. As president, Nixon had gone a step further, forging closer ties with white supremacist regimes across the region because of a belief that isolating them would change nothing.

Reid summarized his concerns and thus his politics when it came to South Africa: "The whole world is neglecting the fact that South Africa is one of the vital 'links' to the entire Western world: It is the most strategic point in the Southern hemisphere, and in Africa." He was especially critical of the Carter administration (and apartheid's critics), which saw "only the racial problems, yet totally neglect[ed] the strategical [sic] value South Africa plays in connection to the United States." Reid advocated maintaining a naval base in Simonstown (near Cape Town, the home of South Africa's largest naval installation) and desired "a complete relaxation of sanctions and embargos" as "the real way to help solve the racial problems." He argued that "ninety percent . . . of all American enterprises in South Africa do not recognize 'color' as their major problem" but rather the real issue was "the lack of concern by the leadership in our country to recognize the strategic position South Africa plays in our free world."[7]

Reid's belief that "I basically stand alone in my ideas about South Africa," revealed not only the depth of his self-absorption but also an ignorance of the growing chorus of conservative voices rushing to defend Pretoria. He further fulminated about alleged American government support for "Marxist regime[s]" in southern Africa. Then he offered his insights on a potential face-to-face meeting with Nixon. "If, sir, in any way I can be of assistance to you, I would be more than glad to share with you any of my knowledge and feelings, as well as the facts and information I have from my experience of living throughout" and "being actively involved in the business community of South Africa. . . . I would truly consider it an honor if in the future I might have the opportunity to meet with you personally."[8] Although meandering, this letter reveals Reid's overarching ideological approach toward South Africa, and indeed in some ways reflects the larger conservative approach to the apartheid question: Ignoring or understating apartheid and its impacts while emphasizing that South Africa was a vital Cold War ally.

Nixon did not seem in a hurry to avail himself of Reid's wisdom and insight. "[M]y schedule for the next several months is heavily committed due to the publication of my book," the former president replied in August. Nonetheless, Nixon invited Reid to contact his office in early December when his secretary could "try to arrange for a visit."[9] There is no evidence that the meeting ever occurred.

On the same day that Nixon penned his demurral, Reid sent a letter to former California governor Ronald Reagan, who a month earlier had received the Republican Party's nomination for the presidency at Joe Louis Arena in Detroit. Reid wanted "to share with you my concern for our great country and its relationship with South Africa." Based on his travels there, Reid believed "the only hope that" the continent had "for any form of stability, is for a strong U.S. position and decisive policy for all of Africa, which, as you know, is currently non-existent."[10] His tone continued to grow ever more urgent. "South Africa is strong, courageous, resourceful, and rich and is the only free Western influence in Africa." And yet, "Our current administration does not even recognize her—how very small of our great country—it is almost embarrassing."[11] Carter had, indeed, taken a more human-rights centered approach to South Africa than had Nixon or would Reagan, though his administration did little concrete to take a more aggressive policy toward the apartheid state.

After laying out arguments about South Africa's strategic significance to the United States, Reid offered himself to the Republican nominee (whose own policies on southern Africa would prove to be very much in line with Reid's). As he had with Nixon, Reid invited Reagan to meet to discuss how "South Africa, its people, its resources, and its courage should be considered and discussed very thoroughly."

He knew "that time is very precious to you at the moment, but perhaps you would be kind enough to let me know a date when it would be convenient for me to have an appointment with you. I am entirely at your disposal for further information or any assistance that you think I may be able to render."[12]

Even if Reid did not get his audience with Reagan—and there is no evidence indicating that he did—he would nevertheless manage to have an impact on US–South African relations, albeit in a more bizarre way than he or anyone could have imagined.

As soon as Ed Lee, the American International Fixtures secretary, thoroughly eviscerated Reid's claims to be able to arrange any sort of tour, he immediately raised the prospects of just such a tour, even if only to declare that the time was not right. Clearly referring to long-standing commitments the Americans had with South African rugby officials, including South Africa's almost sanctified figure Danie Craven, a former Springbok star, coach, and longtime South African rugby chief, Lee promised that "when in my judgment the political and race relations climate is right for a tour by a South African team I will let all of you know." However "the race riots we have been having in Miami, Chattanooga and Orlando show that the climate now and for some time will not be right for such a tour. The racial activists here are very busy indeed." Lee was also cognizant of the South African political situation. "The racial incidents South Africa has been having involving students, Sasol [a South African energy and chemical company that was often a target of anti-apartheid attacks] and government employees are magnified and distorted by the news media here and consequently our public does not know the truth about your situation."[13]

Lee's feelings of empathy toward the South Africans would become a common theme for the American supporters of the tour, most of whom expressed sympathy for what they saw as the deeply misunderstood South Africans and hostility toward the agitating protesters on both sides of the Atlantic. Though they would claim that sport should be separate from politics, most of them held political views that sympathized with apartheid South Africa and condemned its critics. Supporting South African sport was no less a political stance than opposing it.

Lee also recognized a crucial political distinction between the Carter administration and a potential Reagan presidency. "I am satisfied the Carter administration would not grant visas to a South African team now. Hopefully the situation will change in time when, as and if Reagan is elected our next president." For all of these reasons, Lee was also skeptical of discussing a tour of a rugby team from the Ciskei, one of the fraudulent apartheid "Bantustans" that the South African state had set up in order to try to wash its hands of its black population. Such a team "can be promoted as a racially mixed team from a non-South African country," but Lee knew that "if we advertise and promote a tour to bring in gate receipts and possibly get TV coverage and revenue we thereby establish a target for the race activists around which to picket, parade and propagandize." In any case, "South Africa has had a magnificent year of Rugby. The boycot [sic] is broken, you have confirmed your world leadership and you struck a blow against politics in sports and in support of world peace through sports."[14] Equal parts deeply politicized and profoundly naïve, Lee's words would set the tone that almost all American rugby officials would strike in the coming fourteen months.

THE SOUTH AFRICAN PROPAGANDA MACHINE

Doug Reid might have been pleased to discover that he was far from alone in his concerns about South Africa's perception in the United States, a country seeking positive publicity by any means necessary. The South African propaganda machine had discovered a receptive audience in conservatives in the United States, Britain, and elsewhere. Indeed, the abiding National Party commitment to investing in favorable publicity had consequences leading to a crisis of legitimacy among white South Africans, who normally put forth an imperturbable guise about the righteousness of apartheid, that nearly took the entire government down in the late 1970s.

In 1960, South African police had opened fire on unarmed black South Africans gathered in Sharpeville, a township outside of Johannesburg, to protest the onerous Pass Laws, killing dozens and wounding scores more. Most victims were shot in the back and sides. In the wake of the Sharpeville Massacre, the National Party government had become a pariah in the eyes of much of the world. The government tried to counter with a wide-ranging campaign of propaganda to sell that world, and especially conservatives in Great Britain and the United States, as well as to reassure those at home, an image of a kinder apartheid state concerned for all of its citizens and committed to policies of "separate development" that would best serve all South Africans. The government's Department of Information would oversee this sales job. And given South Africa's global polecat status, the department, and the information service of South Africa, which operated abroad, did a remarkable job.[15]

The information service produced numerous publications in order to tell white South Africa's side of things. Presenting apartheid as a benign institution (indeed rarely using the term *apartheid,* preferring the term *separate development*) and selling the putatively independent Bantustans within this framework, publications such as *Progress Through Separate Development* presented a South Africa, as the subtitle explained, "in peaceful transition." "The nations of South Africa"—referring to the quasi-independent Bantustans—"established their separate identities a long time ago and often underlined the independence of their spirit in armed combat. History, however, took its course and the black nations came to be governed by the institutions of the white nation in their midst." In a flabbergasting assertion, the authors maintained, "The purpose of this booklet is to report on the progress that has been made in setting these nations free again."[16] During the years when apartheid was most complete, when control over the nation's black masses most absolute, when the African National Congress, Pan Africanist Congress, and myriad other organizations had been banned, and thus driven into exile or underground, the apartheid state was telling the outside world that apartheid was nothing more than a form of black liberation. It would have boggled the imagination had its intended audience not been so receptive to being boggled. Myriad other publications from the information service and allied organizations reinforced the message that South Africa was merely misunderstood and that the real goal was to maximize African development, an absurd assertion in the 1960s and 1970s, the high-water mark of the propaganda campaigns.

In 1972, the Ministry of Information, overseen by Cornelius "Connie" Mulder, had gotten in the business of actively investing in and even buying media outlets in South Africa and internationally. Mulder, a former minster of sport, had written an academic thesis on, of all topics, hopscotch in South Africa.[17] By the middle of the decade, the government had invested tens of millions of rands into its information campaign, much of it laundered and otherwise misappropriated and illegally expropriated. In large part, the campaign was geared toward countering South Africa's liberal press, especially the *Rand Daily Mail*, a paper that the government had managed to harass but whose voice it had proven unable to silence. The information department pursued the purchase of a Johannesburg English-language newspaper, *The Citizen*, working with a businessman by the name of Louis Luyt.

The ambitions of South Africa's defenders transcended the borders of the republic, as intermediaries tried to buy the right-wing *Washington Star*, with the help of an arch-conservative by the name of John McGoff, a small-time media magnate who had, among other stances, urged his hometown of Williamson, Michigan, to reject hot lunches for school children out of fear that the program represented "federal control." When the owners of the *Star* took issue with some of McGoff's financials and demurred in the prospective sale, he and his South African backers moved on to purchase the *Sacramento Star*. They also managed to plant stories in mainstream newspapers such as the *Washington Post*, and to attempt to exercise influence in American election campaigns.[18]

Almost none of the information ministry's endeavors were aboveboard. And by 1977, journalists, led by the intrepid *Rand Daily Mail*, and a special commission of the government were on the trail of the "Information Scandal." Because of the cover-ups of the original crimes and the discovery of a South African equivalent to "Deep Throat," the secret source of inside information, the Information Scandal would come to be known as "Muldergate." Many assumed Connie Mulder to be first in line to succeed John Vorster as head of the National Party and as the country's prime minister and president. Instead, Mulder had to resign in disgrace, while Information Secretary Eschel Rhoodie was sentenced to prison for his role in these events, but only after going into exile and causing a search for him on the part of state officials and journalists that reached epic and absurd proportions.[19]

More important, so too did John Vorster, who had at minimum given Mulder and Rhoodie the go-ahead, have to step down, first from the prime ministry and then from the state presidency. Rising to take his place would be Pieter Willem "PW" Botha, a man whose nickname, *Die Groot Krokodil* ("The Old Crocodile") spoke to his wily, but also dangerous, ways. Botha, who narrowly won an intraparty election against a weakened yet still formidable Mulder (revealing clearly that without the Information Scandal, Botha would have had no shot at defeating Mulder within the National Party), would lead South Africa through most of the tumultuous 1980s, and would be firmly ensconced as head of party, government, and state at the time of the 1981 tours. Botha would condemn Muldergate while maintaining a great deal of the edifice that allowed for the propaganda campaigns to continue throughout the decade to come. The state purged the sinners even while perpetuating the sin.

Perhaps the most shocking aspect of "Muldergate" is that it was shocking at all. Apartheid was corrupt to the core, and the Information Scandal was neither the first nor the last example of the ways by which representatives of the government, ranging from politicians to police and security forces to the military, would abuse power, break laws, and cover it all up. The remarkable aspect is that it was the one post-1948 scandal that had such dire consequences for its participants, at least until the 1990s.[20] Especially when the principle behind it—selling South Africa, indeed apartheid, to the rest of the world—barely abated even after Muldergate took the Vorster administration down with it.

PLANNING FOR THE BOKS

Lourens Erasmus Smit ("Les") de Villiers, a journalist-turned diplomat-turned head of the South African information services, was among those in the 1970s who identified sport as a fertile ground for softening Americans on the apartheid question. In a full-throated defense of his native land and condemnation of her critics, de Villiers had in the mid-1970s written *South Africa: A Skunk Among Nations*, which included a chapter on the sports boycott that lambasted South Africa's critics for hypocrisy and a range of sins, both real and (mostly) imagined. He loathed the "agitation, threats, disruption and blackmail" used by the anti-apartheid sporting campaigns.[21] And in November 1980, he had an idea. It was an idea that was not entirely new.

It was the same idea that Doug Reid had presented months before.

De Villiers wrote a letter to Ed Hagerty, the editor of *Rugby* magazine, a niche publication in the United States if ever there was one. De Villiers had left the information office after the Information Scandal and founded his own marketing firm, but clearly, he was still interested in the South African cause. He wrote on the letterhead of his firm, which was based at East 64th Street in Manhattan, to Hagerty, whose magazine offices were less than a mile away on Madison Avenue, and made clear that he did not represent either the SARB or any other South African "sport organization."

"I am speaking for myself as an interested South African, wishing to see a rugby visit materialize from my country in the not so distant future,"[22] he wrote. And though de Villiers had no official standing within South African rugby, he was no Doug Reid. He had complete access to the people with the authority to get things done.

De Villiers' idea was that a team drawn at least in part from some of the Springboks on the New Zealand tour that would take place beforehand would play an "extension tour," possibly involving matches between teams on the west and east coasts of the United States, perhaps in San Francisco and New York. As if to alleviate the biggest question that the sponsors would face, he stated upfront that "I have little doubt that it will be a multi-racial contingent." De Villiers had already approached Dr. Louis Luyt, "an accomplished rugby player who represented several South African provincial teams and Captained Orange Free State at one time" to "raise this matter with the S.A. Rugby Board as soon as he receives confirmation of intent and approval from the American R.F.U. regions involved." Luyt, who had become a successful businessman in South Africa, making a fortune as a fertilizer salesman (never have a man and the product he sold been so perfectly matched), and who had been involved in the shadow front to buy *The Citizen*, "would also be available to coach the two teams for a few days before the actual games—should such a mini-tour materialize." De Villiers also thought finances "should be of lesser consideration. Once the local unions have expressed themselves in favour of such a visit, we can approach through Dr. Luyt the S.A. Rugby Board with a proposal which will cover this aspect."[23]

De Villiers included with his letter a testimonial on Luyt's behalf from none other than Springbok legend Dr. Danie Craven, who had known Luyt for many years. Craven praised Luyt's business accomplishments and his distinguished record of service on various boards. He had also "kept his interest in sport, in which he has achieved great heights in several sports, notably rugby, athletics, and boxing. Not only did he represent three of our big provinces, but he took part in our Springbok trials where, for some unknown reason, he was overlooked for national honours. He successfully coached at various levels in his spare time." Luyt was pursuing further education "in law and kindred studies," and these scholarly pursuits had led to Luyt traveling to the United States. It was Craven's expectation that while in the United States, Luyt would also "be used . . . to give lectures on his subject, and to coach sports teams, for not only his ability but his exemplary conduct and firm character will be of tremendous value to the people under him." As a result, Craven was "willing to act as his reference in all respects."[24] In the decades to come, Louis Luyt, fertilizer salesman, would increasingly become Luis Luyt, rugby maven. In 1981, with Doc Danie Craven's imprimatur, his main rugby-related task would be to peddle his bullshit in the United States.

On November 24, Ed Lee, the USARFU International Fixtures Secretary, sent SARB's Alex Kellermann a copy of both de Villiers' letter to Hagerty and the Craven testimonial for Luyt ("de Villiers, Hagerty and Luyt are not aware that I am writing to you") and asked, "Could you consult with Danie Craven and whomever else you think advisable and let me know whether Mr. de Villiers' suggestion has any merit from SARB's point of view? You well know we are most anxious to have South African teams tour here but only with SARB approval."[25]

By the end of 1980, what had begun as fantasy started to become reality. Alex Kellermann wrote to Ed Lee on December 17. Kellermann had discussed the possibilities of a South African rugby tour of the United States with Danie Craven and the issue was to be raised at the SARB's January 23, 1981, meeting. Craven had a few opinions that Kellermann wanted to share. First, he thought that the SARB "would probably prefer a separate tour, as a team returning from a strenuous visit to New Zealand would be tired and a subsequent visit to the United States of America could be regarded as something of an anti-climax." Craven also thought that because the New Zealand tour was scheduled to end on September 12, 1981, "it seems as if a few matches on the return trip would be slightly out of your season." Yet Craven was still flexible, asking, "Would such a visit suit you?" The South Africans had nonetheless chosen "to assume that" Lee's November 24 letter "is an official invitation" but they wanted confirmation. "Please advise whether we can regard it as such, or whether you are merely investigating?"

The American letter of November 24 would thus provide a foundation for the next meeting of the SARB executive committee.[26] A potential Springbok tour of the United States suddenly seemed very real indeed.

A plan for a tour was not yet in place, but it was getting closer as the right people were increasingly in contact with one another. Ed Lee responded to the South Africans, lamenting how slow the mail was between the two countries. He wanted to make clear that his November 24 missive "was purely a letter of inquiry to determine whether a tour of the Springbok[s]" as laid out in de Villiers' November 19th letter to Ed Hagerty "would be considered under any circumstances. It was not an invitation as the USARFU Board of Directors knows nothing about the De Villiers letter." Furthermore, a Pretoria sportswriter named George van Eck and a US-government official in Washington had both called Lee asking him "to confirm or deny reports that the USARFU had issued an invitation to the Springboks for a tour here." He had "of course denied the reports and did not tell them about the De Villiers letter." Lee had come to understand that "Tom Selfridge, US Eagle and Cougar who has just been elected president of the Eastern Rugby Union, has phoned Danie Craven about the De Villiers idea." Yet none of this was done to toss water on the spreading fire. Lee wanted to be clear that the schedule would not be a problem: "September is the beginning of the playing season in most of the USA so tours at that time are quite in order." Lee recognized that the South Africans might desire a separate tour rather than a continuation from New Zealand and did not weigh in one way or the other. In the end, Lee was "confident that we can get the necessary approvals for any tour by any South African side here if such a tour has the approval of the SARB and subject of course to working out the time and details not the least of which is financing. Financing is the big problem. I am no longer worried about politics or racial problems, although visas might be a problem."[27] Why Lee was "no longer concerned with racial problems" must have been directly connected to the inauguration of Ronald Reagan, as neither South Africa nor the United States had reached the day of jubilee on questions of race relations.

Things moved quickly from there. Tom Selfridge of the ERU sent a telegram to Danie Craven in care of Dr. Luis Luyt extending "a formal invitation to play the South African Spring Bucks [sic] on their return from the New Zealand tours 1981."[28] On January 20, 1981, the day of

Reagan's inauguration as fortieth president of the United States, a tele-gram went out from Lee. "USARFU and Eastern RU hereby invite Springboks to play US Eagles and ERU select side September 1981 en route from New Zealand." Lee expected an invitation from a Midwest-ern rugby official to follow soon. It was "necessary that Springboks pay own expenses while in US and expenses of Eagles and ERU to be paid by South African or other businessmen."[29] In February, Lee followed up with an invitation "to Springboks to play Midwest RU Select Side on same basis as USARFU and ERU invitations."[30]

On February 9, Alex Kellermann responded with a handwritten South African post office telegram that said simply, "We accept your kind invitation for three matches in U.S.A." on three tentative Septem-ber dates.[31] That same day Kellermann wrote two letters that gave American rugby officials more extensive feedback. One was to Tom Selfridge, which quoted Selfridge's telegram and explained that "my board has approved the proposed tour in principle, subject to us obtain-ing the necessary permission for a deviation, from the New Zealand Rugby Football Union, and that we are able to obtain the necessary visa to visit your wonderful country."[32] He also enclosed a more extensive letter that he had sent to Ed Lee that same day. To Lee, he quoted and confirmed receipt of all of the cablegrams. He then further explained the way the requested "deviation" to the United States from New Zea-land would likely work. "Just to put you in the picture, when member countries of the I.R.F.B." with which the United States was not affiliat-ed because of its minnow status in world rugby, "undertake tours to each other they sign a tour agreement which allows the visiting team only to travel direct to and from the visited country. However, we have allowed teams to deviate on their way home from South Africa, and there will be no problem from New Zealand."[33]

The South Africans would "foot the bill for the additional airfares, but in order to include the stopovers on the round the world trip, you must let me know in due course what the venues of the expected matches are." He laid out a potential schedule that included a Septem-ber 14 or 15 departure from New Zealand with a September 15 or 16 arrival in the United States. He proposed the match against the Mid-west squad on September 19, a September 22 match against the East-ern Union team, and the September 26 test match against the USA Eagles, with venues to be determined for all three matches. The

Springboks and their support staff would depart on September 28, landing in Johannesburg on September 29. [34] These dates would change a bit in the months to come, but it appeared clear that the mighty Springboks were coming to America.

Little did anyone involved in this planning know that nothing would go quite as smoothly as it all looked on paper. Or that the weeks to come would reveal the galvanizing of an anti-apartheid sentiment that the Boks would face in full force. The United States was a long way in the distance. The immediate future would mark perhaps the most politicized period in the history of sport.

2

STARTING TO PLAY

The Irish in South Africa

HIGH EXPECTATIONS

The Springboks had every reason for high hopes for the 1981 international season, which would see the Irish visit and a tour to New Zealand that would serve as the de facto world championship. Furthermore, there were whispers of a tour to the United States, though, to anyone outside of the offices of USA Rugby, that possibility would remain an afterthought. Although South Africans had watched their country become a global sporting outcast over the course of two decades, the International Rugby Board had not pushed the Springboks or South African rugby to the margins. Instead, it was up to individual national rugby boards to make the decision whether to engage with South African provincial sides, youth teams, universities, the Springboks, or any other teams based in South Africa. Clearly, at least some were still willing to do so.

The 1980 Springboks were awesome. A juggernaut that lived up to the country's exalted rugby standards, the Boks played nine matches in 1980. They defeated a visiting South American side in two tests in late April and early May before the Lions series, which stretched from the end of May to the middle of July. They won eight, their only loss coming in the fourth match against a British Lions team they had beaten three straight to secure the series triumph. There are few meaningless international tests, especially when the Lions come visiting, but the 17–13 loss at Pretoria's Loftus Versfeld Stadium was about as dead as a dead rubber can be with the Springboks having proven their utter dominance and the Lions having nothing but pride for which to play.

This dominance was especially satisfying because when the Willie John McBride–captained Lions had last visited in 1974 they earned their nickname of "The Invincibles" by cutting a swath through their hosts, dominating the first three tests, before the Springboks earned a meaningless draw in the fourth, and winning their other eighteen matches against various provincial and invitational sides. In those still early years of the sporting boycott, most of the Lions ignored or rejected the political implications of touring South Africa, but pressure was increasing. Australian rugby and cricket had disengaged from sporting contacts with South Africa, and Peter Hain and others hoped that the rest of the sporting world, including the Lions, would follow. When a new Labour government came to power in 1974, that pressure increased and the government asked the Lions not to tour South Africa later that year. The request went unheeded by the powers-that-be, but some players and administrators did listen. Two of the most high-profile dissidents had been stars for the 1971 Lions tour of New Zealand and Australia, but Welsh dynamos John Taylor and Gerald Davies, sure selections for 1974, declared themselves unavailable. Taylor was vocal in his loathing of apartheid, Davies more understated, but both took a stand that garnered them considerable criticism in some segments of Welsh and larger British society.

Perhaps ironically, the 1980 Lions tour led to less public outcry than the 1974 Lions tour had. For one, rugby took a back seat to the Cold War politics surrounding the Summer Olympics and widespread boycotts surrounding the Moscow Games. But Britain had also seen a shift in political winds, with Margaret Thatcher's Tories taking control in 1979. Thatcher opposed sanctions on South Africa, and, while the United Kingdom was still a signatory to the Gleaneagles Agreement, whereby Commonwealth nations had agreed not to engage with South African sport, Thatcher's government was mealy-mouthed about its commitments, maintaining a tepid, ineffectual belief in the sporting and cultural boycott while doing virtually nothing to intervene and stop sporting contacts.

After the Lions had departed, the triumphant Springboks traveled to South America to take on a combined team in two tests in October, one in Montevideo, Uruguay, and the other in Santiago, Chile. The South American sides consisted largely of players from South America's rugby giant, Argentina, with a few players from neighboring countries thrown into the mix in no small part because of South Africa's pariah status. Argentina officials were loathe to play and unwilling to host the Springboks officially. The tourists won both matches handily. The Springboks concluded the year by manhandling France at Loftus, 37–15.

Cornelius "Nelie" Smith had coached the Springboks to their greatest heights in 1980 and would continue at the helm in 1981. Born in Bloemfontein in 1934, Smith, the son of a railway worker, did not have much money, but rugby did not require a lot of expensive equipment, and he found that the game came naturally to him. Smith was an accomplished scrumhalf who played for South African universities, Junior Springboks, and for his native Free State, for whom he received sixty caps, thirty-seven as captain. During an era of outstanding Bok scrumhalf play, Smith earned seven caps for South Africa between 1963 and 1965, serving as captain for four of them. He debuted against Australia and a year later played his first match as captain when the Boks hosted France on a poor pitch in the East Rand town of Springs. The 8–6 loss in that match is considered one of the ugliest of all Springbok performances.[1] Indeed, during a rough period for the country's international fortunes, the Springboks lost all four of the matches Smith captained. Nonetheless, his reputation as a great rugby mind did not much suffer.

He entered coaching after the completion of his playing career, taking the helm for his former Free State side, which he coached to their first-ever Currie Cup title, the most prestigious domestic title in South Africa, in 1976. He also coached Griqualand West and Eastern Province. Smith served as a Springbok selector from 1971 through his tenure as Bok head coach, including the ill-fated Lions tour of 1974. At Doc Craven's behest, he moved to the Cape to become the first coaching organizer for the South African Rugby Board in 1978. He was appointed to the Springbok head coaching position in 1980.

Smith was a demanding coach who emphasized fitness and fundamental skills such as passing, catching, and positioning, but he was also deeply analytical and a "master tactician" who would watch films of practices and matches for hours, something that would become standard for coaches by the professional era, but that was practically revolutionary in the 1970s and 1980s. Smith was demanding but not rigid—he expected players to show creative flair and to think for themselves. He also did not punish mistakes that players made when they were trying to be creative and aggressive. He had instilled confidence in the Springboks as he had with every other team he had coached, and their 1980 results were testimony to just how effective his approach could be.

It is little wonder, then, that South African rugby fans looked forward to the 1981 international season, which would see the men in green and gold hosting always-tough Ireland before facing off against the mighty All Blacks. Anti-apartheid activists also were looking forward to the Springbok season, albeit for dramatically different reasons.

ERROL TOBIAS: THE RELUCTANT, CONTESTED PIONEER

Many in the South African rugby hierarchy were tired of playing the role of the globe's sporting polecat. Among them was Danie "Doc" Craven. After graduation from Stellenbosch University, Craven taught at St. Andrews College in Grahamstown from 1936, coaching the school's rugby club even as he was selected for the Boks in 1937. Craven went on to become a Springbok hero as player (as a scrum half, mostly, with appearances as a fly half, center, and even #8), manager coach, strategist, selection authority, strategy tactician, technician, administrator, and elder statesman.

According to some, Craven also did, in his way, want to transform South African rugby, especially in his later years. And indeed, by some accounts, Craven was the driving force behind desegregating the Springboks and was central to Errol Tobias becoming the first black Bok in 1981. Yet Craven had been involved in rugby for decades prior to 1981. His alibi for not implementing change was always a valid, though not airtight, one—that government interference, especially from the Vorster regime, prevented him from doing so. Nonetheless, it hardly would have amounted to heroic behavior for the well-regarded Craven to have frontally challenged the government, held mixed trials, and announced black Springboks in the 1960s or 1970s. Craven knew how great players such as Morgan Cushe (flank), Toto Tsotsobe, "Turkey" Shields, and Johnny Noble (all wings) were, and he had helped bring those players together for the South African Invitation XV, the first mixed South African team, in 1975. Craven deserves credit for this, to be sure, but the Select XV was not the Springboks.

Craven's motivation in selecting Tobias quite clearly seemed to be predominantly about rugby. We have little sense that University of Stellenbosch physical education professor Craven cared much about how the larger integration of black South Africans would be good for his country, but black rugby players would benefit the Springboks. His goal was to maintain South Africa's standing in global rugby, not change within South African society.

In 1995, Louis Babrow, a long-time stalwart with the University of Cape Town rugby club who played for Western Province and earned five caps for the Springboks in 1937, including appearances in the only South African tour victory in New Zealand, felt the need to set the record straight. Babrow had gone on to become a medical doctor, and more important, a vocal opponent of apartheid.

On June 3, 1995, the day that the Springboks defeated Canada 20–0 at Boet Erasmus Stadium in Port Elizabeth on the way to their famous World Cup victory, Babrow unloaded in a letter to a colleague who had been involved in a collection of Craven's recorded reminiscences (what Babrow calls "The Craven Tapes") that served, in Babrow's mind, to further the legend at the expense of the facts. Babrow, Craven's Springbok teammate, confided, "I do not agree with much of what he [Craven] said + much of it is hindsight + lies." Babrow felt that Craven claimed to have opposed racism more than any evidence indicates that he did. "Danie is one of the few people I know who could fool all of the people all of the time," Babrow notes sharply. "He said he fought for the rights of the blacks and coloureds, but [as president of the South African Rugby Board] he stated publicly no black or non-white will ever wear a Springbok jersey." Babrow recalled that at an important intercollegiate rugby competition Craven "personally stood at the gate + stopped eleven of our coloured + Indian students (2 were associate Professors) from entering the main gates used by the whites" and "they had to sit on the little coloured stand with all the drunks + use the toilet under the trees in the open." Babrow maintained that he could "tell you many, many strange things he said + did but I should stop before I go too far which would shock some rugby followers." Babrow, a white man of a certain era, had the rare combination of rugby bona fides and anti-apartheid politics that allowed him to see through some of the mythology that had built up around the sainted Craven.[2]

There is no sense coming to either bury or praise Craven. He did more than most rugby people of his era but less than many and certainly less than he could have from the 1950s through the 1970s. One could simply assert that as a white South African of Afrikaner dissent, he was "a man of his time," but so was Louis Babrow. And Beyers Naude, the courageous Afrikaner anti-apartheid cleric, and Bram Fischer, the lawyer who defended Nelson Mandela at the Rivonia trial, were both Afrikaner men from almost precisely Craven's time. They had all the possible alibis at their disposal and chose to forsake alibi-making altogether. Perhaps, then, Craven's belated discovery that blacks were, in fact, rugby people, warrants a little less hagiography and a little more scrutiny.

But slow change was on the way. Errol Tobias, a coloured center/flyhalf from Caledon, a small town in the Overberg region of the Western Cape, approximately a hundred kilometers from Cape Town, was a strong runner "with an eye for the gap" and rare passing skills.[3] In 1981, Tobias was a thirty-one-year old who had attended Swartberg School and worked in the building industry. He had a successful career in South Africa's always-competitive coloured rugby community and had made his mark at the national level on the 1979 Barbarians tour of England. The Barbarians were an invitational club established in the early 1960s, and the 1979 incarnation was truly a multiracial affair and may have helped to convince the white power structure in South Africa that mixed rugby was viable in apartheid South Africa.

However, there was always a divide within the black rugby communities. The most ardent anti-apartheid advocates called for true nonracialism in sport. In rugby, that manifested in the nonracial South African Rugby Union (SARU), open to all, but unwilling to accommodate those they saw as working within apartheid structures, including, of course, the South African Rugby Board, which oversaw white rugby, and thus provincial and national teams, the South African Rugby Federation (SARF), which was for "coloured" rugby, and the South African Rugby Association (SARA), which was for black ("African," or "Native") rugby, which had previously been the South African Rugby Board but changed its name to avoid confusion with the white board of the same name. To be clear, SARF and SARA rabidly denounced apartheid and rejected the idea that they were collaborationists. But SARU would have none of it.

Tobias came from the federation tradition. This would lead to both his greatest acclaim by putting him in a position to become a Springbok and would lead to the harshest criticism he would face.

Tobias followed the Barbarians tour by becoming the first black player in the Currie Cup for Boland. He and Charles Williams then became the first black junior Springboks, and eventually Tobias earned Bok coach Nelie Smith's selection for the 1980 tour of South America, although he did not earn a test cap.

Springbok selectors were surely aware of the political implications of Tobias' selection, but he appears to have earned his way onto the Bok squad on merit. According to the *Sydney Morning Herald,* Tobias was "on current form, the second best centre" for the touring Boks and although "Foreign critics call him a token black [. . .] there is no question the deceptive and strong inside back is a merit selection in the formerly all-white Springbok side."[4] Rugby journalist Malcolm Brown asserted, "He is very good. I can vouch for that, having seen him make sizzling runs" during the Barbarians tour of Britain in 1979. Brown was, however, well aware that poor performance would revive the accusations of tokenism.[5]

Tobias was part of a generation of black players who approached the top level of rugby in the period from the late 1970s. In 1975, the SA Invitation XV was the first multiracial South African rugby side. They faced a French team that had not lost on tour that year in front of a capacity crowd at Newlands Stadium and emerged with a comfortable 18–3 victory. Although the side was majority white, two players came from the Proteas, the representative side of the Coloured South African Rugby Football Federation (for which Tobias had made his international debut in 1971), right wing John Noble and prop Turkey Shields. The Leopards (or African XV) of the South African African Rugby Board also contributed two players to the SA Invitation XV side, wing Toto Tsotsobe, and flanker, Morgan Cushe. As if to validate the mixed-race squad, Noble scored what one observer has called the "try of the match" just before half-time. Craven was the architect of the squad.[6]

Much like Tobias, Cushe faced criticism for his participation in the multiracial 1975 team from his own black community. Cushe, who passed away in 2013, was a widely respected flank. He also played a

conflicted role in a conflicted era. In the words of journalist Luke Alfred, "Depending on your politics, he was either the worst form of
apartheid collaborator or a subsequently neglected trailblazer, unlucky
not to have been awarded a Springbok blazer, as, say, Errol Tobias
would be" in 1981 and subsequently. Initially, Cushe preferred boxing
to rugby, but eventually he took to the latter sport. Cushe rose through
the ranks of black rugby, including starring for the Leopards before
making his appearance for the SA Invitation XV side against the French
as well as against the mighty All Blacks.[7]

It is perhaps noteworthy that Tobias played a role in the next multiracial South African side to face international competition after the
1975 SA Invitation XV when he starred for the South African Country
Districts XV against a touring American side, the Cougars, at the Border Rugby Union Grounds in East London in August 1978. Predictably,
the South African side crushed the Americans, 44–12, with Tobias scoring two tries and setting up two others as the side's flyhalf. Some observers mistakenly believed that the match against the Americans represented the first multiracial South African rugby team, revealing the
extent to which many of these events played away from the public glare
in what was still very much a closed society.[8]

Morgan Cushe and his cohort represented a generation born too
soon to see the opportunities a generation in the future would reap but
soon enough to experience opportunities that had previously been denied generations of African, coloured, and Indian rugby players; indeed
athletes from all sports. Tobias represented the best fruit from that
poisoned vine, but he was far from alone in facing doubts from all sides,
including his own community. This transgression cut in multiple ways
so that Tobias was seen as problematic by both apartheid supporters
and anti-apartheid activists while he was in his time celebrated by too
few, a standing that has changed in recent years, with Tobias enjoying
broader celebration and praise from within South Africa's rugby community for his pioneering status.

SPORTS "REFORM": HINTS OF CHANGE OR "COSMETIC" PROPAGANDA?

Throughout the apartheid era, and especially in the 1980s, the National Party government, its spokespersons, and its apologists would tout ongoing reforms in sport. By 1981, when feeling particularly emboldened and confident, the government might even go so far as to assert that apartheid in sport was a dead letter. This assertion was a substantial overstatement, even if it was true that the government had been engaging in reform of apartheid sport, especially after the Soweto Uprising of 1976 drew heightened scrutiny to South African policy.

There was no coherent plan in reforming sport. Mostly, it seemed that the government was doing the least it could do in hopes of getting the sports boycott lifted, and oftentimes local, provincial, and national governments acted at cross-purposes and even contradicted one another. So, for example, in 1976, when the National Party government relaxed some policies on sport, policy and practice did not always align. In September, the Federal Information Council of the National Party announced an eight-part policy for sport that relaxed a number of aspects of apartheid sport. One of these changes read, "Where mutually agreed, councils or committees may, in consultation with the Minister [of Sport], arrange leagues or matches enabling teams from different racial groups to compete." The sports minister, Dr. Piet J. G. Koornhof, further was reported to have said on November 16 that South African teams competing internationally "would be selected on merit, on the basis of racially-mixed trials."[9]

Yet in October, the new policy ran into the traditional hurdles. Eight white rugby players in the Eastern Province accepted invitations to play with black players in a match in Port Elizabeth. Dr. Koornhof, the sports minister who had announced the mélange of policy revisions not even three weeks earlier, put forward a "friendly but urgent appeal" for the match not to go on. It was played, and indeed, the white players "were carried shoulder-high off the field by the black players." Koornhof defended himself by saying that the proposed match was still illegal because it was contrary to a sports policy that still did not provide for mixed teams. Furthermore, the white presence at the match was illegal because they had lacked permits to play on public grounds in a designated black area, permits they had applied for but that the government had apparently ignored. Danie Craven, then head of the (white) South African Rugby Board, expressed his displeasure with the actions of the eight white players, calling instead for an "evolutionary approach."[10]

The National Party was itself divided over the question of racially mixed sport at the club or local level. Though provincial congresses had haltingly seemed to approve mixed-sport policies, prominent national leaders maintained that national policy had not changed. Andries Treurnicht, deputy minister of Bantu Affairs, argued that mixed sports clubs would lead to integration. Dr. Connie Mulder, the Transvaal leader of the National Party was unequivocal. "I want to make it very clear that mixed membership of sports clubs is not the policy of the party." Koornhof concurred, contradicting local congresses by saying "Mixed sport at club level remains contrary to party policy" and he provided assurances that "the sport policy would 'in no way threaten the identity and self-determination of the race groups.'" In other words, tinkering aside, apartheid would prevail. Even if "by the end of the year it was generally accepted that mixed sport at club level was not illegal," there were so many exceptions, some immense—liquor laws, the Group Areas Act, the Reservation of Separate Amenities Act—and the reality was that such mixing remained contrary to National Party policy and the preferences of some heavy hitters in the country's highest political ranks.[11]

By the end of 1978 there was no question that many of the reforms from 1976 had begun to take hold no matter the feelings of National Party potentates and no matter the inconsistencies in application. There was more mixed sport than ever, but progress came haltingly. Local authorities exercised the right to deny permits under the Group Areas Act. Powerful political figures maintained their devotion to apartheid and sometimes spoke out of both sides of their mouths. Koornhof, in February 1978, wrote a letter to an International Tennis Federation delegation to alleviate their concerns about the easing of apartheid sport and assured that he wanted his letter to be "a clarification and a confirmation of the normalization of sport on a non-racial basis in SA." In October, in an address before the national conference of the Associated Clubs of SA, the minister of sport declared that "the government accepts that the interests of SA and all its sporting peoples will be served best if sportsmen and sportswomen of the whites, blacks, coloured and Indians belong to their own clubs and control, arrange, and manage their own sports matters . . . A club has the right to decide who shall and who shall not be allowed to join that club." The government also tentatively pursued easing elements of the Group Areas Act and other restrictive legislation, reducing the functions of the ministry of sport in regulating sporting bodies, including issues related to mixed sport.[12]

In 1979, 1980, and the early months of 1981, there was more of the same: reform that represented at best tinkering at the margins. Reform that certainly seemed radical—allowing for national selectors to choose any athlete across sporting codes irrespective of racial designation. Reform that loosened but hardly freed who could be where when. The South African Rugby Board announced that it would consolidate all of the rugby groups (anti-apartheid and anti-collaborationist SARU excluded) under one umbrella. But in the end, these reforms simply flew in the face of the reality that apartheid and apartheid structures—residential and economic, in terms of jobs and passes, in terms of who could be with whom socially, and in terms of the outcomes of the conditions that had created apartheid—continued, tepidly reformed, but for the masses of South Africans, essentially unabated. Further, the government's crackdowns post-Soweto were increasingly violent, the country more and more ruled by "securocrats," the coalition of police, security forces, and military who were on the front lines enforcing apartheid. Apartheid continued and impacted sport in every possible way. Rugby continued to be perhaps the most visible point of pride of white and especially Afrikaner Nationalists. In light of these realities, what was a little pillow fluffing? South Africa remained an abnormal society. How could it possibly stake a claim to having normal sport?

Consequently, anti-apartheid sports organizations were not impressed. The South African Council on Sport (SACOS) continued to press for South Africa's global sporting isolation. They wanted the global community to continue the boycott until sport in South Africa "was fully integrated and all discrimination had been removed." Hassan Howa, the president of SACOS, believed that all of the government's machinations were merely cosmetic as long as the Group Areas Act remained in effect. Tellingly, the government, for all its displays about reform, refused to meet with SACOS leadership. Indeed, in the government's crackdown on the Black Consciousness Movement that culminated in the 1977 death of activist Steve Biko, the BC-affiliated Black

Peoples' Sports Council had also dissolved.[13] All of this is further evidence that National Party reforms were more than anything halfhearted efforts to get South Africa back in the global community's good graces and back onto international playing fields.

Reform or not, however, the rallying cry of the global anti-apartheid sporting forces rang true: "No Normal Sport in an Abnormal Society" recognized that reform was merely cosmetic—as long as apartheid remained in terms of the country's geography and politics, education and patterns or residency, labor laws, and social conditions. As long as apartheid, grand and petty, prevailed, it was impossible to have "integrated sport" because all of the elements that contributed to apartheid had a direct impact on sport.

SLEAZY, GRUBBY, NASTY: THE IRISH IN SOUTH AFRICA

Ireland's national rugby team visited South Africa in May and June 1981, over the objections of many in their home country who opposed such clear collaboration with apartheid sport. As was custom, president Patrick Hillery had been invited to watch Ireland's home matches at Lansdowne Road, the Dublin Stadium that was home of the Ireland Rugby Football Union and thus Ireland rugby's home matches. Hillery refused because of the planned South Africa trip, which he ardently opposed. Ireland's Taoiseach Charles Haughey and his government also made clear their opposition to the tour. Hillery and Haughey, stalwarts in the Fianna Fáil political party, shared the widespread belief that the tour represented an endorsement of apartheid. Brian Lenihan, the minister for foreign affairs, met with representatives from the Ireland Rugby Football Union (IRFU) and asked them not to go forward with the tour "in the interests of justice and Ireland's reputation." Haughey did something similar in May, making both a personal appeal and then pulling together a delegation of high-ranking officials in hopes of getting the union to relent.[14] Bolstering Lenihan's concerns, in February the "Group of 77," an informal body representing more than 110 countries in the United Nations, indicated that they might try to see Ireland removed from its recently acquired temporary seat on the UN Security Council.[15]

Many within Ireland's influential Catholic hierarchy similarly condemned the pending tour. Cardinal Tomás Ó Fiaich issued a statement requesting that the union reconsider its plans. Church of Ireland primate, Dr. John Armstrong, seconded the request, giving opposition to the tour the imprimatur of the Church. They received support from a perhaps unexpected quarter when their South African counterpart, the Archbishop of Durban, Dr. Denis Hurley, wrote, "Be quite clear about it. Both the white South Africans and the oppressed majority of the people of South Africa clearly interpret the tour as an acceptance of the policy of apartheid."[16]

Naturally, the Irish Anti-Apartheid Movement believed that the IRFU's tour plans "border[ed] on the criminal." Ireland's national television and radio broadcaster, RTE (Raidió Teilifís Éireann—Radio-Television Ireland), took as strong a stand as any party to the criticism, announcing in May that it would not cover the tour, reflecting what it understood to be the clear will of the Irish people.[17] Opposition spread across wide swaths of Irish society. All of the main political parties called on the IRFU to call off the tour. So, too, did churches and trade unions, student organizations, and other sporting bodies. A petition circulated calling for the tour to be called off. More than 20,000 people signed it. Lenihan, the minister of foreign affairs, argued, "This is not a sporting event. It is, whether or not the players it organizers choose to regard it as such, a political act."[18]

And the debate played out daily in Ireland's major newspapers. The *Irish Times* and the *Independent* started running letters to the editor about the tour in January 1981 and the volume barely slowed for weeks. There were ardently pro-tour arguments, some of which practically defended apartheid. There were arguments that opposed the tour personally but that argued that it nonetheless should be allowed to go on. There were letters opposing the tour but not arguing for any official action against it, even if they hoped that the IRFU would experience a change of heart. And then there were the anti-tour letters that wanted it canceled by whatever means possible. There were angry letters, sad letters, hostile and aggressive letters. The entire range of arguments about engaging apartheid sport played out daily, sometimes across multiple pages of the country's main broadsheets. On March 2, the *Irish Times*, as part of its weekly competition (no. 615) asked its readers to contribute verse about the tour. They received a "huge response to this competition" and could only publish a sample of the best entries. The winner did not choose a side, but rather took the savvy approach of praising the *Times'* letters page on the Springbok tour issue. Four of the eight published poems were clearly critical of the tour. One was clearly critical of the protests. The others did not take a clear stand.[19]

But none of this sentiment, official or unofficial, mattered. The IRFU ignored, mocked, derided, and pointedly ignored the protests.[20] The majority of players were, it asserted, "gung-ho" for the tour. Rugby officials even tried to paint their willingness to travel in South Africa as somehow a challenge to apartheid. The Irish coach, Tom Kiernan, bizarrely asserted, "I cannot say in any precise way what changes the tour will bring about but I believe that it will harm rather than promote Apartheid," a sentiment echoed by IRFU vice president John Moore.[21] Even more strangely, Kiernan argued, "If you tell me my best friend is being unfaithful to his wife, should I stop meeting him? Where do you start and end with moral questions?"[22] Of course, as Irish journalist Eamonn Sweeney points out, "This idea of the IRFU as cunning stealth warriors against the South African system takes a bit of a blow" given that "the Union's officials would only appear in a TV programme about the tour if no representative of the Anti-Apartheid movement was allowed to debate with them." Given a chance to debate the tour and its merits on RTE TV, the state broadcast network, members of the IRFU refused to appear alongside exiled South African Kader Asmal, the head of the Irish Anti-Apartheid Movement, or anyone in his orbit.[23]

And it was not as if Ireland regularly played in South Africa in a tradition the IRFU was reluctant to break. Ireland had not toured South Africa since 1961, its only visit to the country.

Not everyone involved in Irish rugby was as "gung-ho" as they were made out to be. Several players refused to be part of any team traveling to South Africa, including flyhalf, Tony Ward; lock, Moss Keane; fullback, Hugo MacNeill; and lock, Donal Spring. All four were regular Ireland internationals. Several other players withdrew their names from consideration, though mostly for work-related reasons, a reminder that in the amateur era, players often had to weigh the ability to make a living against their desire for (unpaid) sporting glory. At least two players quit their jobs when it became clear that their employer would not allow them to travel to represent Ireland. The South African Non-Racial Olympic Committee (SANROC) publicly praised Ward, Keane, and McNeill, the first three Irish players to make their opposition to the tour known, with the committee's chair, Nigerian ambassador B. Alporode Clark, sending them letters of commendation.[24]

In Donal Spring's words, which the young lawyer first wrote in a legal aid magazine, "Though I agree with the theory that sport and politics should be kept apart whenever possible, when the evil involved is so fundamental a part of society that it transcends all aspects of human life as in South Africa, one cannot hide behind a banner labeled sport, trade, tourism, etc."[25] Spring was not writing in abstractions. He had traveled to South Africa in 1977 and had seen the "endless supply of servants to cater for the white man's needs." He was appalled by "the racist signposts everywhere—in stations and hotels and on buses" that "spelt it out." He saw "the mixture of hatred and fear that one felt among the non whites side by side with the attempted justification and belief in the supremacy of the white man that was expressed by many of the people we met."[26] His early withdrawal from the tour met with praise from advocates of anti-apartheid sport in South Africa, including from Hassan Howa, a stalwart advocate for non-racial sport in South Africa who said "I can only praise him for what he is doing." Perhaps predictably, Danie Craven said of Spring, "He doesn't know what he's talking about."[27]

For Tony Ward, too, South Africa was not merely an abstraction. The 1979 European Rugby Player of the Year, the handsome young flyhalf had traveled with the Lions on their 1980 South African tour. When he was there, "I got the red carpet treatment," he said, but he and teammate Colin Patterson "scratched below the surface to see what was really going on." He was not impressed. "A lot of things upset me on that tour. You can call me an eejit but my conscience tells me what I should or shouldn't do and as long as my conscience is clear then it's fine." Years later, he knew he made the right decision.[28] His choice is perhaps even more impressive because despite the honors he won after his 1979 season, in 1980, he lost his position for Ireland and was fighting his way back into the national side. In 1981, he was trying to regain his standing in the national team. By choosing not to travel to South Africa, he took a lot of risks, despite his manifest accomplishments.

Moss Keane's decision was a little more muddled. He was a public servant, which meant that government policy against the tour applied to him. Nonetheless, despite the fact that he felt that he could have easily gotten another job, even in troubling economic times in Ireland, in the end, he chose not to go. "I thought of the men and women who fought and died to win us freedom from the apartheid regime that existed in Ireland prior to Independence and came to my decision." It is perhaps not surprising that during the era of the early 1980s the Irish struggle would be on his and others' minds. That said, Keane would prove refreshingly honest years later. "I would be a hypocrite if I said I was absolutely sure of my position" not to play in South Africa, "because I was not."[29]

The fourth holdout was Hugo MacNeill, who was by all reckonings a brilliant university student at both Trinity College Dublin and then at Oxford (and a sterling rugby and soccer player at university and beyond). He was still a student in 1981, and thus, for him, the burden must have been even more immense as he looked at his future sporting career. Nonetheless, MacNeill was paying attention. "I listened to some of the black leaders in South Africa saying 'Please don't come, the Afrikaners don't care about economic sanctions, but they do care about the Springboks." This message rang clear. "The more and more I heard the message it resonated. It was all pointing in one direction. Ultimately, I said 'I can't go, it's just not right.'"[30]

In March, David Irwin, a medical student at Queen's University, Belfast, also announced that he would not be available for selection. He had represented Ireland for the first time in 1980, and between 1980 and 1990 would earn twenty-five caps for Ireland and three for the Lions. Described by a journalist as "one of the best centres in these islands," Irwin justified his unavailability as the result of "examination commitments," but he also was under pressure from the Queens Students Union not to partake in the tour.[31]

Others who wanted to go were not able to because of work. Hooker Ciaran Fitzgerald was a captain in the Irish military. "I didn't go. I didn't have a choice. I put it up the channels and it went to the Department of Defence and the answer was no. That was that. It was a minor disappointment but I was conditioned to it. I knew what was coming."[32] He had made his debut for Ireland in 1979 and not participating in 1981 would not deleteriously affect his rugby career, as he would captain Ireland during two future Five Nations and Home Nations winning seasons and another in which they shared the title with France. He would also captain the Lions when they were whitewashed in New

Zealand in 1983 and would earn eleven Lions caps. He later served as Ireland head coach in the early 1990s. He also won two all-Ireland boxing titles and played hurling.

John Robbie, the great scrumhalf, has thought a lot about that tour as someone who would go on to live and work in South Africa as a rugby player and later as a respected commentator. He was a trainee at Guinness in 1981, and the company initially came out with a statement, which said, "We don't support the rugby tour to South Africa, but we support freedom of choice and if any employee has holiday leave we can't tell them where they can and can't go." From Robbie's perspective, "That settled it. I was clear to travel." But once the Nigerian embassy weighed in criticizing the tour, Guinness changed its view. "One minute I could go, and then the next I couldn't go, so I resigned." Years later, he would reflect on his decision "with some embarrassment:" "There's absolutely no doubt that rugby was used by the South African government to keep morale high. Symbolically, it was wrong to go, I know that now and I admit it. To be totally honest, it was a selfish decision based on playing rugby, which my life was all about in those days. The old apartheid government got great comfort from rugby teams coming because they could say to the people, 'Look, we have friends in the world.'"[33]

Indeed, this quest for rugby friends proved central to the South African rugby strategy as they found themselves increasingly isolated, but Robbie later lamented that he contributed to satisfying that particular itch. "I wish for my own soul that I had said no," Robbie would say years later. Yet "I also think what if I'd taken the correct moral decision and stayed at home? What would I be doing now? I came to South Africa and I've lived here ever since. I became a radio presenter and spoke about the evils of apartheid. The decision to come was wrong, but in many ways that decision was the defining moment of my life."[34] Robbie moved to South Africa soon after the Ireland tour, playing provincial rugby for Transvaal and twice being picked for the Springboks, though he never earned a cap.

Flyhalf Ollie Campbell has nothing but praise for Robbie. "Through his work in the South African media, John played his part in dismantling apartheid. I'm not overstating it. He was a constant voice against apartheid, a really brave campaigner." Tony Ward, who had made the decision not to go, would say "I have great time for John Robbie. Johnny really tackled the system from within. I've got nothing but the highest respect for him."[35] It is clear that in assessing player motives for engaging or not engaging with South Africa, simply determining whether they played or whether they did not is insufficient.

Gerry McLaughlin found himself similarly torn. He taught at Sexton Street, a Christian Brothers school in Limerick. He, too, was given permission to go only to see that permission withdrawn. "There were protests in the school about why I was going. I could understand it." Nonetheless, "I wanted to go on tour so the most honorable thing to do was to resign my job." By his estimation, he paid a steep price upon his return from South Africa. "It cost me a lot financially, that tour. I had no job when I came back, and I had a mortgage to pay. It wasn't easy." Beyond that, "I was blacklisted. I couldn't get a job in a school anywhere in the country. I tried for 30 or 40 jobs and nothing," despite the fact that "I'd been teaching economics for 10 years before that. That's life. It was my decision to tour. I don't blame anyone for it." Much like John Robbie, the trip to South Africa, and the consequences he faced afterward, remained with him. He was appalled by what he saw when he and some teammates visited Soweto. The whole trip proved to be "a lesson for me and the images have stayed in my mind for the last 30 years of how people were treated." The trip would "have huge implications for my whole life afterwards." After much reflection, he concluded that "we're part of one big universe and why should people be treated" the way he saw in South Africa, why should they "not have the same opportunities as our children?" He would go on to continue to play for Ireland and would be chosen for the 1983 Lions tour and would later become a county councilor and then mayor of Limerick, representing the Labour Party. "What I saw in South Africa influenced the rest of my life in some ways. I'm sure of it."[36]

Ollie Campbell too looks back at his younger self with some self-chastisement. "I was twenty-six at the time, probably quite immature in the ways of the world, innocent, really." Certainly, many players from several countries who chose to play against South Africa looking back reflect on their innocence—hand-in-hand with the argument that sport and politics should not mix is an occasional admission that many athletes do not know or care enough about the politics to even have a say, and that their number one priority was simply to play a game they love. This should not provide absolution, but it does provide context. Campbell continues, "It's almost embarrassing to say it now, almost hollow, but all I wanted to do was play rugby. I was living and breathing it, totally immersed in it. That's my excuse and I'm sticking to it." That said, "I have fantastic admiration for the guys like Hugo and Wardy and the others who decided they couldn't travel."[37]

Willie Duggan, another future Ireland captain who may have been the finest Number 8 in Europe, took "the view . . . that we were playing sport, we weren't politicians. What was going on out there was wrong, but it wasn't down to us." His decision to go would occasionally crop up, as when "about 20 years later I was on a job and a woman said to me, 'you're the rugby player who went to South Africa.' And I said, 'I am.' And she said 'I'm not dealing with you," and I said, 'That's fine, no problem, you're entitled to your view.'"[38]

Because of the intensity of the protests against the tour, and fearing that officials at Dublin airport might stop them from departing, the Irish traveling squad had to leave their country incognito, in small groups. Aer Lingus officials had expressed concern that protesters would create "'handling' difficulties," including unwillingness on the part of the country's largely anti-apartheid labor unions to cooperate with the travel plans of a rugby team destined to play in South Africa.[39] So while some left from Dublin, others left from Shannon, Cork, and even Belfast. They gathered in London and, from there, the team departed for South Africa. As Irish captain Fergus Slattery—among the most unrepentant of the players who went on the South Africa tour— recalled, "We slipped out of the country quietly. It was heavy stuff. The government were like all governments. They had their head up their ass. They were saying you should reconsider this tour. What did they know about apartheid? Fuck all."[40]

One South African journalist asserted that the Irish squad "flew out to South Africa in the face of a degree of opposition at home that would have deterred men of lesser fibre."[41] On the other hand, the Irish *Independent* in 2013 called the tour "the sleaziest, grubbiest, nastiest tale in the history of Irish sport." One editorial, in describing the Irish departure, described "one of the most inglorious exits ever" by which "the IRFU team to misrepresent Ireland against South Africa slunk out of Dublin virtually in disguise and certainly, in the eyes of most of their fellow countrymen, in disgrace." According to Kader Asmal, the head of the Irish Anti-Apartheid Movement, they "Skulked out of the country like rats."[42]

Anti-apartheid activists inside and out of South Africa opposed the Irish visit, including the ANC and the UN Special Committee against Apartheid. Denis Hurley, the Archbishop of Durban, explicated what many believed: "This is not a sporting event. It is, whether or not the players or organizers choose to regard it as such, a political act." Ebrahim Patel of SARU, the multiracial rugby body that stood firm against apartheid rugby, identified "shock and anger within the black community. Ireland's betrayal of the black South African people by sending a rugby team on tour will never be forgotten."[43]

As was almost universally the case when a team toured in that era of rugby, Ireland also played a series of "provincial matches."[44] Sometimes these would consist of literal provincial teams, at the time the highest level of rugby after test matches for the national side and the occasional all-star squad, such as the Barbarians. But oftentimes these provincial teams might be cobbled together. In 1981, Ireland faced a number of such squads, and in the words of Ireland rugby historian and long-time *Irish Times* rugby correspondent Edmund van Esbeck, these provincial matches "were most disappointing and some of the opposition provided by the South Africans was ludicrous." Teams such as the South African Gazelles, South African Mining XV, the Gold Cup XV, the President's Trophy XV, and the South African Districts B side "were supposed to emphasize the multiracial nature of South African rugby. All they did was underline what a sham it was." The Gazelles (the Junior Springbok side) beat the Irish 18–15 in Pretoria and the Districts B side also beat the Irish 17–16, but the other three, the teams most cobbled together to put on a contrived face of a multiracial version of South African rugby that only existed in a Potemkin Village version of South Africa, went down to defeat by a combined score of 151–20.[45] The tourists beat SA Mining XV in Potchefstroom 46–7 and walloped the President's Trophy XV in East London 54–3, which represented the most points an Irish touring side had ever scored.

Craven defended the itinerary, despite the scorn that he had received in some Irish circles. "We attempted to meet the requests of the IRFU. Based on a merit selection and multiracial principle, it is true, we could not put provincial opposition into the field that would include non-white players if they were to be selected on merit." But, he continued, "Surely it must mean that, at this stage of our path along what we believe to be the right road, we have problems in that area. Any development of consequence needs time."[46]

Despite this mixed record in the warmup matches, and the fact that Ireland was playing shorthanded as a result of several injuries, as well as the anti-apartheid principles of Ward, Keane, McNeill, and Spring, they nearly stunned the Boks in the first Test match at Cape Town's legendary Newlands Stadium on May 30, 1980, with especially impressive mobile loose forward play (led by captain Fergus Slattery). Errol Tobias would make his surprise on-field debut in Springbok colors on that day.[47] Because South Africa allowed the visiting Irish to choose their preferred green kit, Tobias first appeared wearing a white jersey, not the traditional Bok green and gold. He played center, replacing the injured Willie du Plessis. Tobias was essential in creating one of the Bok tries, making an electrifying break that ultimately led to Rob Louw, Tobias' best friend during his time with the national side, touching down beyond the try line. South Africa emerged victorious in the hard-fought 23–15 contest in front of 40,000 fans at Newlands in a game that also saw Wynand Claassen's debut as Springbok captain.

The following week's test match was even tighter, with the home side squeaking by with a 12–10 win in Durban. Tobias had another fine game, but all the Springbok points came from the boot of Naas Botha, as the Boks escaped with a victory that easily could have gone the other way.[48] Ireland scored the only try of the match and out-rucked and out-scrummed the Boks. Only the sure boot of Botha, who surpassed 100 international points in the match, kept the Boks from losing a game that Ireland could feel hard done by not to have won. Slattery, the Irish captain, later insisted, "Bad decisions went against us," and that Claassen "came over to me after the game . . . and said that we did not deserve to lose. It was very gracious. We were unlucky."[49]

The desultory play of his team aside, Errol Tobias had caught the eye of scouts from New Zealand, who noted "It . . . doesn't matter whether the white Springboks want to play with him or not, because his three brilliant breaks" were all worthy of creating tries. The scout had gone to watch the great Danie Gerber on that day but had "bad news" for the All Blacks: "Tobias is a much bigger threat than Gerber."[50]

The team that had "skulked" out of Ireland "like rats" were feted by their hosts. One South African government minister "hailed" the Irish visitors as South Africa's "best friends," and Doc Craven described them as an example to the rest of the world, though these upstanding sportsmen are rumored to have been unwilling to meet with an Irish citizen who had been evicted from his home as the result of his anti-apartheid stance. Moreover, when the team returned to Ireland, tour manager Paddy Madigan not only raved about "a great tour," he repeated what had by then become a common assertion among apartheid's apologists despite its absurdity: "We had a great reaction from the South Africans . . . as far as rugby is concerned there is no Apartheid in South Africa."[51]

The defeats on the pitch may have served a larger rugby purpose for the Irish, however, as they went on to win the Five Nations Championship in 1982, which included an elusive Triple Crown. This represented Ireland's first Triple Crown in thirty-three years.[52] For South Africa, however, the road loomed, with the much-anticipated tour to New Zealand and the barely anticipated tour to America on the horizon. At least some of the Americans were preparing to confront the Springboks.

3

APART HATE

Planning to Resist the Springboks

PLANNING TO RESIST

The flyers started appearing in the Albany area in July 1981. In coffee shops and libraries, at bars and in restaurants, the one-page mimeographed sheet from "The Capital District Committee Against Apartheid," the address for which was an Albany post office box, called for readers to protest the system of Apartheid (helpfully telling them that it is "PRONOUNCED APART HATE."[1]) By the end of the decade, the crisis in South Africa had become a cause célèbre, with scenes from the townships in particular entering living rooms on the nightly news, on public broadcasting, and in the newly emerging twenty-four-hour cable news embodied by CNN but in 1981 this primer would have been necessary. In 1981, "apartheid" was not yet a household word. Indeed, the Capital District Committee Against Apartheid itself only emerged in direct response to the proposed rugby tour that would bring the Springboks to Albany.

The flyer provides the basic context for the sports boycott against South Africa (getting some details wrong in the process, like claiming that "the boycott has its origins in the 1966 call of the Supreme Council of Sport in Africa for a boycott of the Olympics if South Africa was allowed to participate," though the call to exclude South African sport long antedates 1966).[2] Then, finally, the flyer got to the main purpose:

Stopping the rugby tour. "The South African National Rugby Team (rugby is a ball game developed from soccer) is scheduled to play three games in the U.S. in September: Chicago, Albany and New York. This tour is a propaganda tool of the government of South Africa and its policy of Apartheid." Thus, at the bottom of the flyer, came the call to arms: "Say 'No' to Apartheid. Stop the South African rugby tour."[3] And it served as evidence that this sport, obscure in the United States, revered by white South Africans, would provide a flashpoint for opposition to the South African regime, an opposition that would accelerate dramatically over the course of the 1980s.

In a matter of weeks the tour opposition evolved from being relatively inchoate into a scattered, if still somewhat ad hoc, "Stop the Apartheid Rugby Tour" (SART) coalition including a number of organizations, such as the American Committee on Africa (ACOA) and Richard Lapchick's American Coordinating Committee for Equality in Sport and Society (ACCESS), that had been taking aim at apartheid and apartheid sport for years, and organizations such as The Capital District Committee Against Apartheid that emerged explicitly to confront the tour. ACOA's president, William Booth, chaired SART, though ACCESS continued to be at the forefront of the antitour movement. SART would eventually grow to encompass more than one hundred organizations.

The organizations that would form SART had begun to hear rumblings of the prospective tour almost from its earliest planning stages back in December 1980, even before President Reagan had taken office. Initially, those in the growing anti-apartheid community in the United States who opposed the tour hoped that the Reagan administration would step in and prevent the Springboks from landing on American shores, but this was the stuff of fantasy. Reagan had already committed his administration to a policy of "Constructive Engagement" that was not especially constructive but did rely on a great deal of engagement with Pretoria. Reagan believed that the appearance of the South African rugby team was, in the words of the *New York Times*, "a private sporting matter that" was "not within the jurisdiction of the Federal Government." The State Department had the ability to restrict or even refuse to issue visas, but Reagan was not inclined to pursue that option. The House Foreign Affairs Committee did approve a resolution that would "express the sense of Congress" that the Springboks should

not play in the United States, although the feeling was far from unanimous and the resolution was effectively nonbinding.[4] In the end, even
that symbolic resolution, which received 200 votes of support and 198
of opposition, failed to secure the two-thirds majority required to pass.

The new administration's approval of the Springbok visitors was in
keeping with its already-established policy of Constructive Engagement
toward the Apartheid government in Pretoria. By July 13, when the
Reagan State Department approved the visas for the tourists, the opposition had begun to coalesce. ACOA and ACCESS sent messages to
Chester Crocker at the State Department. William Booth's telegram
from ACOA read, "Urge you to announce refusal entry visas to South
African rugby team planning US trip following New Zealand tour allowing US games would signal indifference to apartheid and to domestic
and international public opinion."[5]

The Springbok American tour might have been planned largely in
secret, but some Africans became aware of the possibility and let their
concern be known. Nigeria's Kaduna News Service issued a news release pleading with the American government to reconsider their issuing of visas to the Boks, which represented "the latest in the spate of
America's flirtations with the racists in South Africa." Writing while the
Springboks faced the daily hostility of the mass protests in New Zealand
the editors believed that it was "still not too late for the Americans to
take the path of reason and adopt the soul-saving device of preventing
the anticipated tour," which they predicted would be met with "hostile"
reactions worldwide. Hinting at American hypocrisy, the Nigerians
noted, "America claims to be the most enlightened and civilized of
nations" yet "regrettably" it was "doubtful if openly fraternizing" with
South Africa, which "promotes hatred, oppression and racial discrimination as state policy," reflected this. The implication quite clearly was
that Americans could be accused of "uncivilized [. . .] behavior." The
growing "rapprochement between Washington and Pretoria is a threat
to the security of the entire African continent," an opinion that had
been made clear at the recent Organization of African Unity meeting in
Nairobi, Kenya. It was "remarkably pitiful that the racists in Pretoria are
having the open collaboration and support of Washington simply because America's foreign policy" was "now based on short-term self-
interests." The Reagan administration's "myopic view of the world in its
policy formulations, particularly as regards Africa fail[ed] to realize

that" without such support "apartheid could surely die a natural death."[6]

The pleas fell on deaf ears, with ACOA noting in a memo that the State Department "gave the usual reasons," that "It is not U.S. policy to interfere with private sports contacts; does not constitute an endorsement of the visit, etc." and that "all the players were screened individually and found 'eligible.'" Prime minister of New Zealand, Robert Muldoon, had earlier indicated that entry visas into his country for the Springbok contingent were conditioned on their receiving visas to the United States. A firmer policy from the American State Department with regard to the Springboks receiving visas could have stopped the entire 1981 tour in its tracks.[7]

The South African Non-Racial Olympic Committee (SANROC) also aggressively opposed the tour. Headed by South African poet, writer, and activist Dennis Brutus, in exile in the United States after numerous run-ins and arrests in his native country, SANROC had early on identified sport as a pressure point to use against the apartheid government. His organization noted that the proposed (but increasingly real) tour represented "a direct contravention of United Nations Resolutions calling for an embargo on all sporting and cultural exchanges with South Africa until the apartheid and racism have been removed in that country." Brutus and SANROC called for "all organisations to condemn this tour and to organize protests," as well as to contact President Reagan "and to call for the withholding of visas to these racists." He also called for the city councils in Chicago, Albany, and New York and the state legislatures in Illinois and New York "to adopt Resolutions condemning these visits and calling for the cancellation of this tour."[8] One day later, on July 15, the Phelps-Stokes Fund, which called for "Education for Human Development" called for the city of New York to prohibit the use of "any public facilities" by the Springboks and asserted its own opposition to the granting of visas to the South Africans.[9] Vladimir A. Kravets, the Ukranian acting chair of the United Nations Special Committee Against Apartheid issued a statement on behalf of his committee condemning the tour, expressing "grave concern" with the American Rugby Union's having been "enticed by South African propaganda" and "deplor[ing] the maneouvres of those sporting bodies aimed at assisting the apartheid regime to break its isolation from international sports" as "such efforts represent an absolute insensitivity to the feelings of the people of South Africa."[10] The multipronged effort to stop the tour had quickly kicked into gear.

But of the organizations that were part of the SART coalition AC-CESS was the most active. Indeed, ACCESS, itself a coalition of more than two dozen organizations, had been on top of the question of apartheid sport generally and of the Springbok place in international rugby—believing there was no place for them—for years. Lapchick took a multipronged approach to tackling the tour. He contacted William Haffner, president of the Eastern Rugby Football Union that was to host the Springboks when they were in New York and Albany, in hopes of getting his organization to turn its back on the Boks. "I want to inform you that your invitation is being viewed as a grave violation of the international boycott against South Africa in sport," and ACCESS, "a coalition of 30 national civil rights, religious, political and sports groups" was prepared "to take action to stop the tour." For ACCESS and Lapchick, the Springboks obviously represented "the apartheid state," and that the tour would be nominally integrated "to deceive overseas audiences as to the true nature of apartheid." Lapchick noted that club sports in South Africa were virtually entirely segregated, and even where multiracial teams were allowed to compete, "after the games end, blacks return to their segregated housing facilities, receive vastly inferior education, work as unskilled laborers, and have no control over their lives." Lapchick wanted the Eastern Rugby Union to cancel their invitation to the Springboks, if for no other reason than that the tour might jeopardize the 1984 Olympics. He also explained that already the Springbok presence in New Zealand had led to massive protests in that country.

In case Haffner doubted ACCESS's potential efficacy, Lapchick reminded him that his organization was behind 1978 protests against the South African Davis Cup tennis team's presence in Nashville, which roused 6,500 demonstrators, and that he was prepared to do the same in Chicago, New York City, and Albany. He also planned to submit the names of any American athletes who competed against the Springboks to the United Nations Center Against Apartheid, a list that would preclude them from competing in other countries. This latter threat seemed ominous, and yet the odds that American rugby players had many international prospects were negligible. Still, "rugby is a new sport in America," Lapchick asserted (wrongly—rugby was a small sport in the United States, not a new one), "We urge you to cancel this tour so that its image will not be tarnished at its birth."[11]

The organization publicly condemned the granting of visas to the Springbok touring party, excoriating the Reagan administration, and arguing that the State Department's granting of visas represented "part of the package being delivered" to the apartheid state by Reagan. "It is consistent with all the moves the Administration has made so far regarding South Africa," which was "suddenly a strategic ally" and so the State Department "now has to convince the American people that apartheid is being softened. What better way to convince the public than by bringing a series" of "South African teams to the United States."[12] Echoing the calls of Phelps-Stokes, SANROC, and other organizations, ACCESS called on the governors of New York and Illinois to deny use of public facilities to the rugby tour.[13] In a mass mailing sent out to coalition members, friendly allies, and dozens of others, Lapchick made his urgency quite clear: "Action Alert!—The South Africans are Coming" and referring to rugby as "the most segregated sport in the most segregated society in the world." The fact that several members of the touring team were members of the South African Defence Force (SADF) and South African Police just made matters more urgent.[14]

All this work and coordination culminated in the formation of Stop the Apartheid Rugby Tour in the second half of July. A planning meeting held at the Organization of African Unity headquarters in New York soon after the Springboks passed through Kennedy airport en route to New Zealand resulted in the announcement of the establishment of the formation of SART. Most of the organized resistance to the tour, especially to the planned matches in Albany and on Randall's Island in New York, would take place beneath the SART umbrella.[15]

Opposition to the tour would expand throughout July, August, and September, with SART establishing affiliates and putting in place structures in Chicago and Albany, the scheduled cities for two of the matches. Valuable support came from a breakaway group of "rugby dissidents" who came from the "rank and file" of the American rugby structure. These individuals formed Against South Africans Playing (ASAP) and helped provide "valuable information on the tour to SART." The local affiliates of SART and the national organization prepared protest demonstrations in those two cities as well as in New York, which was originally to host the Springbok-American Eagles test match.[16]

From the outset, the American supporters of the tour remained both adamant that the tour would go on and obstinate in the face of the growing (but still, on the whole, modest) opposition. SART representatives met with the American rugby officials at the Phelps-Stokes Fund, a meeting brokered by William Robinson, but got nowhere. This may well have been, as SART discovered later and as the *Washington Post* reported, because the Eastern Rugby Union, which had been central to masterminding the Springbok tour, had received $25,000—a sum that represented more than five times the ERU's 1980 budget—from Louis Luyt. Luyt had been a central figure in the Information Scandal, serving as an illegal "conduit for funding secret government propaganda projects, including placement of full-page advertisements in international newspapers on behalf of a 'Committee for Fairness in Sport.'" It was further rumored that ERU president Tom Selfridge had received an additional $50,000 from the South African Rugby Board.[17] The $75,000 represented a pittance—and money well spent—in the context of the international South African propaganda and disinformation campaign.

Similarly, on September 25, 1981, long after the controversies had erupted, the *Boston Globe* reported that South Africa's rugby board had paid the Eastern Rugby Union, the sponsors of the Springbok tour, $50,000, a king's ransom for an American rugby club, even the national side, in 1981. William Haffner, the Eastern Rugby Union's treasurer, claimed to be unaware of any transfer of funds to the union.[18]

And yet, at least some of the most unseemly accusations seem plainly false, or at least to misrepresent exactly what happened. From the outset, American fixtures secretary Ed Lee had made clear that the SARB or its benefactors would have to fund the trip, including American expenses. Alex Kellermann explained the process in a letter to the USARFU:

> The original request came to the S.A. Rugby Board from Mr. Tom Selfridge via Mr. Louis Luyt. It was then discussed by the Finance and Executive Committees of the S. A. Rugby Board and full power was given to Dr. Craven and the Chairman of our Finance Committee, Mr. J. A .J. Pickard, to ascertain from the USARFU the expected shortfall and that they be allowed to transfer a maximum amount of

$50,000 in respect of the shortfall on the U.S.A. section of the Springbok tour.[19]

In July 1981, Kellermann telegrammed Tom Selfridge to let him know that "our bankers have confirmed transfer fifty thousand dollars via Barclays Bank to Schenectady Trust Account Eastern Rugby Union."[20] Kellermann followed up a few days later with a letter to confirm receipt of the funds and to deal with arrangements for the tour.

After the tour was completed, Keith Seaber, a lawyer and the secretary of the USARFU, sent Kellermann a telegram dated October 8. "Executive Committee request you please indicate by return one of the following $50,000 was: 1. Loan to USARFU 2. Gift to USARFU 3. Loan to ERU 4. Gift to ERU 5. In trust to ERU on behalf of USARFU for tour expenses." The SARB responded, "S.A. Rugby Board regarded monies as donation to your Union via trust account of ERU but you advised Craven that USARFU view same as advance and wishes to repay."[21] The USARFU planned to refund the money that had been deposited. It is unclear when or if that happened, though a letter from Kellermann to Keith Seaber, the USARFU secretary, indicated that "at an [SARB] Executive Committee meeting on September 4, 1981, the President of the Board reported that the Secretary of the USARFU advised him by telephone that the $50,000 which the S.A. Rugby Board had paid over to the trust account of ERU in respect of the tour, will be refunded by the USARFU."[22] It seems clear that there was no attempt on the part of individuals or organizations on the American side to use the tour for profit.

The American rugby officials claimed that all expenses would be covered by the Springboks, "local funds" of the American rugby unions involved in the invitation, and any money that the tour earned. However, the American Committee on Africa reported that "a letter leaked by someone from Citibank revealed that the ERFU approached the bank asking for financial support for the tour, with the option of being either a recognized or anonymous sponsor."[23] The letter claimed that Citibank "will benefit from this support in the South African community." The American sponsors also "approached a large number of other U.S. corporations" requesting funding, but this appears not to have been successful.[24]

Everything on the financial side, then, appears to be aboveboard, if in the eyes of some maybe a bit sketchy. For the American supporters of the tour, or at least its sponsors, maybe the Springbok visit really was not about politics. But it also does not appear to have been about money, or at least profits.

SPRINGBOKS IN TRANSIT: NASCENT ANTI-SPRINGBOK PROTEST IN THE UNITED STATES

The antitour protesters had their chance to take on the South African rugby team even before the September tour. As a pariah team traveling from a pariah nation, the South Africans had discovered that much of the Western world had established serious restrictions on or prohibition of South African athletic teams well beyond simply refusing to play them. Thus, when the Springboks left South Africa in July 1981 for the epochal New Zealand tour, they found that simply getting there had become a headache. Australia refused them transit, and given that most points of access to New Zealand required passage through Australia, the Bok tour there almost died aborning.

Except that the South Africans had already come to realize that they could depend upon the friendly and quiescent Reagan administration to facilitate them. As an editorial in the *Cape Times* observed, "There is a readiness in Pretoria to trust President Reagan, a new willingness to cooperate which was never in evidence in President Carter's day. In Washington, in turn, there is a willingness to try constructive engagement with South Africa."[25] Thus, when the United States allowed the South Africans to receive travel visas, the goal was as much to allow them passage through the United States as to allow them eventual return for the rugby on American soil in September. American groups protested the issuing of visas on July 13, to no avail. The State Department announced that there were "no grounds to deny" the visas to the South Africans, and, in one of the most brazen falsehoods in an American summer grounded in falsehoods, asserted "The U.S. government can't decide to issue visas to groups if it doesn't like them; the issuance does not imply approval or disapproval."[26] This was utter nonsense. Indeed, the 1952 Immigration and Nationality Act, better known as the McCarran–Walter Act, had passed after an override of President

Harry Truman's veto and blistering opposition. The law, a McCarthy-era relic, specifically allowed for the exclusion of foreigners for their political leanings and had been used against a host of writers, artists, and others whose politics were deemed a threat to the United States. By the middle of the Reagan years, this list would include "tens of thousands of names." Among those excluded in the three decades after the act's passage were Nobel laureates Pablo Neruda, Gabriel García Márquez, foreign politicians invited by American institutions to speak, and literally thousands of others. And far from providing a brake on this sort of denial of entry, the Reagan administration, with the full support of conservative writers and politicians, allowed these denials to accelerate significantly. The administration could have chosen to deny the South Africans visas to pass through and come to the United States. It chose not to.[27]

With the granting of visas came an acceleration of the opposition to the upcoming tour—on July 14, ACCESS (which had already sent a message in April pleading with New Zealand not to host the Springboks) sent telegrams to the mayors and city councils where the September games were scheduled, as well as to the governors of Illinois and New York, asking that localities and the states prohibit the use of municipal or state facilities for any rugby matches featuring the South Africans.[28]

By the time the Springboks arrived in transit at JFK airport in New York on July 16, ACCESS had organized an early morning demonstration. The team arrived at 6:00 a.m. and found themselves confronted with a small group there "to protest their tour" and to "remind . . . them that they are not welcomed in the U.S." Revelations that four members of the Springbok traveling squad were members of the South African Defense Force and that two were policemen (who were primarily responsible for enforcing apartheid laws) seemed to validate the ire of the protesters. Further revealing the complicity of not only the American government but also American corporations was the announcement that the U.S. Rugby Football Union had sought loan support from Citibank, which was deeply complicit in lending to South Africa.[29]

Errol Tobias, the first black player to don a Springbok jersey, took some particularly ruthless criticism from the protesters, who according to at least one observer on the Bok team, may have represented a mix of ANC and PAC exiles. Some of the protesters shouted at them in Afrikaans, one screaming at Tobias, "Go home, *kaffir* [An ugly racist term in South Africa]!" Although he was clearly upset by being targeted, Tobias screamed back in Afrikaans, "Don't worry, this Hotnot [another ugly racial slur] is only going home a month-and-a-half from now!"[30]

During a layover in Los Angeles, the Springbok touring party managed to find a little bit of rest and relaxation, spending much of a day at Disneyland. Div Visser, a lock from the Western Province, remembered scattered bits of Disneyland decades later. "I just remember all the man-made stuff was impressive" to the point where "I saw this beautiful fish in the water and then later" realized that it was fake. He remembers going on a roller coaster and then "just strolled through all the different presentations." Although he did not remember much in detail from one day of leisure during that tumultuous period, he would recall that Disneyland happened before the New Zealand tour "because we were not injured and stiff from the rugby . . . we were still fresh and fired up for lots of rugby."[31] This was likely the last peaceful day the South Africans would experience.

On July 17, another demonstration confronted the Springboks, this time as they prepared to leave Los Angeles International Airport where the South Africans were finally to fly directly to New Zealand. The Boks had briefly encountered the United States, but not for the last time.

In the midst of the Springboks touching down in America twice, the SART coalition was launched (a communication campaign), with each constituent group involved in the alliance sending a telex to Los Angeles mayor Tom Bradley calling for a public statement denouncing the stopover of the South Africans in Los Angeles later that day. Los Angeles was scheduled to host the Summer Olympics in 1984, and anti-apartheid groups had come to realize that as a consequence they held some leverage in dealing with city officials. When ACCESS contacted Los Angeles councilman Robert Ferrell to ask him to make a statement on the Springbok passage through his city he agreed, presenting it on July 20, after the Bok party had already passed through the City of Angels.

ACCESS got a similar resolution to that in Los Angeles before the New York state assembly—too late to have an effect on the Springbok passage through the United States, but indicative of the rising concern with the Springboks and what they embodied.[32]

THE FINAL PREPARATIONS

By July 1981, Alex Kellermann was in regular contact with American rugby officials, including "almost daily" telephone calls and "a number of letters going backwards and forwards" between him and Tom Self-ridge, who had clearly become the American point person for the Bok tour. The identity of the membership of the executive committee of SARB that would visit the United States was still in flux, and sadly, Hannes Pretorius, who along with Kellermann had met with Doug Reid at the Daniel Malan Airport in Cape Town in July 1980, had died from a heart attack back in January. Kellermann and Selfridge planned logistics such as team lodging, with the South Africans preferring a suite for the Springbok manager, singles with a bath for the two assistant managers, the team doctor, as well as for the team's captain, Wynand Claasen, and vice captain, Theuns Stofberg. The other twenty-eight members of the touring team would require double rooms ("with bath"). If there were not sufficient single rooms for Claasen and Stofberg, the Americans could book one more double room. They also wanted a "team-room with seating for 35 persons, for their exclusive use," information about the hotels at which the teams would be staying, and "a full list of the entertainment which the team must attend and which you have cleared with security."[33]

But before the Boks would play rugby in the United States, they had to face New Zealand. In rugby terms, All Blacks–Springboks represented an epic clash, the greatest the sport had to offer on planet Earth. The Springboks had no idea that the clashes on the field would pale in comparison with what would happen off of and all around it.

4

THE 1981 SPRINGBOK TOUR TO NEW ZEALAND

A Country Divided

TROUBLE COMING

"I can see nothing but trouble coming from this." That was New Zealand prime minister Robert Muldoon's response when he was told that the New Zealand Rugby Football Union was going forward with the invitation to the Springboks to tour in 1981.[1]

And go forward they did. Fifty-seven days. Sixteen matches, two of which were canceled. Three test matches. A government assertion of $7.2 million dollars spent on policing and other security (that might have been underestimated substantially). Nearly 2,000 people arrested, with 1,520 charged for 2,254 offenses, an estimated 35 percent of whom escaped conviction. Barbed wire around playing fields. Police in batons and riot gear. Glass and nails strewn on pitches. One airplane flying over the pitch dropping "flour bombs." Families, friends, coworkers, neighbors, and one society profoundly divided.

The 1981 Springbok tour was an epochal moment in the history of New Zealand. At least one assessment calls it "the most divisive event in New Zealand since the 'Great Strike' of 1913," a general strike that lasted from October 1913 through January 1914 and was characterized by violence, disruption, and broad social upheaval. Far more than just a conflict over sport, it revealed deep fissures in a society that saw itself as civil and friendly and reasonable, liberal in outlook and conservative in temperament. Yet New Zealand long had its own racial divisions over the place of Maoris in the country and more broadly the place of all Pacific Islanders, many of whom had immigrated and who found themselves second-class citizens. These tensions had manifested in many ways, including in rugby, where the country's national team had oftentimes accommodated South African demands not to play its Maori players. The 1981 tour arguably divided New Zealand unlike anything before and certainly more than anything since.

The conflict over allowing the Springboks, a clear embodiment of apartheid, to tour was exacerbated by the fact that the Springboks were not just any other team. They were the All Blacks' main rivals, their most legitimate competition, a team that managed to have a winning record against them despite rugby being unquestionably New Zealand's number one sporting passion by a long way. And in an era when the teams did not play every year, when tours were planned years in advance and anticipated for just as long, test matches between the two sides were a big deal. To complicate matters, in South Africa, many anti-apartheid advocates chose to publicly support the All Blacks whenever they clashed with the Springboks, a form of everyday resistance against an increasingly draconian apartheid state.

SPRINGBOKS VERSUS THE ALL BLACKS

From the first Springbok versus All Blacks match in August 1921, the first in a three-match series of tests in New Zealand, to the eve of the first 1981 test in Christchurch in August 1981, a span of almost exactly sixty years, the two teams played thirty-four times across nine series, five in South Africa and four in New Zealand. The Springboks won nineteen matches and five series, the All Blacks thirteen matches and two series, with two matches and two series resulting in draws.

Prior to the Second World War, New Zealand had accommodated South Africa's requests that they leave their Maori players at home when they visited South Africa and exclude them from selection when the two teams met in New Zealand. The issue received some mention among liberals on the eve of the 1949 tour, but to no real avail, as the biggest story that emerged from that first apartheid-era tour was a humiliating four-test sweep defeat at the hands of the Springboks on South African soil. Critics were even more vocal on the eve of the 1956 tour, but once again, with little concrete impact, as the emphasis seemed to be on revenge for the 1949 humiliations.

But after the 1956 tour, increasing numbers of New Zealanders realized that there was no viable way to separate sport from politics. Initial New Zealand resistance to engagement-as-usual with the Springboks emerged over the Maori question and not more generally on South Africa's apartheid system. By 1959, the planned 1960 tour of South Africa ran headlong into "No Maoris, No Tour" protests and petitions endorsed by both New Zealanders and South Africans. The Sharpeville Massacre of March 21, 1960, merely served to exacerbate antitour protests. In that event, police opened fire on anti-pass law protesters organized by the Pan African Congress, killing dozens and wounding scores more, the bulk in the back and sides, indicating that they posed literally no threat to police as they fled the chaos. Sharpeville had direct impact on the global anti-apartheid sports movement as it revealed just how brutally intransigent the apartheid regime was. The 1960 tour nonetheless went on, with no Maori players for the All Blacks, the last time this would happen in the engagement between the two teams.

From 1965 on, Maoris would be allowed, at the insistence of New Zealand rugby and government officials, though during the 1965 tour South African politicians, including Prime Minister Hendrick Verwoerd, indicated that a planned 1967 New Zealand tour of South Africa would not allow Maori players, tossing a match into the kindling of controversy and leading observers to believe that they might have seen the end of rugby engagements between the two countries. When Maori players would join the All Blacks in future South Africa tours, South Africa would designate them "honorary whites." It was clear that South African officials knew that an unyielding approach to the Maori issue would result in no longer being able to play New Zealand, which would make them increasingly irrelevant in world rugby. And indeed, the 1967 Springbok tour would in fact not go on as the New Zealand Rugby Football Union, under pressure from New Zealand's conservative National Party prime minister, Keith Holyoake, canceled it, sending a clear message to South African rugby that change needed to happen or else the Springboks would lose their chief rugby rivals.

The 1965 Springbok tour of New Zealand and the 1970 All Black tour to South Africa (in both cases the host team won three tests of four) saw increasing protests on the New Zealand side. The 1970 All Blacks included three Maoris (Sid Going, Buff Milner, and Blair Furlong) and a Samoan player (Bryan Williams). In 1969, students at the University of Auckland formed Halt All Racist Tours (HART), an anti-apartheid tour movement that would take center stage in the debates over New Zealand engagement with South African sport and especially rugby. It is worth noting that while Maori inclusion was the initial rallying cause for the protests, HART and the anti-apartheid tours movement more broadly was dominated by Pakeha (white) New Zealanders. In 1973, the Springboks were scheduled to tour New Zealand again, but the tone of antitour activists was clearly different, more assertive, and more radical than in prior years, and Norman Kirk, the newly elected Labour prime minister, who in the run-up to the election claimed that he would not interfere in any planned South African tours, changed course, and canceled the scheduled 1973 Springbok visit, handing CARE, HART, and their partner organizations a victory.

1976 AND ALL THAT

The 1976 tour of South Africa would prove to be the most problematic yet. The protest movement in New Zealand and worldwide had been emboldened, especially after events in the UK and Australia between 1969 and 1971 and the successes of HART in getting the antitour movement on the political radar beyond the Maori question. Indeed, after the cancellation of the 1973 tour it was clear that the very idea of sporting contacts with South Africa had become problematic and that tinkering—allowing Maoris and Pacific islanders to play, the granting of "honorary white" status, marginal reforms to apartheid—would no longer be sufficient to forestall serious criticism. On the pitch once again, the hosts, this time South Africa, won the test series three matches to one. But for most in South Africa, worldwide rugby could not have mattered less in the winter of 1976, as two weeks prior to the first provincial match against the Border Invitation XV in East London in the eastern Cape, the country had once again exploded, this time as the result of the Soweto Uprising. That eruption of popular protest began in the massive South-West Township outside of Johannesburg, where black students had risen to protest the implementation of Afrikaans as a medium of instruction in all schools. Of course, the protests were about so much more. They were about apartheid's indignities, about its injustices, about its crimes against humanity. Thus, once again, South Africa's apartheid policies drew global attention and made the New Zealand decision to tour the country look all the more dubious.

At the same time, perhaps no country's defenders were as adroit at counterpropaganda as South's Africa's by the mid-1970s. Thus, even as pamphlets calling for the All Blacks not to tour in 1976 gained wide currency in New Zealand, as 1976 progressed so too did a glossy, professionally produced pamphlet, "Rugby in South Africa: The Facts," touting legitimate changes in South African rugby in recent years, overstating the extent of those changes, most of which were modest, and underplaying the comprehensive nature of apartheid at the local, provincial, and national levels that had caused anti-apartheid sport activists to develop the slogan "no normal sport in an abnormal society."[2] At roughly the same time, a "Friends of the Springbok Association" opened in New Zealand. Based in Auckland, the organization sought to cultivate ties between those who might have friends and family in South Africa but also to sell a particular image of South Africa for those who might be inclined to provide support for the country and perhaps spread a friendly message.

The New Zealand tour took place on the eve of the 1976 Olympic Games in Montreal, and more than a score of African nations had made clear that New Zealand's engagement with apartheid Africa was unacceptable. Once New Zealand chose to tour South Africa and the International Olympic Committee refused to ban New Zealand's Olympic team from participating in the Montreal Games, twenty-nine countries withdrew from the Olympics as a direct consequence. Newly emboldened, and in most cases, relatively newly independent African nations took their nationalism and their opposition to apartheid seriously and put their principles ahead of their Olympic dreams.

MULDOON

Prime Minister Robert Muldoon had believed that the NZRFU would ultimately call off the tour in light of heightened global and local scrutiny of apartheid. As he wrote President Kaunda of Zambia, "My Government has made it very clear to the New Zealand Rugby Union that we do not wish the tour to take place. Over many months we have told the Rugby Union, both publicly and privately, that the proposed tour will do immense damage to New Zealand and . . . the whole Commonwealth." But he had also promised not to intervene in such decisions on the campaign trail, and he did not want to reverse course as Norman Kirk had done.[3] His deputy prime minister and foreign minister, Brian Talboys, was vocally and ardently against the Springbok tour, but he had been unable to convince either the NZRFU to cancel the tour nor was he able to get Muldoon to act more assertively.

Muldoon, one of the longest serving prime ministers in the history of New Zealand, could be abrasive and hypersensitive to criticism. He was rarely reflective or apologetic about his actions. And this, more than anything, would come to characterize his leadership when it came to the Springbok tour. He would lash out at his critics, including African heads of state, claiming that they ignored violence in their own backyards, a dangerous bit of whataboutism that could come across as condescending and occasionally racist. In the words of a South African anti-apartheid publication, "Muldoon was determined to use the tour to whip his political opponents and demonstrate his firmness to those rugby-mad New Zealanders who support him and who think the world is oval-shaped and can be kicked around."[4]

Muldoon believed that once he had failed to convince the NZRFU to rescind the invitation to the Springboks, it was his responsibility to let the tour go forward. Many of his critics believed that had he more forcefully referred to the Gleaneagles Agreement and insisted that it was binding he may have been able to twist the NZRFU's arms. But he also turned the clashes over the Springbok tour into a law-and-order issue, an assertion that usually proves to be more sloganeering than policy any time it is invoked.

PREPARING FOR BATTLE

HART and affiliated organizations—Citizens Against the Tour (CAT), The Citizens Association for Racial Equality (CARE), Citizens Opposed to the Springboks Tour (COST)—kicked into gear nearly as soon as they knew the Springboks were arriving in New Zealand, printing flyers and holding organizational meetings and strategy sessions, launching letter-mailing campaigns and staging preparatory rallies. While the largest focus would inevitably fall on the test matches in Christchurch on the South Island and Wellington and Auckland on the North Island, every one of the planned matches with provincial and other local and select sides would meet with protests.

New Zealand had cultivated a reputation for racial harmony and many protesters felt it important to use the Springbok tour to raise awareness of Maori rights and racial issues in the country. Others drew parallels with anticolonial struggles. And not a few drew comparisons between South Africa, New Zealand, and the US civil rights movement. And of course, there would be plenty of hangers on, those who may have opposed apartheid, liked the idea of protest, and wanted to be in the center of the promised action. Some were there for the carnival atmosphere.

The antitour movement was deeply committed to nonviolence, to direct-action protests, civil disobedience, and to a wide range of demonstrations. Yet violence occurred for lots of reasons: indiscipline, newcomers to protest not necessarily committed to nonviolence, a percentage of radicals committed to the cause but not to the tactic, the presence of pro-tour folks happy to use violence (and to thus garner a response) and the presence of police, especially the newly created Red Squad (formally the Red Escort Group), and Blue Squad (a far smaller organization that operated predominantly in Wellington), both of which oftentimes exacerbated and frequently initiated violence. They were the first New Zealand police squads in the country's history to be equipped with full riot gear, including visored helmets and the so-called "side-handle" or "long baton," all of which managed both to limit accountability, as police were virtually anonymous, and to encourage violence, as police with militarized equipment tend to use that equipment. In the minds of many antitour protesters, the Red Squad and the police more generally were simply "New Zealand's top street gang."[5]

Meanwhile as the tour approached All Blacks captain Graham Mourie made an announcement that reverberated across the rugby world: he simply could not play against the South Africans. He had not been the first All Black to declare his opposition to apartheid, but, as the first captain to do so, he was the most prominent. Mourie had suffered a rib injury at the trials for the 1976 Springbok tour but has acknowledged that he would have gone had he been selected. "At that stage of my career," he recalled, "any purer motives of morality, responsibility to my country and the greater game of rugby were quickly sublimated by the desire to be an All Black."[6] This is an understandable sentiment from a young athlete who had spent a considerable portion of his life with dreams of making the national team, with playing at the highest levels of sport. But it also is what makes his decision to not play in 1981 so admirable.

Mourie had gone from not making the All Blacks team for 1976 to being named captain by November 1977. When the All Blacks left for South Africa in 1976, he was twenty-three years old. By the time he made the decision in 1980 not to tour South Africa the next year, he was twenty-eight. As the tour approached, he continually "evaluated the information available" but "it was increasingly becoming clear that the situation in South Africa and its ramifications for New Zealand rugby were decidedly not to my liking." He had been given an opportunity to travel to South Africa for an invitation game as part of a "world" team but could not go because of a previous playing commitment with his provincial club, Taranaki, which toured Europe and Japan at roughly the same time. He later expressed that he wished he had gone to be able to see apartheid up close. Through 1979, he continued to weigh his options, asking other internationals what they thought, but also assuming that because of Gleneagles either the NZRFU or the government would call off the Springbok visit.[7]

He reflected in a notebook that he was keeping at the time that he had announced that day, November 17, 1980, that he would not be playing against South Africa, "a decision that I had in reality made some time ago, but never brought to the light of day." Mourie feared that by not playing, "I was betraying a cause which had been very good to me" but this was overshadowed by the fear he would face if he did choose to play: "Fear of being dishonest to myself. A question of conscience. A question of not being selfish (of admitting that I would love to play against the Springboks)." Moreover, Mourie also believed "the tour is wrong—for morality, for rugby because the controversy and the effects of the tour will be bad for the game."[8]

Naturally, Mourie found a great deal of support and faced considerable criticism for his decision, effectively reflecting the state of the debate in New Zealand in 1981. But he did not look back and, after the Springbok tour, he returned as All Blacks captain, a position he would maintain until September 1982.

All Black center Bruce Robertson announced his opposition to the tour, arguing that he had been disillusioned by witnessing apartheid up close on the 1976 tour. A host of former All Blacks echoed Robertson's sentiment, including Ken Gray; Bob Burgess; Mick O'Callahan; former All Black captain Chris Laidlaw; John Graham; Bevan Holmes; and, perhaps most significantly, Wilson Whineray, who had captained the All Blacks from 1958 through 1965, which included two Springbok tours.

Other players made different choices, but not necessarily lightly. Fullback Allan Hewson's own household was a house divided: his wife was ardently against the tour, "a problem," Hewson's biographer writes, "which undoubtedly arose in many New Zealand homes in 1981." And as in the Hewson home, most of them "squared up to it as best they could. They felt trapped: that whatever they individually did, they couldn't win." This was Hewson's dilemma, one he handled as best he could. "He earnestly defended his right to play rugby against anyone, just as he acknowledged the antitour people's right to protest within the law." His wife Pauline's objections were straightforward. "I objected to the principle of apartheid and I didn't agree with the tour. I wasn't prepared to march against the tour but nor did I attend any of the matches. I made my protest by staying away." She claimed that at least one All Blacks wife went a step further, actively participating in protests. Hewson asked a basic question. "I appreciate why many people oppose contact with South Africa, but would the abandonment of a rugby tour promote the cause of the oppressed people there? I would say rugby contact has done more than isolation would have."[9]

Other All Blacks took the approach that they were rugby players and play they would, especially against the Springboks. "As a sportsman I defend my right to play against whoever I wish," the giant, outspoken lock Andy Haden argued in a book of reflections on rugby that he published even as his All Black and Auckland playing career was ongoing. "The simple criteria I have always applied is, do they play rugby? Their country's politics are irrelevant." This was not, he emphasized, "a bridges-building philosophy; I don't even offer that as an excuse. Very simply, I am a rugby player and see no cause to discriminate between would-be opponents." Perhaps refreshingly, Haden rejected one of the main clichés that infect these sorts of discussions. "To say that politics and sport should not be mixed is too idealistic. They are inexplicably mixed and they always will be." Instead, he believed that "The sportsmen of today must face that and prepare accordingly, appreciating that sport is of major importance for politicians, if a dangerous platform for a politician to tread."[10]

The Springboks, meanwhile, were under no illusions that the tour would be easy, though they also surely had no idea what they were in for. Captain Wynand Claassen wrote in a posttour report to the SARB, "All of us realised from the start that" the entire New Zealand trip "was going to be a difficult tour. On the field of play without doubt, but events off the field would demand far greater commitment from every player and member of the touring party."[11]

JULY 22: THE DAY OF SHAME

Critics of the tour would dub the first official match day, Wednesday, July 22, the "Day of Shame." The Springboks, who had arrived on July 19, would play Poverty Bay and would win by a 24–6 score. Errol Tobias, who would play in none of the tests, scored his first try in New Zealand in this match, confirming in his mind and in the mind of Abe Williams, but, he also believed, in the eyes of New Zealanders, that there should no longer be any question about his role on the team. Indeed, after Williams asserted that the New Zealand scouts had posited that Tobias posed a bigger threat to the All Blacks than stalwart Danie Gerber, Williams was no longer allowed to speak with the media.

But the real story was not what happened in the match. Much of the attention was on events at Gisborne, a small city on the northeastern part of the North Island, where the game was played. The media had amassed there after all, and there were protests, and police countermaneuvers, and all of the expected drama featuring friends of rugby and foes of apartheid, protesters and police, "anti's" and "pros." Claassen noted that the Springbok party "were all rather surprised to find the place surrounded by barricades with a large police force contingent in attendance."[12] Before long barricades and massive police presence would be part of the daily routine for the players.

Events connected to "The Day of Shame" were hardly limited to Gisborne, and indicative of the nationwide nature of the demands to stop the tour, there were simultaneous protests and counterdemonstrations, marches, and rallies in virtually every city and town in New Zealand, including large events in Christchurch, Wellington, and Auckland.

Geoff Chapple of the organization Mobilisation to Stop the Tour (MOST) has written a book about the 1981 tour in which he has addressed the issue of the protests and the allegations that those who opposed them were merely committed to "law and order." The Day of Shame served to bring out these dynamics. For Chapple and his colleagues, the goal was, simply, "to stop the tour." Thus "the only way forward for the movement was through the law." This "meant disruption" and "to stretch the police and make the tour itself unmanageable." This "meant establishing as goals and targets the institutions which had brought the tour on." Those who had been at the center of organizing the tour understood these dynamics, "but how far the movement at large would come on in support of those goals, or into mass civil disobedience, was unknown as the Day of Shame dawned." As the day reached dusk, "it was clear a new history had been posted right across New Zealand. Stop the tour. The goal was alive, the law, as it had to be, was under challenge, and the police hadn't coped."[13]

Thousands had marched in the major cities, hundreds in a dozen or more other municipalities. They carried signs with slogans like "Stop the Tour" and hung banners from windows and chanted the anti-apartheid slogan from South Africa, "Amandla!" They danced and sang and chanted and shouted. "It was a people's protest of a size and style New Zealand hadn't witnessed before," according to Chapple. "The boom of crowds in every city, but above all else those crowds were now acting alone. They had been dismissed as impotent by the formal political process. Now they were divorced from that, alone and potent. The police were shut out."[14] In other words, "law and order" was a political slogan, an alibi, and thus irrelevant to protesters who felt excluded from the tenets of law and order and who felt as if any disorder fell on the government and its police force.

A WIN FOR THE PROTESTERS: HAMILTON, JULY 25

Hamilton also saw protests on the "Day of Shame," but its day in the limelight would come on Saturday, July 25. On that day, protesters had geared up for the first major on-pitch challenge, and early on, about 350 protesters tore down a fence and stormed the pitch at Rugby Park in Hamilton, New Zealand's fourth largest city and metropolitan area, and one of the heartlands of New Zealand rugby. Counterprotesters who either had become activists for the tour or who simply wanted to watch rugby grew ugly, tossing bottles and other projectiles at the protesters. Then came the rumors that Pat McQuarrie, a fifty-nine-year-old rugby man, one-time accomplished fighter pilot, and a staunch opponent of the tour, had gotten hold of a plane and was planning to fly it near, over, or around the stadium. McQuarrie had lost his pilot's license in 1976 after dropping flour bombs (bags of flour that exploded like bombs upon hitting the ground) on a visiting South African softball team in 1976. The fear of what McQuarrie might do, coupled with the police's inability to move the protesters from the rugby grounds, despite increasingly aggressive measures, including beating protesters who were hemmed in by hastily erected barbed-wire fences, led officials to cancel the scheduled match between the Springboks and Waikato, one of the signature provincial clubs in New Zealand.

The events in Hamilton marked one of the clearest successes for the antitour movement. "Looking at the setting sun" while departing the venue after the cancellation of the match, Springbok captain Wynand Claassen later wrote, "I wondered whether it was setting on the Springbok tour of 81 as well."[15]

A GAME IN TARANAKI, THE ACTION ON MOLESWORTH STREET: JULY 29

July 29 saw another day of protests in more than one locale. The Springboks played Taranaki in New Plymouth, on the west coast of the North Island. The South African visitors would once again win handily, 34–9, in yet another match that would virtually disappear amidst the maelstrom. New Plymouth was, if anything, even more of a rugby stronghold than Hamilton. Part of the rural rugby spine of New Zealand, New

Plymouth was a smaller community that had both a smaller protest movement and, in some ways, as is often the case in rural towns, a potentially more combustible politics than might be found in more cosmopolitan cities. Contrary to expectations, perhaps, the goal at each venue was not necessarily to stop each game. It was simply to have a presence and to keep the momentum moving. Even a national movement required local leadership, and local leaders in New Plymouth had not even really been in contact with the leadership of HART or other organizations. As one HART leader tried to explain to a journalist who wondered why the chaos of Hamilton was not being replicated in the hinterlands of New Plymouth, "The trauma here is dangerous. You mustn't consider what was done in Hamilton can be attempted in New Plymouth."[16]

There was a closely monitored protest march in New Plymouth. Police told local protest leaders that they could march "to a point thirty metres from the main gates" of the stadium. Several hundred protesters reached that designated point. A Red Squad officer told local protest leader Gordon Webley, "If they don't move away, we'll move them and hurt them," and so they did, beating protesters who were already obeying the demands to move away. In the words of longstanding New Zealand anti-apartheid activist, antitour leader, and 1981 chronicler Tom Newnham, "Clearly the police were itching to get stuck in. This action at New Plymouth was the beginning of the arbitrary and quite unlawful police actions which became common practice for the remainder of the tour."[17]

The main action, the international story, on July 29 played out 350 kilometers away, a five-hour drive or so, on Molesworth Street in Wellington. There was a protest march on Parliament and things got ugly. COST had called for protesters to gather by 5 p.m., and emboldened by events in Hamilton, 2,000 or so answered the call, despite Wellington not being the scene of a match that day. Some of the protesters had a laugh, one group of students from Wellington Girls' College beginning a chant, "Stop the Royal Wedding!" referring to the nuptials between Prince Charles and Lady Diana that were to take place in a matter of hours. The protest leaders, including Trevor Richards, had set up an amplification system against police commands and were trying to mobilize the unwieldy group. The leaders, including Richards and Alick Shaw, a future deputy mayor of Wellington, joked about storming Parliament but instead announced a change in course, to march from Parliament to the South African consul. Shaw also advised children not to join in and encouraged adults to "form ranks 10 across, arms linked with the strongest people on the outside." He commanded, "The demonstration should at all times be orderly, peaceful, disciplined and non-violent."[18]

Before they could even really commence the march from Parliament onto Molesworth Street, the police took to their own megaphone and demanded that the march disband. Some protesters took the advice and dispersed, but many did not, including several students from Victoria University who remained steadfast. The protesters who remained, and many who had broken ranks of the lines but remained in the area, chanted things like "1, 2, 3, 4, we don't want your racist tour; 5, 6, 7, 8, stop the tour, it's not too late!" Others shouted, "Free Nelson Mandela!" "Remember Steve Biko!" and "Amandla!"[19] They stood defiant. Many began to march.

And they got the hell kicked out of them.

The police, "in what was, in essence, a retaliation for the Hamilton debacle," descended on protesters and unleashed their batons, on protesters who may have been breaking the law but also on hundreds who were not. The response to Hamilton had, in part, been what amounted to "an open cheque," both in terms of literal expenditure on the police but also in terms of police behavior.[20] The protests in Wellington would, in the minds of many participants, lead to the radicalization of the protest movement. Part of this radicalization would be a rejection of nonviolence in at least some circles. Future protesters would arrive with protection of their own, bicycle and motorcycle helmets, jerry-rigged shields, and even armor. The police had become militarized. Some protesters would respond in kind, even if in a pathetic simulacrum. The events in Wellington marked something of a point of no return for the protesters because of the actions of the police, and by implication, the government.

THE FIRST TEST: CHRISTCHURCH, SATURDAY, AUGUST 15

There would be more than two weeks between the events in Wellington and the first test of the tour in Christchurch, the second largest city (behind Auckland), and third largest metropolitan area (behind Auckland and Wellington) in New Zealand, located on the east coast of the country's South Island. During that time, the Springboks played four matches with four wins. They defeated Manawatu 31–19 in Palmerston North, a small city in the south center of the North Island where 5,000 protesters ran up against a massive police presence. Real violence was prevented when the protesters followed the instructions of the police, though Alick Shaw made the point through a loudspeaker that "in Molesworth New Zealand police had behaved rather too similarly to the South African police."[21] Days later the Springboks crushed Wanganui 45–9 in Whanganui on the southwest coast of the North Island where protesters similarly confronted increasingly assertive police.

They moved to the South Island where they defeated Southland 22–6 in Invercargill, the southernmost and westernmost city in New Zealand and one identified as "a city with deeply embedded racism" by John Minto, one of the founding members of HART. The police presence was the biggest yet on the tour, certainly relative to the small number of a few hundred protesters, and their newly aggressive tactics were on display. Minto and a small group were arrested early on Saturday morning after their arrival, spending six hours in jail before being released with no charges pending. Minto's arrest had been particularly aggressive. A young constable growled, "Ah, Minto, I'll have you," "grabbing him, spinning him around and pulling him by the hair along the footpath" before he "pushed [Minto's] head down and rammed it into the side of the police car." In the midday protest, which the arrested group was able to attend, a new chant emerged, which "echoed throughout New Zealand for the next five weeks": "Two-Four-Six-Eight—racist Tour—Police State!"[22]

Finally, the Springboks defeated Otago 17–13 in a tightly fought match in Dunedin at rugby-mad Otago's infamous (for visiting squads) Carisbrook, better known as the "House of Pain." Because of the location of the University of Otago, there was a robust protest movement in the city but the police presence was roughly as large as the five hundred or so protesters gathered for the Springbok arrival and the match at Carisbrook. Police broke an agreement to allow a march to continue peacefully to the stadium when it forced the protesters to stop barely 200 meters after they started. The "breach of faith by the police" resulted in "considerable anger" from protesters. A small group of a little more than two dozen made their way into the stadium and were mildly disruptive on the terraces but were arrested fairly quickly after being forcibly removed from the stadium.[23]

Christchurch was the area in New Zealand where in the minds of many tour opposition was strongest. The HART movement there was strong and resilient, providing not only substantial local leadership, but considerable national presence. It had seen a succession of marches and protests before the tour. Students at the University of Canterbury provided both leadership and sheer numbers to the movement. Yet a kind of paranoia had descended upon Christchurch as it would the other major cities where test matches were held. In the words of Geoff Chapple, "It was as if the atmosphere of some dark and cataclysmic star had begun to descend on the city." The result was that "the prevailing goodwill, or tolerance, citizen to citizen, gradually disappeared. Everyone was addressing their neighbor, or the stranger approaching down a city street. Friend or enemy?" In this climate it felt as if "The mere act of wearing the distinctive red, white, and black HART Stop the Tour badge became a bravery."[24]

A few days before the Christchurch test, Prime Minister Muldoon was interviewed on Australian television and naturally he was asked about the Springbok tour. First, he asserted baselessly, "We have this professional protest movement, the rent-a-demo people, and for the first time in their lives they have got support from areas that would never have supported them before on other issues. That's what worries me most." After asserting that he would never and could never have denied the South Africans visas, especially after his election campaign promises, he asserted that he was "afraid of extreme violence, that kind of thing, and Christchurch is the place where I'd be worried about it." When asked if this was "a real possibility" he replied, "Well, it must be because of some of the people that are down there." His interviewer asked, "if someone was killed on Saturday, would that be enough to convince you that the tour should be canceled?" Muldoon, suddenly not into speculation after maintaining that the prospect of an explosion was "a real possibility" "because of some of the people that are" in Christchurch, clucked, "I think you are introducing a hypothetical, emotional element should have no part in a discussion like this." When challenged on this point and asked if an explosion that killed people would cause him to reconsider, he said no, praised the police force, and effectively said nothing could change his mind about the tour.[25]

The Springboks arrived in the city for the Test on an unscheduled Air New Zealand flight, transferred to several vehicles, had a police convoy accompany them, and took several evasive maneuvers before departing onto the highways. They thought they had fooled journalists and protesters. And briefly they had, as police had done everything to ensure that the Springboks eluded observers, including one HART member being threatened with charges of "obstructing police by following them" when he figured out the mechanics of the convoy whisking the Springboks from the airport. In the words of Geoff Chapple, they had "stumbled into the *Alice in Wonderland* atmospheres of the tour."[26]

Because of protests, or at least the fear of protesters, some of the Springboks asserted that they had slept on the floors of squash courts at Linwood Rugby Club and had arrived at Lancaster Park just after 9 a.m. on the day of the test. As one South African confided to a journalist, "We have no chance now, that is not the way to prepare for a test against the All Blacks."[27] The reality was that their accommodations were fine. According to an NZRFU liaison, the lodgings were "about as good as a hotel," even if, in the words of two writers who covered the tour, "their sleeping arrangements could not have matched the comfort of an enormous double bed" that they might have experienced in Christchurch's city center.[28] They would soon learn that at least in the major population centers, makeshift lodging would replace the swanky hotels they may have come to expect. The protesters might not be able to halt the tour, but they would prove capable of disrupting it.

On August 14, the Friday before the Saturday test, an explosive device went off near Lancaster Park, the stadium that would host the first test. It had been packed in a container of sand, had been noisy and woken people up within two kilometers of the blast, and had done no damage whatsoever. That fact did not alleviate tension in the buildup to the most important match of the tour so far.

While the more than 6,000 marchers outside the stadium were mostly peaceful, a significant number managed to get into Lancaster Park and access the field, only to be met by a squadron of police who spared no brutality, leaving "a frightening jumble of bodies piled in a heap."[29] One small group, known as the "Mongrel Mob," attempted to bring down the goal posts using ropes, something they had successfully done in the days preceding the test, but they were not quick enough.[30] After the "brief invasion" a clean-up squad followed and recovered tacks, shards of glass, and fish hooks.[31]

While the All Blacks took the first of the best-of-three test series, protests continued apace outside the stadium as well as in cities across the country, especially the major centers. If the Springboks had not been aware of the magnitude of the movement against them, they were beginning to realize it now.

THE SECOND TEST: WELLINGTON, SATURDAY, AUGUST 29

In another fortnight, the second test would take place. In between were three scheduled matches. The first of these was scheduled for August 19. That match was cancelled for a remarkable reason: "To give the police a rest,"[32]

Protests resumed on Saturday, August 22, when the Springboks, remaining on the South Island, crushed Nelson Bays in Nelson. Prior to the match, protesters had managed to sneak an unarmed gunpowder bomb into the Rutherford Hotel, where the Springboks were staying. As if to further underscore their incompetence, the next day police mistook a journalist's portable typewriter for a bomb in the hotel lobby and blew it up.

On the day of the match, police "snatched" up a handful of vocal protesters for offenses allegedly committed prior to that day. Little came of most of the charges. As the match kickoff approached, a protest march, numbering perhaps a few hundred, split into three groups. One stopped as requested on a bridge 300–400 meters from the entrance to the stadium. Another group ended up near the barbed-wire defenses of the stadium. A third group ended up within viewing area of the stadium but were blocked by the Maitai River. Things were so easy for the police, in fact, that members of the Red Squad were able to sit together in a row on the edge of the field and watch the Springboks administer a hiding to the severely outmanned Nelson Bays side.

The August 25 match against the NZ Maori, the only nontest that the Springboks did not win, was also relatively quiet on the protest front. Some of the biggest tensions surrounded not the Springboks, but the NZ Maori side, who were seen as betraying the Maori cause by engaging with the Springboks. "You are selfish in both attitude and action," read a statement issued by a delegation led by Auckland grad student Des Kahotea, representatives of Maori organizations, and the Maori Women's Group. "As descendents of the indigenous people of Aotearoa, you trample over the indigenous people of Azania (South Africa) by collaborating with their oppressors."[33] Both protesters and supporters had found the Springbok hotel, but the former were not too aggressive, and in fact, several chatted with Abe Williams, who supposedly "dispensed advice to the protesters." The team was even able to wander the deserted streets of Napier, but that quiescence was sure to change in Wellington, despite the government's renewed effort at undermining the protest movement by releasing the results of an "investigation" in which it was purported that there were fifteen "subversives and radicals" operating within the antitour movement.[34]

In Wellington, as in the other major cities (and not a few of the minor ones), the antitour protests would represent the highlights, the apex, but for weeks before the Test hundreds of people met every Monday evening for planning sessions organized and led by the Wellington-based COST. The meetings were to "assess the previous week's activities and to plan for the following week" and they were "turbulent, democratic, and noisy." Twice a week for two months leading up to the Test match hundreds and sometimes thousands showed up for regular protests—not just in Wellington, but around the country—and in Wellington an estimated 8,000–10,000 protested on the day of the Test.[35] The Springboks hurried up to Wellington the day before the test match, again foregoing luxe accommodations to stay in the social room of the Athletic Park grandstand, described by one journalist as a "cold, cavernous place, certainly not the place to prepare for a test that, if it was lost, would ruin the tour."[36] Their conditions were arguably better than those the All Blacks faced, at least on test day, as the New Zealand team had been brought from their hotel early in the morning to sit and wait in the chilly Athletic Park changing rooms while the Springboks could "laze around until mid-day."[37]

Journalists and support staff were also encouraged to head to Athletic Park early in case of trouble or delays. Once they got to the stadium, "It all seemed routine, barbed wire around the edge of the field, the helicopter aloft, the police warning that there were demonstrators within the ground."[38]

The protest did not disappoint. The police were out in full force—1,600 or so, fully equipped in riot gear. Barbed wire surrounded the pitch and other sensitive areas. In the days before the match, police had raided the HART and COST offices in hopes of learning their plans. The morning of the match a bomb was detonated. COST and HART leaders might have heard wind of it, but they did not want to know much to ensure plausible denial, though this approach also indicates that they were playing with fire, and that for all of the talk of nonviolence, there were those willing to engage in not only violence, but potential terrorism. Fortunately, no one was hurt, though transportation was seriously hindered in what might qualify as a success for whoever laid it. Protesters set up human barriers to block roads. There were marches seemingly everywhere, some quite clearly planned, others obviously impromptu. There was much violence from the police and considerable violence from rugby supporters, some of them politically committed to the tour itself, many of whom simply wanted to see rugby. There was singing and chanting and there were signs. There was dancing. There was fear and there was running. There were tense standoffs. Both sides seemed organized, in some cases embracing and adopting the tactics of the others. It was chaotic and occasionally bloody.

Yet the test match went on, and the Springboks pulled off a 24–12 victory.

It was cold and raw and rainy, with a stiff southerly breeze befitting a New Zealand winter. The field was wet and soft; 31,000 fans were in the stadium. The Springboks started off strong with two Botha penalties and a try and conversion giving the Boks a comfortable 12–0 lead. By the twenty-second minute, another penalty goal made it 15–0. The teams traded penalties to make it 18–3, with the deadly Botha accounting for fourteen of the Boks' eighteen points. The Springbok loose forwards were dominating and the Boks controlled set pieces. In the second half it was more of the same, and while the All Blacks fought back as hard as they could, the Springboks, given little chance after their form in the first test and the circumstances that they had faced with the protests and their general tour conditions, emerged with the win. Botha had scored twenty of the points with five penalties, a drop goal, and the conversion on Gerrie Germishuys' try.

The third test in Auckland on September 12 would be the decider.

THE THIRD TEST: AUCKLAND, SATURDAY, SEPTEMBER 12

A group of protesters awaited the Springboks' arrival in Rotorua, a city on the shores of Lake Rotorua located in the north central part of the North Island, on August 30, storming the tarmac when they thought the Springbok flight had landed. It was instead a plane carrying police, which, in the wry words of journalist Don Cameron, "rather ended the demonstrators' activities for the day."[39] The Springboks finally arrived with rather less fanfare at the airport but protesters outside their hotel chanted denunciations as police eyed them warily.[40]

Following their 29–24 victory over Bay of Planty, the Springboks made the short trip to Auckland on September 3. Meetings between civic leaders, rugby officials, and protest leaders resulted in some compromise offers, but nothing came of it, in no small part because "the demonstration machinery had been winding up for many days and Saturday was the time for action, not words." Although the test at Eden Park would not be for another week, the matchup against Auckland in that storied stadium would provide a trial run. And though the Springboks defeated Auckland handily 39–12 on September 5, the protests raging outside the stadium served as a clear omen that the next week would be intense. In the meantime, the Springbok party would spend the next few days in Whangārei, New Zealand's northernmost city, some two hours' drive north of Auckland proper, where they defeated North Auckland in their final midweek match before the third and deciding test. Protests in Whangārei were "noisy but quite peaceful" in part because relatively few protesters but an awful lot of police had headed north.[41]

In contrast, Saturday, September 12, the day of the third test, forever to be known as the "Flour Bomb" match, was the most chaotic, dreadful, violent, and frightening day of the entire tour. In the words of Trevor Richards and others, "Outside Eden Park and throughout sections of the city, Auckland resembled a civil war zone. . . . Barbed wire, road blockades, half the country's police force, many with helmets, shields and long batons, confronted 7,000 anti-apartheid supporters. The battle raged for much of the day." The violence was such that "some who marched were lucky to come away with their lives. One man was hit with a riot squad baton with such force that one end of it flew in the air as the baton snapped."[42]

Moreover, in Auckland, two men would carry out Pat McQuarrie's threat to fly over the rugby stadium. Indeed, as Richards writes, "Internationally, what is remembered most, especially amongst anti-apartheid activists in South Africa and around the world, is not the violence as much as the daring act" of Marx Jones and Grant Cole. Early the afternoon of the test, as police and protesters and protesters and tour supporters clashed throughout Auckland, the two left Dairy Flat, a rural district about thirty kilometers north of Auckland, in a Cessna 172. "This is radio anti-apartheid," Jones radioed ground control just after 2:10 p.m. "Please inform the police and the Rugby Union they've got just 10 minutes to stop the third test." Their warnings went unheeded, the test was not stopped, "and for the next 90 minutes the Cessna 'bombed'" Eden Park with "flour bombs," heavy sacks of flour. The plane would continue to distract and disrupt and inspire equal parts fear and bemusement among the crowd, officials, staffs, and players, leaving the pitch "scarred with white smears of flour" and flyers. A group of protesters tried to rush the pitch, but they had "no chance," as "the police snared them against the barbed wire" ringing the field "just as we used to trap rabbits in the corner of a close-netted fence when we were kids."[43]

With thirty-two minutes remaining in the second half a flour bomb connected directly with the head of All Black Gary Knight, a prop who had represented New Zealand as a wrestler in the Commonwealth Games in 1974, winning a bronze. He slumped to the pitch but somehow continued. This led to a brief moment of levity, when referee Clive Norling told medics attending to Knight not to pour too much water over the flour-covered Knight, "or you'll have him covered in pastry!"[44] Nonetheless, as All Black wing Stu Wilson noted later, "If a flour bomb had to hit someone it's as well it was Gary Knight. If it had hit" fullback

Allan Hewson "it would have turned him into instant blood and bone fertilizer for Eden Park."[45]

Referee Clive Norling also called All Black captain Andy Dalton and Springbok captain Wynand Claassen together and suggested calling off the match, to which Claassen responded, "No way!"[46]

The match would continue.

Toward the end of the eighty minutes the teams were drawn 22–22. The heroes for the Springboks had been wing Ray Mordt, who scored three tries, and Naas Botha, who kicked two penalties and two conversions, though when Mordt pushed across his third try to tie the match at twenty-two, Botha missed the conversion, possibly distracted by either an injury delay or by the presence of the Cessna that "swoop[ed] only 10 metres above the crowd on the open stand as Botha step[ped] back."[47]

In the waning seconds, referee Clive Norling of Wales—whose "self-appointed star-status" in the words of All Black Murray Mexted, made players from both teams worry every time he blew the whistle—called a controversial penalty on an esoteric matter (or series of esoteric matters as his explanation changed several times during and after the match).[48] Initially, Norling called for a free kick, which he then inexplicably changed to a penalty. Even today in New Zealand this is celebrated as a just and brave reading of the rule book. Though All Black captain Andy Dalton, when once asked by a South African journalist about the improbability of the decision, "smiles a knowing smile" and responds, "I must say that I thought that was a really reasonable decision." Then, perhaps a bit less provocatively, "Look, it was a very close series. If I was a South African, I would probably be on the same wavelength about the last penalty, but I'm a New Zealander and, for me, it was a good decision," though he was smiling again when he said this last bit.[49] In South Africa, the decision is seen as perfidious cowardice of the rankest sort.

New Zealand's Allan Hewson was to take the penalty. There could be no greater pressure moment in all of sport. Andy Dalton tossed Hewson the ball and simply said, "Kick it." At that point, in the words of Hewson's biographer, Ian Gault, "The loneliness of the long-distance goalkicker was never more vividly exemplified than at Eden Park at that moment." Hewson certainly grasped the moment. "I tried to keep cool and concentrate only on the kick. I kept saying to myself 'It has to go over, it has to go over.'" Hewson slotted the kick. "The kick felt good and I can't describe how good it felt watching the ball curl inside the right-hand upright. I knew then we'd beaten the Springboks."[50] A few desperate seconds passed, the final whistle blew, and the All Blacks had won 25–22. "I tried to imagine my feelings had Allan Hewson missed that final penalty kick," Andy Haden wrote later. "A surge of desperation swept over me. That goal had indeed meant more than just a scoreboard victory for New Zealand."[51] However, as Wynand Claassen would write, "It was sad that a series like this one, so closely contested, and with so many problems, should end in this way." After each team had won a test "convincingly," and after the All Blacks dominated the first half of the third test, the Springboks the second half, "What a shame that all this should be spoilt by one last controversial kick awarded by a 'showman with a whistle.'"[52]

The green Cessna made a total of fifty-eight passes over the stadium, dropping about sixty flour bombs. Several times the plane dropped below 300 feet, with one witness claiming that it flew below the top reaches of the goal posts at least once. Marx told a reporter that he "did it to fight apartheid" and gave the reporter an envelope of money to pay for the charter as he was being taken away by police. The protesters loved the sight of the plane. Another protest organization had arranged for a small plane of its own, which dropped off eight balloons bearing a placard reading "Biko." As one rugby supporter said upon seeing the tribute to the slain Black Consciousness leader, "There was a hushed silence when we saw it coming. All my mates around me suddenly went quiet and it was then I felt that I should be out there with [the protesters]."[53] Meanwhile, Allan Hewson credits the flour bombing for the All Blacks victory: "It fired our players, transforming them into unbeatable giants. The Springboks were never going to win from that moment."[54] But Andy Haden argues that the All Blacks were "unaffected" by the "Cessna's incessant buzzing of the field in Auckland."[55]

On September 13, the Springboks departed New Zealand on the fifty-seventh day of their tour. Demonstrators at the airport carried banners and signs and bellowed chants like "Seven, eight, nine, ten; racist tour, never again!" And, as the plane carrying the Springboks took off, a few protesters wept with joy. One rolled up one of his banners under his arm and muttered "good riddance!"[56]

The cost to New Zealand, monetary and otherwise, was nearly incalculable. The government admitted that it cost $7.2 million in public money to defend the tour, but there were myriad costs not bound up in that figure. As for the New Zealand Rugby Football Union? It cleared $900,000, tax free.

THE AFTERMATH

New Zealand would not play South Africa again until the Springboks (perhaps prematurely) emerged from isolation in 1992. Indeed, protesters began mobilizing against a planned 1985 tour of South Africa almost as soon as the Springboks flew out of the battered country in 1981. Even as this was happening, well into 1982, more than a year after the Springbok tour had ended, New Zealand police continued to arrest and harass those who had been involved in the events of 1981, and in most cases were active in the work to prevent the 1985 tour. A New Zealand high court decision refused the All Blacks the right to travel. In 1986, a "rebel" New Zealand team, the Cavaliers (more on them later), consisting of a number of All Blacks who would have traveled to represent their nation in 1985, toured South Africa to much consternation, but even for the Springboks' greatest rivals, formal ties with South Africa had grown toxic.

In the words of Robert Muldoon's biographer, Barry Gustafson, the 1981 Springbok tour of New Zealand "was about more than apartheid, sport or South Africa." It also represented "a generational and attitudinal clash between the traditional, semicolonial values and perspectives held by an older generation and especially those living in rural small-town New Zealand" and, "the more liberal, internationalist, post colonial-values and perspectives toward which a younger generation and especially those living in urban Auckland and Wellington were moving."[57] But it also resembled an epochal early clash of what later generations might call the "culture wars" in which political sensibilities manifested in debates over popular culture, sport, and other areas of daily life that in the abstract are not overtly political but that can easily become politicized.

Mary Baker, one of the prominent antitour figures in Christchurch, would later write to a friend that the tour had "revealed a lot of racism in our own country. I am certain that many pro-Tour people (with the exception of the really ardent rugby lovers) are also anti-Maori and Polynesian in New Zealand itself." For all of the drama of the tour, "All the issues facing us of unemployment, growth strategies, of the National Party, etc. have been overlooked in this battle."[58] That would have been the case, of course, whether the tour had been stopped successfully, had never been allowed to take place, or had gone on with no protests at all.

Many of the antitour opponents hoped that at minimum Muldoon's intransigence, which only grew as the tour progressed, would result in his government losing power in the 1981 elections that would take place after the tour. Muldoon's National Party did lose seats, three in total, leaving him with a majority of just one seat in Parliament. But he would remain in power for another three years.

Andy Haden remembers driving away from the Eden Park stadium after the epochal third test. "I certainly wasn't sorry the tour had ended" and he felt "slightly hungover from the events of the day and night before I felt an enormous relief that the chapter of events of the previous two and a half months were closing. The pages of history could be turned to saner times."[59]

In August and September 1981, the Springboks played rugby matches across New Zealand. The putative highlights were the three test matches. New Zealand won two games to one. And in the words of Trevor Richards, "that is about the last thing anyone remembers about it."[60]

THOUGHTS OF AMERICA

Throughout the Springbok tour of New Zealand, articles would periodically crop up in the New Zealand press over the potential pending tour of the United States. Sometimes portrayed as an oddity, sometimes as an absurdity, sometimes as a joke, and always within the context of the ongoing politics, the tour to the United States was understood for what it was, a ridiculous effort for the Springboks to gain something akin to legitimacy, yet also a legitimate political challenge in which the Springboks, and thus South Africa, would achieve the imprimatur of the Reagan administration and thus a certain level of credibility, if not endorsement. But the prospects of a US tour still seemed vaguely ridiculous to most observers. Little did they realize just how ridiculous things were about to get.

The Springboks in the lineout against the USA Eagles. *Courtesy of Wessel Oosthuizen*

The Springboks warm up in Racine. *Courtesy of Wessel Oosthuizen*

The Springboks and Midwestern All-Stars in action in a game the South Africans won 46–12. *Courtesy of Wessel Oosthuizen*

Match action in Racine (Errol Tobias, the first black Springbok, is in the middle of the image). *Courtesy of Wisconsin Rugby Library*

Giant Springbok lock, Loouis Moolman, preparing for the postgame festivities.
Courtesy of Wessel Oosthuizen

An American rugby fan in all his finery. *Courtesy of Wessel Oosthuizen*

The intrepid media descend upon Racine. *Courtesy of Wessel Oosthuizen*

Springbok assistant manager, Abe Williams. *Courtesy of Wisconsin Rugby Library*

**EASTERN RUGBY UNION
OF AMERICA, INC.**

PROUDLY WELCOMES

**THE SOUTH AFRICAN
SPRINGBOKS**

GREATEST RUGBY TEAM IN THE WORLD

EASTERN PENNSYLVANIA RFU
FLORIDA RUGBY UNION
GEORGIA RUGBY UNION
METROPOLITAN NEW YORK RFU
NEW ENGLAND RFU
NORTH CAROLINA RFU
POTOMAC RFU
UPSTATE RFU
VIRGINIA RFU
PALMETTO RFU
MID-SOUTH RFU
LOUISIANA RFU

The Eastern Rugby Football Union Welcomes the Springboks. *Author's collection*

Protester Marvin Happel is arrested for disrupting the match in Racine. *Courtesy of Wisconsin Rugby Library*

The program for the Springbok match against the Midwest XV. *Courtesy of Wisconsin Rugby Library*

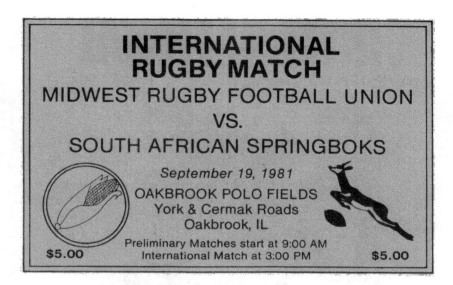

INTERNATIONAL RUGBY MATCH

MIDWEST RUGBY FOOTBALL UNION
VS.
SOUTH AFRICAN SPRINGBOKS

September 19, 1981

OAKBROOK POLO FIELDS
York & Cermak Roads
Oakbrook, IL

Preliminary Matches start at 9:00 AM
International Match at 3:00 PM

$5.00 $5.00

The original ticket for the Springbok–Midwest XV game that was secretly moved to Racine after protests convinced Chicago officials to forbid the match from being held in their city. *Author's collection*

The USA Eagles take on the mighty Springboks. The Springboks ran away from the outmatched Americans, winning by a final score of 38–7. *New Zealand Rugby Museum—Palmerston North*

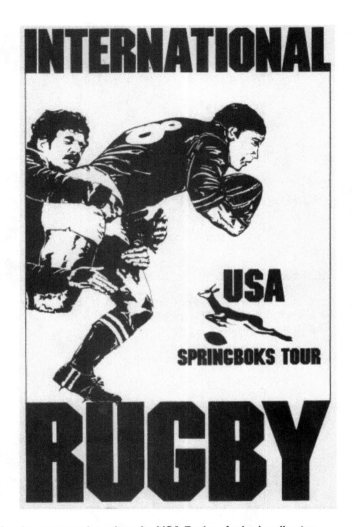

A flyer for the test match against the USA Eagles. *Author's collection*

UNITED STATES OF AMERICA
RUGBY FOOTBALL UNION

David Chambers
President,
6103 Diamond Head Drive
Austin, TX. 78746

September 26, 1981

UNITED STATES EAGLES vs SOUTH AFRICAN SPRINGBOK
ROCHESTER, NEW YORK

On behalf of the Board of Directors, let me take
this opportunity to welcome each of you, and especially
our guests, the South African Springbok. The Springbok
are renown in the International Rugby community as one
of the top teams in the world, and their visit to our
shores marks another highlight in our short history of
international play.

Today's game will provide the opportunity for the
best rugby players of the United States and the best
players of South Africa to display their athletic talent
and to compete against each other on the field of play.
The opportunity to compete in sport for the pure sake
of sport, must always be preserved, and that is a goal
of the United States Union.

I hope that each of you enjoy today's game and that
special camaraderie which has always been a special
part of rugby football.

Sincerely yours,

David E. Chambers

USA Rugby welcomes the Springboks. *Author's collection*

5

CLOAKS, DAGGERS, AND RUGBY

The Springboks in the Midwest

"'Top Secret' was stamped over the Springbok tour of the United States yesterday as they headed into a mystery tour unprecedented in this history of major sport."[1] —*Cape Times*, September 14, 1981

SURF SAFARI

The Springboks flew straight from New Zealand to the United States, desperate for some rest, relaxation, and, above all, a break from politics. According to Springbok captain Wynand Claassen, they spent most of their eight-hour layover in Hawaii "mingling with other tourists in shorts and t-shirts," and while they "didn't spot" Tom Selleck's Hawaii-based television hero, Magnum P. I., they "did give the T-shirt trade a big boost as the boys made up for the shopping time they were denied in New Zealand."[2] A handful of players even took some time to surf the beach at Waikiki. These included hooker Shaun Povey, and lock Div Visser, Errol Tobias, and loose forward Rob Louw. Louw was well-known among the Boks for his iconoclastic liberal views, and he was possibly the only member of the white Springbok party to befriend Errol Tobias in any meaningful way (the two were roommates on tour, an arrangement that Louw would surely have had the ability to approve or veto).

But the team's much-needed respite proved short-lived. By the end of the New Zealand tour there was growing speculation that the Springboks touring party would face protesters in the United States, too, something most would have doubted two months earlier. "There is a continent-wide chain of protest groups linked to a command center run by the co-ordinator of Sart (Stop the Apartheid Rugby Tour), Dr. Richard Lapchick, waiting for the Springboks," one South African newspaperman reported. Lapchick was happy to feed this rather grandiloquent overstatement of his capacities. "We are ready," he said, "we are waiting, watching. Be assured, we will be in close attendance the moment we get word" of where the scheduled events would take place. Lapchick also believed he was "under close scrutiny," as his home had been broken into the week before the South Africans' arrival, his files related to the tour rifled through, though by whom he never has known.

Regardless of what Lapchick and SART could actually achieve, American tour supporters were determined to go forward. Tom Selfridge of the Eastern Rugby Union, who announced that "under no circumstances" would the tour be stopped, nevertheless expressed concern about neo-Nazi organizations that had claimed they were going to serve as "bodyguards" for the team. "Rugby people and only rugby people are being invited," he insisted.[3] The editors of the *Chicago Tribune* wanted a small affair for the Boks in their city. "If all goes as planned" the Springboks would "slip into town, play a secret game in a secret field, and slip out of town again with nobody but a few local ruggers the wiser." They hoped the Springbok entry would be surreptitious because otherwise, "We're likely to go through a scrum version of the Skokie Nazi march," a reference to the infamous 1977 incident in which the National Socialist Party of America fought to march through the predominantly Jewish Chicago suburb of Skokie.[4]

David Hall, an official with the Chicago Lions, maintained his "original posture that the game will go on" although he had "really gotten upset about" the fact that organization had become difficult. "Because everything's got to be kept quiet. The press has really screwed up everything for the rugby community."[5] Presumably, this was a reference to global events surrounding the Springboks, especially in New Zealand, because the American press had still been largely silent on an event most of them had no clue was happening. It is perhaps telling that organizers who claimed that they celebrated free assembly rights for a rugby team wanted to decry the press covering the events surrounding that very same match. It would not be the last time on the tour that such hypocrisies would come to the fore.

TOM BRADLEY AND THE STATE DEPARTMENT

The Boks were initially supposed to fly from Honolulu to Los Angeles, but early criticisms and small protests against the tour coupled with his own anti-apartheid convictions had caused Los Angeles mayor Tom Bradley to make public his opposition to the Springboks' visit to the United States. Bradley, Los Angeles's first African American mayor, also had a distinguished pedigree as an athlete. He had been an all-city football and track athlete in high school before taking an academic scholarship to UCLA, where he was a member of the track team and a teammate of sporting pioneers Jackie Robinson, Kenny Washington, and Woody Strode. Robinson, a four-sport star at UCLA, would go on to the most fame when he desegregated Major League Baseball for the Brooklyn Dodgers in 1947. But in 1946, Robinson's UCLA football teammates, Washington and Strode would break the color barrier in the NFL that had been in place since 1933.[6] A week before the Springboks were to arrive in the United States Bradley voiced his opposition to the tour in a letter to Secretary of State Alexander Haig.

> If the South African rugby team is allowed to play the matches in this country, it would be in violation of a United Nations sports' boycott against South Africa. Because of this and because of the possibility of violence such as occurred in reaction to the team playing elsewhere, and the threat by African nations to boycott the 1984 Summer Olympics in Los Angeles, I strongly urge that your office withdraw the visas issued for the purpose of permitting the South African team to compete in the United States.[7]

Bradley received letters and telegrams both of support and in opposition to his public statements on the Springbok tour.[8] His concerns about the Los Angeles Olympics certainly were legitimate—after all, twenty-six African nations had boycotted the 1976 Montreal Olympics in the wake of the 1976 All Black tour to South Africa. If they were willing to boycott Olympics being held in Canada because of New Zealand hosting the Springboks, surely many more countries might be willing to boycott Olympics held in Los Angeles because of the United States playing host to the Springboks. *Sports Illustrated*, the most popular and respected sports magazine in the United States at the time, reported on the Springbok trip to America and concluded that Americans might look at the decision to host the South Africans with dismay because "a small group of their countrymen, combining a simple lack of sophistication with a kind of petulant obstinacy" had "at the very least put the Los Angeles Games in jeopardy and at worst crippled forever the Olympic Movement."[9] When Peter Ueberroth, president of the Los Angeles Olympic Organizing Committee appeared on Ted Koppel's widely respected nightly news program, *Nightline*, and maintained, "I think that the South African tour will cause the African nations to band together and talk about a boycott for 1984," which might be joined by other nations, the threat became clear.[10] Juan Antonio Samaranch, the head of the International Olympic Committee (IOC) also "had gone out of his way to say how displeased he was that the U.S. rugby authorities had chosen to jeopardize the L.A. Games." If nothing else, the decision to host the Springboks might provide "just the peg" the Soviet Union needed to boycott the 1984 Olympics in a tit-for-tat for the 1980 United States boycott of the Moscow Games.[11]

Bradley's opposition to apartheid extended beyond municipal self-interest and prompted a large contingent of the California delegation in the US House of Representatives to support the "sense-of-the-Congress resolution in opposition to the visit. In a floor speech Congressman Mervyn Dymmaly argued, "Whether we like it or not, politics, in this instance, cannot be separated from athletics. To countenance the appearance of a South African team in the United States would be one more symbolic expression of approval of South African apartheid." Because a two-thirds majority was required, the 200–198 vote in favor of the resolution failed.[12]

On October 20, long after the Springboks had come and gone, and the controversy was largely forgotten, Bradley received a response from the State Department's acting director of the Office of Intergovernmental Affairs and Public Liaison, Edward Marks. Marks underscored the fact that the invitation to the Springbok team, "which is not sponsored by the South African Government," came from the USA Rugby Football Union, "a private organization independent of the U. S. Olympic Committee and other American sporting bodies," and insisted that "It has been for some time policy not to interfere with such private sporting exchanges." Marks then put forward a clear summary of the administration's emerging policy of "Constructive Engagement" with Pretoria:

> The United States abhors apartheid, a policy of the South African Government which President Reagan has termed "repugnant" to the basic values of our own democratic and multiracial society. Although apartheid is a hindrance to relations between the U.S. and South Africa, the answer is not to walk away from the problem nor to engage in preaching or public posturing. The United States is firmly committed to support for peaceful, evolutionary change leading to a stable, nonracialist society in South Africa. We will support change not in the spirit of confrontation, but of constructive help. [13]

And with that, the State Department washed its hands of the Springbok tour.

In the words of Hodding Carter III, who had served as Assistant Secretary of State for public affairs in the Carter administration, the Reagan approach was one "that seems to wink at institutionalized racism and hint at close partnership with" the South African government. [14] The winking had been none too subtle. Chester Crocker, the architect of the administration's Constructive Engagement doctrine had already declared that "in South Africa, the region's largest country, it is not our task to choose between black and white," a declaration of moral relativism that, in the words of syndicated columnist and longstanding civil rights reporter Carl Rowan, "effectively took the side of the white minority that has the weapons, the dogs, the police, and other instruments of oppression." [15]

ANONYMOUS IN CHICAGO

With Los Angeles off the schedule, the Boks flew instead to Chicago, where, according to Bok captain Wynand Claassen, the players "were pleasantly surprised" by the media reception at O'Hare Airport. "American news people were," in Claassen's words, "better informed . . . than their New Zealand counterparts." [16] This seems unlikely given that New Zealand reporters were well versed in both questions of apartheid and the meaning of rugby and apartheid sport. If anything, the American media coverage reveals that it was hardly informed at all about the tour and its implications. Despite the secretive nature of their ever-changing travel plans, the Springboks encountered several television cameras, photographers, and reporters at O'Hare. "We're tired," Professor Johan Claassen, the team manager, said to reporters, "but we're happy to be here."[17] For all the experience Claassen had in dealing with the media barrage in New Zealand, he seems not to have developed the sort of savvy answers to be expected of someone whose job was, in part, to liaise with the media. When confronted with political questions, his pat response was "I'm sorry, we're here to play rugby." This sort of tone deafness made a liberal observer like Rob Louw "cringe." Louw believed that "if only the right people had been there to discuss our situation honestly and openly we would have had the whole world as our audience." Claassen, "a dour, staunch Afrikaner" who had "inflexible ultra-conservative views and would allow no deviation from his own straight and narrow path," was not, suffice it to say, the right person. His poor mastery of English only exacerbated matters, making him look "callous" and "naïve."[18]

Meanwhile, Chicago politicians "had picked up on the scent of publicity." Shortly after the Boks landed, the Chicago City Council voted unanimously, 37–0, on a resolution introduced by Mayor Jane Byrne, to "publicly denounce the intent of the South African Springboks to play in Chicago."[19] One city alderman even announced plans to propose a resolution to ban the Springboks from so much as appearing on public property, thus effectively confining them to their private digs, though that appears not to have come to a vote. This all seemed to come rather late in the game given that officials surely knew that the Springboks were coming to town, but it is quite possible that the city council had not been prepared for a rugby match to be controversial. They would be neither the first nor the last to be caught unaware of the implications of the Springbok tour.

Even some South Africans, who otherwise supported the tour and did not fall into the category of anti-apartheid activists, were beginning to question whether the tour should go on in America. The Afrikaans-language Nationalist newspaper *Rapport* wrote an op-ed in which it questioned whether the American tour was worth the trouble, especially after the international attention the events in New Zealand had brought. The editors of *Rapport* worried that anti-tour sentiment might embarrass not only Reagan, who was proving to be a good friend to the apartheid government of South Africa and who would face re-election in 1984, but also the US Olympic Committee, which would host the 1984 Olympics in Los Angeles and faced boycott threats. If Reagan found the need to halt the Springbok tour, might it harm US–South African relations?[20]

Although nowhere near as sympathetic to the National Party as *Rapport*, the editors of the liberal *Cape Times* echoed some of these concerns but showed some cognizance of the larger global political implications of the Bok tour:

> South Africa's vital interests could suffer damage. Some of these interests are rather more important to South Africa than any overseas sports tour. It may be that the best thing for all concerned would be to bring the Springboks straight home without the scheduled American stop-over. Irrespective of what happens in South African sport, the international climate will not improve significantly for this country until its domestic political dilemma has been resolved and a non-discriminatory system of government by consent is in force.[21]

Sportswriter Dan Retief, one of the journalists on the Springbok tour, perhaps stumbled upon the reason for the Boks to undertake this trip after so many arduous, beleaguered weeks on the road. He noted that the United States was not only a potential sleeping giant in the rugby world, but also that it offered the Springboks, and by extension South Africa, "a valuable ally in a hostile world."[22]

Despite growing opposition and doubt, the tour would go on. The Springboks stayed in the Chicago Athletic Association's (CAA) downtown headquarters, practiced at Grant Park, and even engaged in some sightseeing. The Boks were impressed by their accommodations. Wynand Claassen described the CAA as "a posh club where one can only stay on private invitation," and their stay as "absolutely delightful after the cares and strains of New Zealand."[23]

Once again, the Boks took time to shop. "Everything was so modern, so unbelievably well-organised, so efficient and there was such a variety of things to buy." Claassen took note of his teammates' expenditures. They bought "everything from [W]alkman tape players to golf clubs and it came to a staggering 10,000 dollars." Claassen was one of the most enthusiastic shoppers, earning the nickname "Pakkies (Parcels) Claassen." Team practices were "less frequent and less arduous and a light-hearted spirit prevailed" in no small part because they did not expect to face top-rate competition in the United States. They would "just stroll down to an open area in the enormous public park next to Lake Michigan to pass the ball around for a bit." Instead, they shopped and watched the Chicago Cubs play the Philadelphia Phillies in their "famous ivy covered . . . stadium. With our baseball caps and American t-shirts I'm not sure even the members of New Zealand's Red Squad would have recognized us."[24]

They also were able to watch the Chicago Lions rugby club—arguably the Midwest's premiere rugby club—play an Irish "touring side" in what Claassen called an "'American Style' rugby union match." What he meant by this indicates just how low rugby ranked on the American sporting consciousness. "We were amazed to see how inventive the Americans had to be to play rugby. Without a ground of their own," the Lions, "undaunted, merely hired a piece of the park next to Lake Michigan and turned it into a rugby field—within a half an hour." He explained that "a guy in a Volksie" [a Volkswagen, popular in South Africa as well as the US at the time] who had "the rugby 'kit,'" drove up and set about laying out a field. Within minutes lines had been laid down and soon the collapsible posts had been assembled and hoisted into position." What followed was a "rousing game of rugby, and right after the final whistle down came the posts while the lines were being erased." Tenemure College defeated the Lions 7–3. This led Claassen to wonder "how well the Americans would do if they had" South African caliber "facilities and opportunities. In fact, just about the only thing South Africa is more advanced in than the Americans is rugby, and judging by the enthusiasm we came across that won't last for much longer either."[25]

That evening, on September 16, the Springboks were the guests of the Lions at a local tavern, a "temporary watering hole" that they used while their clubhouse was being renovated. There they watched the biggest sporting event in the world that week—even in South Africa it was the biggest sporting story of the week "eclips[ing]" the Springbok tour in the words of one South African newspaper—the Sugar Ray Leonard versus Thomas "Hitman" Hearns fight for the undisputed world welterweight championship.[26] The bout turned out to be one of the all-time great fights, with Leonard winning in a fourteenth round technical knockout at Caesar's Palace in Las Vegas. The Springboks bet among themselves as to who would win, with Wynand Claassen winning his bet with Carel du Plessis, a wing/center and future Bok coach who would soon earn the nickname "The Prince of Wings." Claassen noted that Leonard came back in the fight "almost as we had in the third test in Auckland."

In Chicago, the Springboks also attended a reception held in their honor at the city's South African Consulate. Claassen notes that this experience too highlighted differences between their experiences in New Zealand and the United States. Something went awry with the team's transport to the event and rather than arrange for a new ride they chose to walk the mile or so to the Consulate building. "We were dressed in our green dress blazers and we never could have gone out on the street like that in a New Zealand city. People stopped to ask us who we were and why we were all dressed up so smartly. No-one knew anything about South Africa or had heard about a game called rugby—this in spite of the fact that we had been on television and that the newspapers had carried articles about us."[27] Heroes among white South Africans, pariahs among large numbers of New Zealanders, these big-shouldered gents were simply anonymous in the City of the Big Shoulders. "It soon became clear," noted Claassen, "that it was very easy to vanish into the masses and that we were free to roam the streets, exploring the city of Chicago."[28] In the words of Dan Retief, who covered the Bok tour for the South African press, "Naas Botha," the Boks' star flyhalf, "rates about as much attention as you would get if you said to the average Pretorian: 'Do you know Luther Elliott of Los Angeles?'" a name Retief chose at random from the telephone directory.[29]

However, their location soon came to be known to a small number of protesters. Occasionally they had to leave via the CAA back entrance to avoid picketers who congregated outside the building at lunchtime and in the afternoons. A coalition of black activists, for example, made clear their opposition to the tour by calling the Springbok presence "an insult to black people the world over."[30] During another protest, city alderman Danny Davis declared that playing the game "would be an insult, an indignity." Phumzile Zuma, a representative of South Africa's African National Congress, told a rally at Federal Plaza, "We cannot divorce politics from sports."[31] Nonetheless, Wynand Claassen asserts, "Nothing much materialized." Despite the threats of "massive demonstrations" that Jesse Jackson had promised, "a very small group of protesters pitched up outside the club and they peacefully walked in a circle, displaying the slogans on their placards." But this had no effect on the Bok players. "This protest lasted for about 30 minutes and we missed it altogether, only realising that it had taken place when watching the news on television that evening."[32]

In addition to pushing the Chicago City Council and the mayor to condemn the Springbok presence, Jesse Jackson, who had been in Memphis working with Dr. Martin Luther King, Jr. when King was assassinated in 1968, was one of the leading forces behind the burgeoning anti-tour protests. Jackson, the head of People United to Save Humanity (PUSH) and coordinator of the Black Coalition Against the Rugby Tour, an arm of SART, had indeed promised to disrupt and, if possible, halt the tour. Jackson, an ordained minister, reflected the traditional role of the church in the civil rights movement, and he held a "final count-down rally" in a Chicago Baptist church days before the match. "Our aim is to drive the Springboks out or drive them underground," he told the crowd. "We have nothing against the players themselves, but these young men are being used to make a political statement to build a political bridge between South Africa and the United States."[33]

But if Jackson held no malice toward the Springbok players, he did aim his venom at one specific target: Ronald Reagan. "The President seems determined to make South Africa a cause célèbre. He is attempting to turn back the hands of time and that may yet expose his lack of knowledge of foreign affairs." Further, he accused Reagan of trying to create a "white pro-fascist bloc" with the National Party government in Pretoria. "What our people are saying," Jackson announced, "is that South Africa must join the human community if it wants to be respected. It must allow people human rights."[34]

But the American rugby officials were not going to relent. Ed Lee, the USARFU Fixtures secretary who had been central in planning the tour, served as a spokesman for both teams. He announced to the media, "We not only intend to play, we're determined to play." Given that American teams, though not the national side, had played in South Africa, it was only courtesy to allow the Springboks to play in the United

States. "Besides," said Lee, "they're the world's greatest rugby team, and it's an honor to play them."[35] Although most New Zealanders would surely have disagreed with that assessment, having just taken two of three tests from the visitors, the larger point stands: from a purely sporting vantage point, it absolutely was a coup for the American minnows to be able to play global rugby sharks like the Springboks. Ed Lee, like Johan Claassen, may have been deeply committed to the virtues of rugby, but both men were tone deaf to the politics surrounding the Springboks.

Rob Louw, meanwhile, was surprised by some of the racism he saw in Chicago. At one point when he and Tobias were walking the streets, a black man asked Tobias, "Hey man, what you doin' with that white spook?" He was shocked to discover this American "apartheid." He also learned that sports provided a way out for many African Americans. "Errol and I were shocked to hear that racialism is strong in America."[36] They may have been even more shocked to know about ongoing protests over school integration in Chicago on the part of both black and white parents, who were distressed about a desegregation plan that was about to be implemented in the city. American hands were far from clean on matters racial in 1981.

Further complicating the black–white narrative was the fact that Abe Williams, the coloured assistant manager of the Springboks, publicly put forward his support for the tour. "They have called me a black bastard and Uncle Tom in New Zealand. I just feel that I'm a rugby man and an educationist. I am just trying to do my bit to change society." And while he "fully underst[ood]" the opposition to the tour he planned to "simply ignore" protests because "at this time in our life in South Africa, it's important to have discussions, to get across to other people and get a look at other societies. It's the only way to change attitudes."[37] Perhaps, ironically, Williams thus conveyed the diplomatic possibilities of the tour far better than any of those whose job was to conduct public relations.

A BAD SPY MOVIE: WHERE WOULD THE MATCH TAKE PLACE?

The first match of the Springbok tour was scheduled to be played in Chicago, against a Midwest XV All-Star team, but the public statements and mass meetings from Jesse Jackson and his Operation PUSH coalition, caused officials to move the game. This political opposition also set in motion a series of events worthy of a James Bond film (or maybe one featuring Inspector Clouseau).[38] According to *Sports Illustrated,* "It was as if John LeCarre was collaborating on the subterfuge with the Marx Brothers."[39] Jackson, whose Chicago home base was embroiled in the controversies over school desegregation, and thus especially sensitive to racial issues, vowed "to track down the location of the match and disrupt it."[40] The local members of Stop the Apartheid Rugby Tour (SART) struggled to figure out the match site. "We will check out all our leads," said Laura Brock of SART, who promised to stay by the phone "directing the efforts of a chain of Bok-hunters" in Illinois, Wisconsin, and Indiana.[41] On the other side, Neo-Nazi groups declared themselves in support of the tour and claimed that they would "arm themselves and police the game."[42] One elite hotel in Wisconsin, the Abbey on Lake Geneva, had already cancelled the Springbok squad's reservations when it became clear that there might be disruptions from protesters. South African journalists who were staying at the Playboy club and hotel in Lake Geneva (rumors had spread among the players that they had been scheduled to stay there as well) were "very disturbed" and "increasingly fed up with their isolation and lack of information."[43]

The *Cape Times*, in their editorial questioning the wisdom of the American leg of the tour, noted, "There is something pretty much awry when a game of rugby must be played in a secret venue with only invited guests present."[44]

Very few guests would end up being invited.

Officials eventually settled on Racine, Wisconsin, a city on Lake Michigan, about eighty miles north of Chicago and just about twenty-five miles from Milwaukee. Even before it was known that Racine would play the role of impromptu host, the Racine *Journal Times* published an editorial advocating the cancellation of the game not only to avoid violent clashes between protesters and supporters of the tour but "more importantly on moral grounds." An op-ed on the same page, however, made the opposite case, on the grounds that "rugby is rough enough without being tainted by politics."[45] These would be the essential opposing arguments as the conflict over the Springboks raged throughout the coming days, and by and large capture the two sides of the debate about South Africa sporting isolation more generally. One side believed that South African teams represented their country and thus, its abhorrent politics, and that those policies were in fact embedded in South African sport. The other equally ardently argued that politics and sport should not mix.

Wisconsin's governor, Lee Dreyfus, had no opportunity to weigh in given how quickly events accelerated, but claimed he would have no objections to the Springboks playing in his state. "I'd love to see them play a racially integrated American team and have us beat the pants off of them."[46] Dreyfus had the delusional belief that American rugby could muster up a "Jesse Owens moment," whereby a superior integrated American team would humiliate the apartheid Springboks. But liberal members of the Midwestern rugby establishment believed such posturing to be both ignorant and "preposterous."[47] From a rugby perspective, it was absurd to think that the American national side could beat the Springboks, never mind that a Midwestern all-star team could somehow humiliate them. But beyond that, as Robert Buchanan, president of the Madison-based Wisconsin Rugby Club in 1981, recently noted, with the presence of Errol Tobias and Abe Williams in the Springbok traveling team, "The Springboks had as much diversity as the Midwest Select Side."[48]

The clandestine maneuvers to get the teams and fans to the game approached "bad spy movie" dimensions "with all the secrecy and intrigue."[49] The absurd lengths the organizers went through to maintain the secret even inspired a parody account in the Racine *Journal Times.* The editorial imagines a phone conversation between "Roy Rugger," captain of the Bumps and Bruises rugby team and the British-accented "Deep Throat." Deep Throat's mission was to make sure Rugger was able to get to the game. The directions he gave barely were more absurd than the real events: "Take Highway 50 off I-94 until you get to an old red barn with a Drink Milk sign on it. Then turn left. . . . There will be a gravel road 15 yards from the barn . . . take that road 2.36 miles and then hide your car in some raspberry bushes on the right [and] take

36 paces and stop at an old hollowed out stump. . . . Then make the sound of a whipperwill." Once Rugger heard "a wolf howl," he would "proceed another 51 paces and wait for your contact . . . a short man dressed like a grizzly bear" who would guide him to a clearing where the match was to be played. Rugger was curious as to why there was so much secrecy surrounding a rugby match, and Deep Throat explained, "We don't want any of these protesters hanging around . . . they ran us out of Chicago and made such a fuss in New Zealand, we had to have 148 of them arrested. And all because of apartheid." This last assertion caused a clueless Rugger to ask, "What position does he play?" and Deep Throat to slam the receiver down in exasperation.[50]

But even the most tongue-in-cheek satire could not match the actual planning leading up to the underground September 19 rugby match. As late as Friday, officials were still making concurrent plans to hold the match in several locales. A small number of organizers privy to the plans made a series of phone calls late Friday night to inform a small inner circle to meet at a Howard Johnson's restaurant on Highway 50 in Kenosha County at 8:15 Saturday morning. There, they would receive directions to the field where the match would take place. Dave Canfield, the father of two players for the Libertyville, Illinois, rugby club who were among the Midwest XV, received a call at 12:30 a.m. on Saturday and was told to drive north on I-94 the next morning to the Highway 50 exit in Kenosha County. "I was told there would be a 1954 Oldsmobile there, and that there would be a man wearing a green rugby shirt in the car," Canfield explained to a reporter. "We were supposed to show him a ticket." The yellow tickets were for the original game that was supposed to have been played at the Oakbrook, Illinois, polo field. Canfield continued, "Then we were supposed to say 'Are you Checkpoint Charlie?' That was the password. Then he was to ask if we would open our trunk." Even when demonstrators thought they had figured out the ruse and approached the man in the Oldsmobile they did not know the password and so were sent off in the wrong direction.[51] The Oldsmobile at the Howard Johnsons in Kenosha was overseen by "a bunch of conspiratorial kids in the jerseys of the Racine Rugby Football Club" whose "looks were stern but it was clear that they were bubbling with fun. And just as obvious was the fact that they had little idea of the extent to which they were being betrayed by their elders in the sport."[52]

The man responsible for organizing the Midwest XV match, Tyke Nollman, the president of the Chicago Lions, established a "hot-line" that would allow people to get details that would eventually lead them to the match. He also announced different venues to the press at different times to sow seeds of confusion and to keep the scent cold for demonstrators. "Was it rugby or hide and seek?" asked a Racine *Journal Times* headline. "The only thing missing was a self-destructing tape recorder," added the article detailing the extent of the covert planning.[53]

Despite these efforts, a fair number of spectators found out the location of the game. The Midwestern rugby community was small and virtually everyone within it knew one another. For those in known clubs, such as the Wisconsin Rugby Club in Madison, organizers and the club president, Robert Buchanan, "organized . . . a simple phone tree." The WRC organized an "early morning meeting time for ruggers in the Madison area." Buchanan had been told that they needed to be prepared to respond quickly because there would "be barely enough time to drive from Madison to the 'hidden match's location.'" Buchanan chose Pitcher's Pub, which was adjacent to his club's field, and provided the number for both the bar and the pay phone in the lobby, in case he could not get into the bar. "When the call came to me, I passed on the location and we all quickly jumped into our vehicles" and drove the hundred or so miles to Racine. "We never heard of 'Check Point Charlie.'"[54]

The Racine police also appeared to have been given notice of the match. Furthermore, "scores of spectators" who arrived in cars with Illinois plates apparently followed the Springbok bus from Chicago.[55] "Check Point Charlie" thus has become part of the mythology surrounding the match—not entirely untrue, but finding the mysterious interlocutor also hardly represented the sole determinant for whether one could get to the match or not.

Dave Canfield could not understand the opposition to the match that caused so many hassles. "I only wish people in this country would become that excited about curing cancer, having peace, or curing MDS. But all this over a young man's game. I think it's kind of ridiculous."[56] Canfield's arguments may have been red herrings—it is difficult to imagine that protesters were taking busy time away from curing cancer to demonstrate against rugby any more than, say, the parents of rugby players were when they went to watch a match or the players were when they played in it—but they represented a common view of some of the advocates of the Springbok tour.

RUGBY IN RACINE: THE MIDWESTERN XV AGAINST THE SPRINGBOKS

Away from the drama, the Springbok players tried to prepare as normally as possible. They were up early, grabbed boxed lunches and coffee, and boarded buses for the mystery setting. The South African media members had received a call at 6 a.m. and were told that they would be picked up in an hour. They stopped at the first Howard Johnson's they saw for an early morning breakfast, and then found themselves "barreling over the rolling cornfields of Wisconsin."[57] Wynand Claassen noted that "again we realized that the American mediamen were real professionals, for they had a television crew posted outside of both entrances of the club waiting for us to emerge." When the touring party left through a back exit "they were onto us and we raced off with them following behind with the cameramen leaning out of one of the windows. By the time we reached our destination he must have had yards of film of the three busses racing down the highway." If at least some in the media had not been left behind in Chicago, however, the "clandestine departure had the effect of throwing off the demonstrators, and by the time they had organized themselves to go in search of the ground the match had been played and we were already on our way back."[58] Or nearly so, anyway.

The Midwestern players, support staff, and supporters were nearly as in the dark as the South Africans as the match approached. Before heading to Wisconsin, the team that was set to play on Saturday practiced in Lincoln Park in Chicago. According to the Midwest manager, Stu Pippel, "There was a fair amount of media in the area trying to get 'THE' story and put different slants on it." There was little story to get from that group, however. "To be honest, the squad members, coaches, and administrators of the Midwest Union had been given no information as to who, what, when, how or where for the match." Pippel recalled a reporter asking one of the players, Joe Scheitlin, "who are you with" to which he replied, "We're with each other." In Pippel's assessment, "No story here for that reporter."[59] Joseph Sauer, the Midwest Rugby Football Union vice president and a reserve player in the match, recalled that the planners had stumbled upon the pitch that they used "in Racine next to a National Guard base and the Lake Michigan shore" and it was likely one "used before by the Racine–Kenosha Club and interestingly it was in a poorer part of town." The day before the match, the Midwestern Rugby Football Club side that was to face the Springboks found a field upon which to practice and then "wound up spending the night in a dumpy motel" on Highway 94 in Racine.[60] At the time, Sauer thought that "the media had blown the Springbok visit so out of hand that minor protest groups seemed monstrous and public officials all over the place declared they were out to deny a group of amateur sportsters the constitutional right to assemble." Yet Sauer admitted his group's subterfuge, including their ability to "spoof all kinds of media people and protesters" and admitting that they never told public officials the final details "just so they wouldn't over react."[61] This kind of thinking would be common among the American advocates of the tour, who would claim their constitutional rights but would do everything in their power to deny the similarly embedded rights of protesters and the press, never mind public officials. Sauer certainly was just a young man wanting to play a rugby match against elite opposition with whom he would never again be able to share a pitch, but the selective commitment to constitutional rights would become a hallmark of the efforts to host the South Africans.

Stu Pippel doesn't "remember hearing any of the Midwest team debating whether the match should be played. I think most of us were considering it a huge honor to play against the Springboks without even considering what repercussions or consequences may lie ahead." But over time he "often wondered if any of the Midwest players ever had 2nd thoughts about it. Whether the Midwest and USA Rugby condoned apartheid by playing the match became an issue for me."[62] In the words of long-time Midwestern rugby stalwart, Buck Buchanan, "A half dozen of my friends wanted to test themselves against some of the better rugby players in the world. I wanted to be there for support." After all, "In reality, having the Midwest Select Side play against an international team in Wisconsin had seemed too far fetched to us to be even remotely possible."[63]

The match was played on an American football field at Roosevelt Park, meaning that the goalposts were placed on the dead-ball line at the back of the gridiron end zone rather than on the try line, a peculiarity that struck South African observers as comical. The field was also considerably narrower than a world-class rugby pitch, and the lines were painted in a way nearly unrecognizable to the Springboks. Bok player Okkie Oosthuizen "spent some time wandering around the touchline and asking his teammates 'which one is the 22?'" referring to the 22-meter line that is standard on all rugby pitches and serves several important purposes, especially in determining possession.[64] Roosevelt Park stood between a National Guard armory "with tanks and artillery on display" and "a building that looked like a clubhouse." That building was the Dr. John Bryant Center, a vital institution in Racine's black community. "In a piece of crassness equaled only by their original invitation, the administrators of American rugby had chosen a predominantly black section of Racine for the Springboks' debut."[65]

The match took place at 9:15 a.m., thus marking the only time a Springbok side has ever played a match in the morning local time, a bit of trivia that nonetheless illustrates just how odd the trip was for the South Africans. The game kicked off fifteen minutes late, which was "not uncommon in the happy-go-lucky world of U.S. rugby."[66] At least part of the reason for the delay was that it took a few minutes to track down that most essential object for the game, a ball, as neither team nor the referee was in possession of one. Ultimately, a ball was found, with some asserting that the Midwestern Rugby Union used one of their own but others believing that the Springboks provided a ball. Any one of these oddities would have stood out, but the combination of them, in addition to the covert nature of the game itself, made the whole situation seem absurd, causing Johan Claassen to mutter "This is really something to see."[67]

The Boks, who had been forced to change behind a building, "started slowly" and "in fact trailed by six points before pulling away to win" according to Wynand Claassen, who did not play in the nontest match and "found the best seats in the ground by clambering up a tree."[68] The South Africans started off the game playing against a brisk wind, effectively "running uphill." The Boks wore their customary green and gold jerseys, the Midwestern Thunderbirds white jerseys with "a mielie" [a South African word for corn] "badge" on the front.[69]

Joe Scheitlin scored the first try of the match for the Midwesterners, "most likely because the Springboks," who would have had to be up inordinately early to get from Chicago to the field, warm up, and be ready to play, "may not have been fully conscious at that ridiculous kick-off time," according to Pippel.[70]

The Boks rebounded from the early deficit and paltry 18–12 half-time lead and easily defeated their white-clad opponents, 46–12, with Colin Beck, Theuns Stofberg, Edrich Krantz, Louw, and Hempies Du Toit each scoring a try, Carel du Plessis, a future Springbok head coach, scoring two, and Gysie Pienaar kicking two penalties and six conversions. Billy Chung kicked the two drop goals that gave the Midwestern side their early 6–0 lead and converted the Scheitlin try. By eleven o'clock, the match was over. Ed Lee, the American spokesman for the visitors, claimed after the match, "I'm delighted that it came off the way we planned it. We had a good sporting event."[71] The Midwestern coach, Jim Perkins, "was very proud of the effort put forth by the Midwest players."[72]

Attendance was sparse. Wynand Claassen claimed to count "exactly 247 spectators scattered around the touchline," including a few South Africans based in the United States, numbers roughly confirmed by Rob Louw and a reporter from *Sports Illustrated*.[73] Representatives of the USA Rugby Union and the Midwest Union hosts still "sold programs complete with lineups," the proceeds from which would help defray costs of the Springbok tour.[74] It is worth pointing out that for the Springboks, 250 spectators at a rugby match contributed to what Rob Louw called "a pathetic situation."[75] According to a South African reporter on the scene, "except for the accents" the fans there "could have been supporters for a third-league match on the South African platteland." One American observer described the crowd as "all middle-class white folk, most of them young, some with babies in strollers. . . . It would be hard to imagine a less threatening way to start a weekend."[76] The attendance was small, but it also represented the largest crowd anyone could remember at a rugby match in the Midwest, with at least some fans coming from as far away as Iowa and Ohio, apparently from rugby clubs privy to inside information from the tour's supporters. While beer flowed freely among the crowd throughout the morning, Roosevelt Park was a long way from Cape Town's Newlands Stadium.

The only player from Racine among the Midwestern All Stars was William Chung, a twenty-three-year-old from Korea with permanent residence status in the United States who played for the West Side Harlequins of Milwaukee and had scored the bulk of his side's points on the strength of his kicking. He had mixed feelings about the match but was happy to have experienced the competition against an elite side. He also argued (though Buck Buchanan is dubious) that his team was racially diverse. His teammates included a black player from Indianapolis and a Hispanic player from Fort Wayne, Indiana. When asked how the Springboks were as competitors, he responded, "They were huge. They averaged over 200 pounds. I weigh 160 pounds . . . I was surprised at how well we did."[77] Chung had South African connections—he had lived in Durban. He was not the only person with South African ties on the Midwest squad. Freddy Schofield, a chiropractor, had played with his friend Rob Louw for Western Province Schools, and Judex Oberholzer was from Pretoria.

"AN AFFRONT"

Despite the care taken to avoid protests, "a number of demonstrators managed to get to the ground and they caused a brief delay midway through the second half."[78] Joseph Sauer, the player–vice president of the MWRFU had heard a rumor that "supposedly my red Ute was spotted from the highway just as I left that motel by an antagonistic Milwaukee rugger and he alerted the Chicago protesters that we were gathering in a couple buses that something was happening in the Chicago area."[79] Stu Pippel believed that "the way the protesters eventually found the match site was that a woman who lived across from the pitch called a relative in Chicago who was one of the protesters."[80] But this was all speculation—the protesters, like those fans who gathered, probably had a number of ways to discover what was happening in Racine, even if at first they were slow to gather.

Of the protesters who found the secret site, two were arrested, Marvin Happel, a forty-five-year-old member of the Racine School Board, and Joseph L. Harris, a thirty-eight-year-old civil rights leader. Police restrained Happel when he walked onto the pitch during the game, warning him that if he attempted to do so again, they would arrest him.

Once released, Happel started right back onto the playing field so officers loaded him into a police vehicle. Harris, too, went to jail for walking onto the field and interrupting the game. These disruptions only caused play to be stopped for about five minutes or so. Wynand Claassen remembered the match being played largely "without incident" with the one interruption that he noticed "being when a lone protester," likely Happel, "walked onto the field brandishing a bat-like object. He tried to talk to the players but was quickly removed by security guards."[81]

Although early on the planners had successfully flummoxed much of the media, by the end of the match "there were television crews everywhere." The BBC conducted a report from the match, describing it as "one of the most extraordinary rugby matches ever played," predicting "repercussions that will last for years."[82]

The players moved quickly on from the game. They "pulled on their tracksuits and piled into the bus for the trip back to Chicago with a brief pit-stop to grab a few six-packs of Michelob." Back in the anonymity of the city the Springboks had "a pleasant banquet with the Midwest XV that evening, and then the whole lot of us went out to explore Chicago's night life."[83] The players from both teams, at least, maintained the customary sense of postmatch collegiality and fellowship (and drinking) that historically has characterized rugby.

The banquet was held back at the Chicago Athletic Association, where the Springboks had escaped ahead of the protesters in the wee hours of that morning. It was "quite the affair," according to Stu Pippel. However, "To no one's surprise the Midwest Union had no funds to cover the substantial cost of the dinner," so at the next meeting of the MWRFU "it was decided that each member club would be assessed a $200+ fee to cover the cost of the Springbok tour." Those clubs that did not pay the fee were threatened with sanctions ranging from exclusion from Midwest-sponsored events to losing access to referees. "You might imagine the uproar that created, particularly among some of the more 'activist' universities and colleges," such as the University of Wisconsin–Madison, which "drafted a letter to the Midwest Union essentially saying 'go f**k yourselves.'" Pippel "actually found [himself] supporting the UW club on its stance."[84]

Almost immediately, Racine city officials decried the fact that they had no knowledge that the game would be played at Roosevelt Park. In a shocking lack of awareness, the organizers had decided to hold the match at a park adjacent to a predominantly black neighborhood. One black protester asserted, "If we'd known the game was being played here, we'd have had hundreds, maybe thousands here."[85] For all their talk about the rights of the rugby players to play, the organizers did everything that they could to abnegate the rights of those who wanted to protest a game being held in a public park. They wanted all the benefits of the Springbok presence and wanted none of the responsibilities or burdens. They wanted to assert the separation of sport and politics while denying the rights of others to exercise their concerns about the inherently political nature of the Springbok tour.

Tensions among the crowd rose as locals realized what was happening and as protesters caught up to the game. One neighborhood resident, James Cotton, whose home was located across from the park, noticed the cars pulling up to the facility. "Nobody really knew what was happening. You could tell everything had been kept secret because the crowd didn't start gathering until 30 or 35 minutes after the game had started. The police weren't even here until after it began." James' son, Henry, who also lived nearby, said playing the game in the park showed "total insensitivity." He explained, "This park is on the fringe of a black neighborhood. The feelings of the people here just weren't considered." Somebody had to know what was going on before they showed up here. Times are bad enough right now without having something like this happen right in your neighborhood." Yet another black observer called the game "the most blatant affront to the minority community in Racine I've ever seen." Charles Swanson, a local black attorney who had been subdued by police for walking onto the field wielding a stick during the match, later explained, "I had to do something even if I were disbarred or arrested. It was very insulting for them to bring them here. We cannot tolerate that here . . . to bring them to the only black park in Racine." Happel, the school board member who went to jail for his on-field protests, also believed the game represented "an affront" to Racine's black population. "It only emphasizes what we have been saying all along, that South African team tour represents a racist policy."[86]

Corinne Owens, who was active in the Racine branch of the NAACP, was "shocked" when she discovered that the game was being played in her hometown. "When I heard, I made some phone calls and took off in my car" but by the time she arrived people were leaving. "If I had been down there earlier, I probably would have been one of those arrested." Although she wanted to make it clear that she only spoke for herself and not her NAACP branch, she was certain that they would hold a meeting in response to the events. "I can't believe the city would allow the game to go on. There's racism there somewhere. I think it was pretty sneaky." Owens had support for her arguments from George Stinson, the vice president of the Racine NAACP who saw the game as "an insult to all people seeking social justice" because it was played near a community center named after John Bryant, a black doctor and civil rights leader in the city. "It's an affront to us, it's an affront to his name, it's an affront to all the people of Racine." One member of Racine's black community got into a skirmish with white fans and later told a reporter simply, "I don't like punks from South Africa coming into my neighborhood." Martha Pettit told police she was shoved and kicked while she carried a picket sign at the field. [87]

Sister Lois Vanderbeke of the Dominican Sisters in Racine was one of a dozen or so of her order who turned up to protest as soon as she heard the news that the game had begun in Racine. "We feel this is a fraud to the community," she explained. "Somebody had to know about this beforehand. We feel we have been taken by our local government . . . by our national government, which we know has been doing it all along." A woman described as having a "British accent" shouted at Vanderbeke as she carried a picket sign. "You have apartheid in this country too! I've been here three years and have seen it. You're just not as honest about it." This childish "you do it too" argument was common among supporters of apartheid South Africa and seems especially ill-aimed given that Vanderbeke asserted that many more people would have joined her in protests had many of them not been in Washington, DC, for a Solidarity Day rally. It is a stretch to believe that the highly motivated activists who made up the still-nascent anti-apartheid movement in 1981 were not equally outraged by American racism. Indeed, after the match, protesters chanted "Segregation here, apartheid there, end racism everywhere," and some carried signs reading "Smash US/ South Africa racist axis." Other slogans and signs called for "Apartheid ambassadors get the hell out" and "Drive Springboks out." Counter-protesters tried to drown out the anti-apartheid activists and others loudly cheered the players as they exited the field after the game. [88] The protests might have been even greater, but a busload of demonstrators from Chicago arrived a half-hour after the game had ended.

The debate continued in Racine for several days, keeping rugby, South Africa, and the anti-apartheid question at the forefront of local discussions. The Midwest XV players defended their decision to play the match and used the familiar justification about not wanting to mix sports and politics. Given that the opportunity to play the Springboks also represented a once-in-a-lifetime chance to play a world-class team, their self-interested justification is, at least in the context of a purely sports-driven argument, understandable.

Local officials, meanwhile, had to deal with the aftermath of the match, a situation exacerbated by the fact that every local politician was just as caught off guard by the location of the game as was the rest of the nonrugby community. The sentiments of Jack Molbeck, assistant director of the city's parks and recreation department, most clearly expressed what many other officials felt: "I'm pissed off. They didn't have permission to play in the city of Racine. They definitely didn't have permission to play in Racine." Indeed, Molbeck had explicitly refused permission for the Racine–Kenosha Rugby Club to hold a game at a different park on Saturday. It soon became clear that the Racine City Council planned to act in response to the stealth playing of the Springbok match.[89] "The more I think about it, the madder I get," exclaimed an outraged alderwoman, Dorothy Constantine. "I'm appalled at the insensitivity of our rugby people, to put this game in a neighborhood which couldn't exist in South Africa."[90] Several Wisconsin legislators also expressed opposition to the Springbok presence in Wisconsin. In the words of Representative Thomas Crawford, a Milwaukee Democrat, "It is important to recognize the South African team for what it is—a political statement and display of pride in the South African system."[91]

The editors of the *Journal Times* condemned both the apartheid regime and almost everyone involved in the staging of the game in their city. "First, and most importantly, is the abhorrent South African policy of political, economic and social abuse of an entire race of people." In light of this reality, "Saying that sports is either not political or should be kept out of politics is exceptionally naïve." Therefore, "The second wrong was the sponsorship by this area's rugby group. It was deceitful." The editorial continued:

Knowing full well that a permit for the game had already been denied by the city of Racine, knowing that the team represented one of the more hateful governments in the world, knowing that there was potential for a serious confrontation they did not notify police of the match; plus, our rugby group sneaked the South Africans onto the field located right next to one of Racine's racially mixed neighborhoods. It would be hard to use enough adjectives to describe the profound insensitivity exhibited by the organizers of the match. [92]

But the editors had a few harsh words for the protesters as well: "As much as South African policy is objectionable, as much as the match being held in Racine is objectionable, so, too, is the conduct by some protesters." They singled out Marvin Happel, Joseph Harris, and Charles Swanson, who, they argued, "did nothing to effectively illuminate the issue." On the other hand, "The placard carriers along the sidelines, who pointed out South Africa's racism, were well within acceptable bounds. So were the protesters who debated and argued." The last line of the editorial read, "The eyes of the world got a brief look at Racine Saturday. It was not the city's finest hour." But the main takeaway came in the penultimate paragraph:

The tour by the South African team has been farcical. Team members have had to sneak around the countryside because of the antagonism exhibited by so many Americans. That should send team members back to South African [*sic*] with a message: despite the lack of moral con[vi?]ction [*sic*] by the Reagan administration (which only decries inhuman policies when there is no economic impact) unofficial America is not tolerant of that country's intolerance. [93]

Meanwhile, that week the city leaders responded. The Monday after the game the parks commission unanimously passed a ban of the Racine–Kenosha Rugby Club from playing in city parks. For the order to go into effect, the city council had to approve it in a special meeting called by mayor Stephen Olsen. Geeta Sharma-Jensen, a native of India who had lived in Racine since 1971 and had been a reporter for the *Journal Times* since 1975, when she earned a master's degree in journalism from nearby Marquette University, wrote a column opposing the proposed ban. "I cannot help feeling that if such a ban is allowed, it could one day boomerang and land in someone else's lap—the collective lap, for example, of the very people that city officials are attempting to mollify." She opposed "tak[ing] away the freedom of those Americans who seem unruffled by South Africa's lack of human rights. . . . For, we must not forget that if the Kenosha–Racine rugby club is barred from a city park, who's to say that one day blacks or any one else may not also be barred for similar reasons."[94] Cooler heads prevailed when officials realized that a ban of the club might well violate both the United States and Wisconsin Constitutions and, in the end, the city council chose to censure the local rugby club, a largely symbolic effort, though a couple of organizers faced prosecution for violations of parks regulations.

Readers of the *Journal Times* weighed in as well. Michael LaMartina thought that perhaps the protests against rugby proved to be a distraction from the fact that American policy toward South Africa was itself remiss. "While rugby has become the focus of the anger and moral outrage that many of us truly feel towards South Africa," he wrote, "it is, I suppose, comforting to many, because they can more easily continue to ignore the official policy that our government and industry exhibit, which serve to justify apartheid more surely than a hundred rugby teams or a thousand exhibition games ever could." Sam Bort effectively rejected the logic of the *Journal Times'* condemnation of the most assertive protesters, arguing that Happel and Harris "deserve the respect and admiration from all those people who cherish freedom and oppose racism. They had the fortitude to try and disrupt the game. If many of us hadn't gone to Washington, D. C. that weekend, either the Racine County jail would've been filled, or the game would have been stopped."[95]

Paula Peppers reflected a different perspective. "When people object to a nation's political policies, they rally together and attack the people of the nation. It would make more sense to attack the leaders of the nation—not the residents." She also questioned whether there was any malice attached to the fact that the organizers held the game in such close proximity to a black neighborhood. "The fact of the matter is that we live in an integrated society and there are very few fields anywhere that are acceptable for rugby playing where there are not any black residents nearby."[96]

Additionally, the *Journal Times* wanted readers to see the issue "as others see it," and so the paper shared opinion pieces from two other newspapers, both of which supported the right of the Springboks to play in the United States.

The *Wisconsin State Journal* argued, "There will be no avenues to understanding if there aren't ways for South Africans to meet others in the world, people to people, in friendly athletic competition or in other settings. . . . Let the South African ruggers play." The editors of the paper noted that the South African team included "two blacks." "Let them know how we feel about their nation's racist policies in conversation before and after the games. After all, we are only emerging from more than a century of discrimination ourselves. . . . We have much more to talk about, much to learn."

The *Milwaukee Journal* took a different tack. "The First Amendment shouldn't be battered on the playing fields of America. And Wisconsin citizens should have more than a passing interest in that concern." And while the editors acknowledged the possibility of violence marring public matches pitting American sides against the South Africans, they insisted that "fear of disorder does not justify denying either the players' right to assembly or the protesters' right to decry the rugby tour as symbolic of a racist regime."[97] Both of these arguments are reasonably subtle and, as we shall see, the *Milwaukee Journal* view would prevail from a purely legalistic standpoint, at least when the issue moved to Albany.

A few moments before the end of the peculiar match, Springbok coach Nelie Smith, who had "been stone-faced and silent long enough" and "permitted himself a smile" turned to an American rugby official and said "We're nearly home and dry, eh?"[98] The Springbok tour had left its mark on the Midwest. But the events in Racine merely served as a preview of the tumult that would take place in Upstate New York.

6

ALBANY I

Facing Off in the Courts and Against the Colonials

TOM SELFRIDGE AND THE 1981 SPRINGBOK TOUR

The events in the Midwest would prove simply to be a warm-up for a pair of matches in the Albany area, where Tom Selfridge, the chairman of the Eastern Rugby Union (ERU), had "achieved overnight fame as he battled for the right to stage" games involving the Springboks.[1] Selfridge had represented the United States in its first three test matches in the modern era starting in 1976, facing Australia, France, and Canada, and earned five caps in total for the Eagles. In 1980, soon after his playing career ended, he had been elected president of the ERU, the largest of the four regional rugby unions in the United States. He would later go on to be inducted into the USA Rugby Hall of Fame largely based on his work as a pioneering player, administrator, and advocate for the sport.

Selfridge had played against a South African team when the US Cougars select team toured that country to virtually no fanfare in 1978. "We played a game in one of the first fully integrated stadiums," Selfridge later recalled. "People could sit wherever they wanted to. The particular rugby union we were playing against owned their own stadium and that board of directors chose to do that." Selfridge also spoke about having "the opportunity to play a game against the first integrated South African team."[2] In both cases, it is unclear what Selfridge means by "fully integrated," as so many aspects of South African life were dominated by apartheid that "fully integrated" somewhat loses meaning or worse becomes an assertion of naïveté. Selfridge and the Cougars did play against the SW County Districts, whose ranks included two "coloured" players, Hennie Shields and Errol Tobias. Nonetheless that playing experience, and the "lavish hospitality" the South Africans had provided, along with the chance to play one of the world's greatest sports teams, had encouraged Selfridge to pursue the South African matches in New York.[3]

Even if Douglas Reid believed he was the man to organize a Springbok tour that would benefit both nations, Tom Selfridge, a far more self-aware and practical man with actual influence in American rugby circles, was truly capable of pulling off such a feat. It was his Eastern Rugby Union that got the $25,000 from fertilizer salesman and rugby impresario Louis Luyt, and it was Selfridge who found himself as the organizer, chief spokesman, and unquestioned authority for a tour that he could not have imagined would garner him national and international attention. In fact, the US leg of the tour hit its most significant early public visibility in early August, while the Springboks were still bogged down in New Zealand. The August 1 Sunday *New York Times* published Selfridge's opinion piece defending the Springbok visit, and a piece by Richard Lapchick of ACCESS, and Franklin Williams, the president of the Phelps-Stokes Fund and a former ambassador to both Ghana and the United Nations, who were in opposition to the tour.

Selfridge's argument was essentially twofold: that American rugby simply wanted to play the highest level of competition possible, and that the Springbok visit represented an unprecedented opportunity; and that politics and sport should not mix. Simply put, he "invited the Springboks to play here in an effort to give our athletes better competition and upgrade our sport." Maintaining that his main concern was "development of the sport" in the United States and "attracting world-class athletes," Selfridge claimed, "If the Darth Vader Rugby Club were coming on tour to the United States, I'm sure we could arrange plenty of matches." Denying the very real linkages between sport and politics and the explicit links between apartheid and sports in South Africa, Selfridge further stated that, "Saying that the Springboks represent more than just a sports team is like saying that George Steinbrenner or Tom Landry run the cities of New York or Dallas." Such reasoning revealed a truly shallow understanding of the connection between Afrikaner nationalism, white supremacy, and the Springboks, for in the most literal sense, the Springboks have always been presented as representing "more than just a sports team" by their supporters.[4]

It also represented a willful or naïve misreading of the history of sport. Selfridge's assertion, "The statement sports and politics do not mix is very true," was not, and never had been, true. Further, Selfridge's belief that "the real issue comes down to the rights of a private, independent sports organization being allowed to schedule and play its games against any other similar organization. The Springboks are not politicians. They do not set or make any policy in South Africa." But Selfridge ignores the main criticism of the anti-apartheid sports movement, which was that there could be no such thing as normal sport in an abnormal society. The Springbok players, other than voting for the National Party and, in a number of cases, literally working for the state in numerous capacities, may not have directly set policies, but they did benefit from those policies. The Springboks absolutely reflected and represented apartheid South Africa.

Just as Selfridge misjudged the relationship between politics and sport, so, too, did he fall for the illusion that South African rugby officials and the government hoped would fool supporters of the tour, such as in his claim that "the team is multiracial, selected on ability and open to all players in South Africa." Errol Tobias absolutely belonged on the Springboks but his presence, and that of Abe Williams in the management team, provided a shield against the very legitimate criticisms that South African rugby was anything but committed to merit in selection either at the national level or across the spectrum of South African rugby.

Doubling down on his desire for a separation between sport and politics, Selfridge closed his piece with a simple suggestion: "The people who do not like the policies of South Africa or the United States should go to the seats of government in Pretoria or Washington to protest, and allow the sportsmen to play their games in the stadiums of Chicago, Albany and New York City."[5] This idealistic flourish was also naïve in the extreme, as anyone who had seen the bloody aftermath of the Soweto Uprisings of 1976 would have understood what it meant to advocate that critics of the Springboks or South African policy go and protest in Pretoria. Indeed, government-sanctioned violence would only increase as the South African government developed the "Total Strategy" to crush opposition throughout the 1980s.

Naturally, Lapchick and Williams saw through this sophistry, revealing a far greater understanding of the realities of South African society and sport than the propaganda that advocates of the tour spoon-fed willing recipients. To be fair, Lapchick had written Selfridge before the tout "as we did to all those supporting apartheid sport. Like all the others he claimed he did not support it."[6] Beyond the simple fact that the tour violated the global sports boycott against South Africa, they pointed out the realities of South African society for the black majority, which "struggles to survive" and which had "little leisure time to practice sports." "Even if they had the time," the authors noted, "blacks have very limited access to training facilities or proper coaching. Ninety-nine percent of those few who play do so at the club level where sports are segregated." And while "some national and international teams are integrated" it was, in the words of Lapchick and Williams, "not hard to see through the window dressing."[7]

Focusing in on the 1981 tour, Lapchick and Williams debunked any myths pertaining to the presence of Abe Williams and Tobias on the touring side. They all but accused Williams of being a sellout. "We can listen to [Williams] tell us through the press to be patient with South Africa and allow the considerable evolutionary progress to continue. He can then point to [Tobias] to show the progress. South Africa is 13 percent white, yet 29 of the 30 men on the rugby team are white. Progress? The painful reality is that although Williams can travel to New Zealand and America with the Springboks, he cannot go to most white hotels in Johannesburg to have a drink with his newfound pals." To be fair to Abe Williams, 1981 Springbok Div Visser recalled many years later, "Abe was and is a great ambassador for our 1981 squad and we all love him."[8] Lapchick and Williams rightfully pointed out that "Apartheid is being hardened." Indeed, it would continue to "harden" in the decade to come. Ultimately, for the two anti-apartheid writers, if moral outrage was not enough to stop the tour, the prospect of widespread social upheaval should have been.[9]

Lapchick and Williams would garner support in the *Times'* letters to the editors. Ronald Gutfleish of Englewood, New Jersey, rejected that the Springboks did not carry with them political implications and that sport and politics could or even should be separated. "The South

African Springboks serve an important political function," and "if the tour is allowed to go on, the South African government will portray the fact that we are hosting the tour as support for its political system" and the tour "will bolster an oppressive regime, proving once again that sports and politics cannot be separated."[10] Paul Duguid of New York City rejected that the Springboks were merely a private club. "In nothing but name are the Springboks a club. They are as much a club as the American League All-star team is a club. The Springboks are the South African national team, selected from across the country to represent the country as a whole," he explained. "Playing for this team is, indeed, referred to as 'representing your country.'" Yet the Springboks could only muster one coloured and no black African players. "You can see why they want to call their team a club, when in fact it is a national team representing the apartheid system."[11]

DENIED!: PLAYING POLITICS AND THE POLITICS OF PLAYING

The first Springbok match in New York was to pit the visitors against the "Colonials," an ERU all-star squad. This game was scheduled for Albany's Bleecker Stadium, but even before the Springboks surreptitiously took the field in Racine, New York governor Hugh Carey pressured Albany mayor Erastus Corning II to call off the game, setting in motion a series of political machinations and court challenges that culminated in a trip through the gantlet of the United States court system and an exploration of the meaning of the First Amendment of the United States Constitution.

On Thursday, September 17, Mayor Corning cancelled the match, but he made it clear that he was acting at Governor Carey's behest. Carey declared that there was "imminent danger of a riot," and therefore "determined that the rugby game should not be held in Albany." Speaking at the Albany City Hall, Corning articulated that the decision was Carey's, not his: "[Carey] did not recommend that I cancel the game—he prohibited it, period. He made a unilateral decision not to play the game in Albany." Indeed, earlier Corning had argued that it would have been "wrong to prohibit an individual or group from taking part in a public athletic event because of their beliefs or the policies of their government." Moreover, he was not even convinced that Carey had the authority to cancel the game, declaring "I don't know whether he has the power or not, but he has taken the power."[12]

For his part, Carey believed that he was acting "consistent with my constitutional obligations as governor. . .to ensure that the laws are faithfully executed." Carey said that he had been informed that, "Local law enforcement resources are inadequate to protect the well being and lives of the people of this state and the properties of the state and its people if the proposed game proceeds." He also argued that while he had the authority to call in the National Guard, the possible violence "may not be adequately countered by such measures and, indeed, may even be exacerbated by such measures." Carey's chief of staff, Robert J. Morgado, told a local reporter that members of the Ku Klux Klan from Connecticut and the Communist Workers Party from New York—strange bedfellows if ever there were—planned to disrupt the game, but claimed he was unable to release the confidential report.[13]

Carey apparently did not think about how poorly it reflected on him as the chief law enforcement authority in his state that he could not maintain safety and security at a rugby game, protesters or no. Furthermore, there is an irony attached to the fact that Carey's arguments were similar to those put forth by Orval Faubus, the governor of Arkansas who attempted to forestall the Little Rock Nine from entering Central High School. New York City mayor Ed Koch had earlier used "similar grounds to cancel a scheduled appearance of the Springboks in New York City" in what amounted to a preemptive strike, but he had faced no legal challenges.[14] Indeed, the American Committee on Africa described Koch's decision as Stop the Apartheid Rugby Tour's "first victory" in their campaign against the Springboks.[15] Rochester, too, rejected a Springbok match, though the NY-CLU worried that Koch was granting a "heckler's veto" by succumbing to his fears that demonstrations might get out of hand and would require at least 2,000 police. Nonetheless, the early successes in keeping the Springboks off New York fields caused a *New York Times* writer to muse, "Even better than beating them on the field, say those protesting the American tour of South Africa's national rugby team, is keeping them off it in the first place."[16] The Americans were never going to beat the Springboks on the pitch. But keeping the Springboks off it seemed a possibility.

The Eastern Rugby Union immediately announced that it would go to court to appeal the decision to cancel the game. Joining them would be the NY-CLU. They would argue that Carey and Corning did not have the authority to prohibit the game and that doing so was unconstitutional. "If a black African team wanted to play and the Ku Klux Klan threatened to disrupt it, the governor would be the first to offer the protection of the state police," NY-CLU executive director Dorothy J. Samuels argued. "The only difference here is that the group is an unpopular group."[17] Steven R. Shapiro, an attorney for the NY-CLU had argued before the court against Carey's decision. "What began as an athletic contest has been elevated into an important test of constitutional principles. This case is not about apartheid. The South African Springboks could just as well be any other unpopular group."[18]

Albany lawyer Lanney E. Thayer, who represented the Capital District's Coalition Against Apartheid (CAA), which had actively opposed the tour in the weeks leading up to the Springboks' arrival, supported the ban in court. While his opponents emphasized First Amendment rights, Thayer believed the Fourteenth Amendment prohibition against discrimination took precedence over the First Amendment claims. He believed that if Albany held the game in a public facility, the city "would be condoning, supporting and sanctioning South African apartheid." In South Africa, he argued, sport "is an arm of the system of apartheid."[19]

The question of whether a rugby match could count as speech proved to be a fascinating one, and one without precedent. It would seem that in order for the Springbok game to have been protected under the First Amendment, there would have to be an explicit recognition that the game was in fact a political endeavor. Yet the defenders of the Springboks assiduously insisted that theirs was an apolitical tour, that the Boks were independent of their country's government, and that sports and politics should be kept separate. An amicus brief that the New York Civil Liberties Union filed tried to reconcile this seeming paradox by asserting that the political beliefs of the players were secondary. The lawyers for the Eastern Rugby Union "asserted that the controversy surrounding the tour ha[d] itself turned the game into a political event, thereby cloaking it in the broad protections of the First Amendment."[20] But this is a peculiar argument—the very people creating the controversy did not want the game to be played, while those claiming to be apolitical wanted to be able to benefit from the political protections guaranteed in the First Amendment. Had the protesters promised not to show up, thus obviating the ostensibly political "cloak," could the governor have then cancelled the match? And would the advocates of the tour have accepted this argument? Or were they the ones cloaking the deeply politically implicated Springboks in apolitical garb?

Beyond these inconsistencies, the various courts and judges clearly embraced the rugby union's arguments. And, as journalist David Margolick's analysis in *The New York Times* made clear, the Supreme Court "has recently shown an inclination to extend constitutional protections to forms of entertainment, as well as political and ideological speech."[21] Invoking a recent ruling that nude dancing constituted "a form of public expression and could not be prohibited by a local zoning ordinance," the NY-CLU insisted that "there is no obvious reason why nude dancing viewed through a coin-operated booth in an adult establishment should be entitled to greater protection" than what had clearly become a highly politicized sporting event.

Legal scholars were divided over these questions as well. Lawrence Tribe, the famously liberal Harvard Law School professor, argued that "Neither rugby nor soccer are speech-protected by the First Amendment." Furthermore, he believed that by "allowing the possibility of violence against those lawfully exercising their First Amendment rights at the game, any decision by the governor to permit the match would 'turn freedom of speech inside out.'" Geoffrey R. Stone of the University of Chicago Law School similarly argued that the anti-apartheid groups who opposed the game did not make the game itself a constitutionally protected form of speech because the match was "not designed in any sense to communicate ideas to people."[22]

But Tribe and Stone hardly enjoyed unanimous support for their views. Gerald Grunther, a professor at Stanford Law School, argued that the events "at the periphery" of a sporting event can in fact have serious political implications, and that to be entitled to the rights of the First Amendment, "You don't have to be a street-corner political orator." Furthermore, he maintained, "The fact that a South African team is playing on American soil is the communicative thing. It makes South Africa legitimate in some peoples' eyes." Grunther further argued, "The mere possibility that government officials were reacting differently to the rugby match than they might have to a civil rights demonstration should trigger real worries for anyone concerned with First Amendment principles."[23] But again, the civil rights demonstrators would not deny their explicitly political speech. The advocates of rugby denied that they represented any kind of politics. Ironically, a Springbok team that outwardly endorsed South African policies would have likely presented a better First Amendment argument than one that almost to a man denied any interest in or connection to politics.

Grunther made a compelling case for why Carey's protestations that peoples' safety was at risk were not sufficient, invoking case law from the famous champion of liberal causes, Supreme Court justice William O. Douglas. "[A] function of free speech under our system of government is to invite dispute," Douglas wrote in 1949 in *Terminiello v. Chicago*. "It may indeed best serve its high purpose when it induces a condition of unrest, creates dissatisfaction with conditions as they are or even stirs people to anger."[24] Building on Douglas' argument, Grunther asserted that the potential for violence at a Springbok match represented "an arena where there is some affirmative obligation on the part of the government to go out and protect the speaker to the best of its ability."[25]

Howard G. Munson, a federal district court judge, ruled that Governor Carey could not prohibit the match. Munson rejected Carey's assertion that he did not have enough time to call out the National Guard if he felt the need to do so. More importantly, Munson wrote,

> By enjoining the scheduled sporting event, the Governor of New York seeks to destroy the very constitutional freedoms which have enabled more than a century-long struggle in this country to ensure racial equality. Surely the American citizens must realize that the benefits of such a constitutional heritage must not be commanded by executive privilege and extended or withheld on the basis of popular demand.[26]

Munson believed that Carey's claims that there might be thousands of protesters, that there might be instigators of violence, and that he could not contain such threats, were not backed by evidence. Even after assessing a report that the governor's attorney claimed validated Carey's claims, Munson remained unconvinced.[27]

On Tuesday, September 22, the day of the first New York match, a three-judge panel of the United States Court of Appeals for the Second

Circuit in Manhattan, with jurisdiction over New York, Connecticut, and Vermont, upheld Munson's decision. The state's lawyers immediately appealed to United States Supreme Court justice Thurgood Marshall, the legendary NAACP Legal Defense Fund lawyer and the first African American Supreme Court justice, who was the justice designated to oversee matters before the Second Circuit. Marshall provided the ironic coup de grace by buttressing the side of the rugby supporters, in what surely stood as an endorsement of the right of the team to play rather than the politics underlying the challenge. Marshall issued a one-word ruling on Carey's order: "Denied."

Whatever the debate among legal scholars and others, and whatever hypocrisy it might have revealed about the political and politicized realities of the Springbok tour, the courts made it quite clear that in this case, the Springboks had a clear First Amendment right to play in Albany. Selfridge had emerged victorious. An observer writing for the *New York Times* the next week noted, "The South African Springboks, who come from a country where an unexpected edict can make it a crime for siblings to speak to each other . . . found themselves the beneficiaries of free speech guarantees."[28]

SPEAKING OUT AND CRACKING DOWN: PROTESTING THE SPRINGBOKS

The supporters of the Springbok tour had rejected the imminent threat of violence when they argued before the courts. The Springboks themselves did not. Star flyhalf Naas Botha could not deny his team's belief that "the unthinkable possibility of the Boks being attacked by a maniac with a gun was always present in a country littered with such unstable people."[29] This was not exactly a ringing endorsement of the American reputation. Yet, perhaps ironically, their fears were exacerbated by encounters with American law enforcement, not with protesters or critics. Rob Louw, the Springboks' liberal, iconoclastic flanker, had been warned along with the rest of the squad about potential violence from massive demonstrations. "We were starting to fear for our lives," he recalled. "Some of the players were even scared to look out of windows. We were conscious of the many cranks in New York City." Yet his most disquieting encounter was with a local police officer in Albany entrusted with their safety: "He spoke with a real Telly Savalas accent. He had revolvers all over his body. He showed them all to me. He even had one strapped to his ankle." He told Louw "that police had intercepted some demonstrators on their way to Albany," something that would not have been illegal amidst debates about the First Amendment, and that "these demonstrators had an unbelievable collection of guns and ammunition." But, Louw stated, "This was never in the news. I wonder why. Maybe the policeman was a crank?"[30]

Upon their arrival in the Albany airport, some among the South African contingent had found themselves facing a crowd of 150 or so protesters, "mainly black," chanting, "'Go home, racists!'" The press bus faced the brunt of the protests, as the media had been left on a coach on the tarmac for more than an hour while officials figured out a way to spirit the players and staff away from the protesters unseen, which they were eventually able to do.[31] Meanwhile, the team had been told that there might be up to 10,000 protesters from Stop the Apartheid Rugby Tour (SART) attempting to prevent or disrupt the match on Tuesday. "But the only rumblings came from the sky" as that afternoon the skies opened up and it rained from Monday afternoon through the game Tuesday evening.[32]

The debate over the tour had played out in the Albany *Times-Union* throughout September, with wide-ranging perspectives filling more column inches as the month progressed. Furthermore, alongside accounts of the Springbok controversy were increasing numbers of stories about South Africa more broadly. The concerns about the Los Angeles Olympics played a large role. Prominent speakers such as Donald Woods, who had written about and become friends with murdered Black Consciousness leader Steve Biko were invited to speak in Albany. Local unions stood against the Springbok visit. Journalists, politicians, and the public debated the possibility of violence, and the political and legal machinations took center stage as a national and international story suddenly had become the year's biggest local news and a local news story suddenly had gone national and even international. With all of this coverage, until the day of the match, when the newspaper had to explain the basics of the sport to its readers, very little of the reportage, analysis, and opinion had anything to do with rugby or the sports pages.

At 1:17 a.m. on the day of the first Albany match, about nine hours after Munson levied his decision, a bomb went off at the headquarters of the Eastern Rugby Union in an office building located in a shopping center in Schenectady, about twenty miles northwest of Albany. Schenectady police investigator James McGrath said that the bomb had been placed a few feet from the rugby union office's door and that the force of the blast went away from the door so that, out of the $50,000 of damage, $50 worth was to its intended target, the ERU office. Though the building was vacant and no one was hurt, the explosion undermined some of the anti-tour cause. Before the bomb detonated, someone had called local disc jockey Dale Lane of radio station WWWD, to warn that the explosion would occur. Lane figured the caller was a "wacko."[33] Tom Selfridge was initially quoted as saying that there was no evidence that the bomb was aimed at the rugby union. "It could be a demonstrator who doesn't like some other business in Canal Square," where the explosion occurred. Meanwhile the anti-tour coalition leaders disavowed the bombing as well, with a spokesman dismissing the attack as "the work of some looneys" and maintaining, "ours will be purely a peaceful protest."[34] Eventually the radical "Black Liberation Army" claimed credit, leaving a "communiqué" saying, "Don't play games on African people's graves."[35]

Not even two hours after the bombing, police arrested three of the people who had been active in leading the protests. Police burst into the apartment of activist Vera Michaelson with pistols and shotguns drawn and pointed. Mike Young, who had been especially active with SART, was charged with illegal possession of a weapon, and Aaron Estis and Michaelson were charged with possession of marijuana and firecrackers. Their colleague, John Spearman, had been arrested earlier for being in an allegedly stolen car, despite the fact that he was driving Young's vehicle, which had not been reported stolen. Spearman was later charged with possession of a weapon as well. At their arraignment, the judge refused to set bail, instead announcing that the four would be held for seventy-two hours. Only two days later, after the match, did two of the accused have the opportunity to post bail at $10,000 while the others were released on their own recognizance.

Stop the Apartheid Rugby Tour initially refused to take a position on the merits of the charges as they did not know all of the facts. However, they stated "unequivocally that the holding of the 4 activists without bail for 72 hours was clearly aimed at sabotaging the struggle against the Springbok Rugby Tour," as doing so "meant they could not attend

Tuesday's massive rally against the Springbok game, nor could they participate in further attempts" to contribute to "opposition to Saturday's proposed Springbok game," which was to be the test match against the US Eagles. Nor did SART miss the irony attendant in the arrests and withholding of bail: "The Springboks, the national team from the world's most racist country, are accorded all sorts of 'rights' to come and spread the poison of apartheid, while those who are demonstrating against them are denied even the most basic rights."[36]

SART had pulled together a coalition of more than one hundred civil rights, anti-apartheid, religious, political, and sports groups under the leadership of American Committee on Africa (ACOA) president William Booth, to oppose the Springbok appearances. Another coalition of almost twenty organizations sponsored demonstrations against the September 22 match. They did not operate on the sly, announcing their plans for what they hoped would be a widespread protest against the match. The coalition statement condemned, among other things, "the Reagan Administration's collusion with South Africa," the violation of the sports boycott that the Springbok matches represented, and the fact that "both governments," South Africa's and the United States', "encourage systematic police brutality and attacks on black people and racial polarization in an attempt to pit us against one another," envisioning a true transnational movement because, "From D.C. to Johannesburg, we also find a rising tide of unified struggle against these crimes." They obviously wanted to halt the match, but they also hoped for more than that, such as an end to "diplomatic recognition and relations with the white minority government of South Africa," Congressional action "to end economic, military, technological, cultural and sporting links to South Africa," and condemnation of South African "aggression against its neighbors," including demanding the liberation of Namibia. SART called "on our fellow Americans to learn about these issues and join with others in pressuring our elected representatives to concretely support the liberation movements inside South Africa and Namibia in their struggles for freedom."[37]

This was not the only coalition or organization active in opposing the matches in upstate New York. Richard Lapchick had some ACCESS members engaged. The NAACP participated, as did the newly formed Capital District Coalition Against Apartheid. Boji Jordan, an exiled member of South Africa's Pan Africanist Congress (PAC), lived in Albany, and offered the support of other PAC exiles in the area. Religious leaders formed coalitions to protest the tour and letter-writing campaigns inundated Albany's city hall. The US Olympic Committee also weighed in, expressing fear that engagement with the Springboks could cost them the 1984 Los Angeles Summer Games. Even American rugby's tiny circles were enlisted, as a breakaway group of players and supporters across the Eastern Rugby Union established Against South Africans Playing (ASAP) and, according to ACOA, these "'rugby dissidents' . . . provided" SART with "valuable information on the tour."[38]

Joining the US protest movements, a coalition of African, Asian, and Latin American voices also condemned the Springbok tour. The organization of African Unity (OAU) called for the isolation of the United States, and the Tanzanian Olympic Committee sought clarification on the US Olympic Committee's possible connections with the Springbok tour. African countries and organizations, which had successfully advocated for the widespread African boycott of the 1976 Montreal Games because of New Zealand's All Black rugby tour of South Africa that year, similarly threatened the 1984 Olympics. The African Supreme Council for Sport condemned the US government for allowing the Springboks to visit, for the ERU taking Louis Luyt's money, and for embracing "the ridiculous pretext" that because the Springboks were on a "private" visit the United States government somehow had no oversight capabilities.

PROTEST AND PLAY: THE SPRINGBOKS VERSUS THE ERU ALL STARS

After all of the buildup, the night of the match between the Springboks and Colonials finally arrived. That Tuesday evening, the city provided enough police presence to ensure that the event went off smoothly. The crowd was small, with estimates of about 300 or so showing up inside the facility while 1,000 or so protesters massed outside. One account noted, "More came to jeer than to watch the Springboks play."[39] Demonstrators had marched from two Albany locations, the state capitol, where more than a thousand had gathered, sang songs, and chanted, and the campus of the State University of New York at Albany, and met at the stadium, where the NAACP's Clara Satterfield offered a scathing critique of the courts' decisions. "It's nice to hear that the judges and the mayor have learned how to read the Constitution," she told the crowd. "Now that they know the First Amendment, maybe they will learn to read down to the 13th, 14th, and 15th. Racism is alive and well in Albany." A group of approximately fifty protesters from the Revolutionary Socialist League broke into an area near the Springbok clubhouse and taunted the riot-gear-clad police. The rest of the protesters "shunned" this splinter organization. [40]

The cold, driving rain probably kept some of the least committed spectators and demonstrators at home and, according to observers, may have taken "the sting out of what briefly threatened to be an angry confrontation between state troopers and the more militant protesters at the entrance to the ground." [41] Springbok captain Wynand Claassen believed that "the rain caused many demos to stay away and only about 1,000 turned up to sing songs and parade around the ground." Claassen observed, "The US police seemed less concerned than their New Zealand counterparts about avoiding a confrontation, and their numbers included marksmen armed with rifles and State Troopers carrying batons which looked like oversized baseball bats." [42] Rob Louw also noticed the "massive police presence, some of them marksmen carrying rifles," though he, too, believed the rain was the biggest deterrent to the protesters. [43]

The folk singer Pete Seeger was among the protesters "confined to a knoll 100 yards away" and whose shouts could be heard on the pitch. Seeger led protesters in the South African song, "Wimoweh." Dennis Brutus, the exiled South African poet based in America who had denounced the Springbok tour on behalf of the South African Non-Racial Olympic Committee, also spoke. Perhaps one of the grandest ironies of the whole Springbok tour is that even as the Reagan administration was providing visas to the Springboks, it was in the act of refusing to renew Brutus' visa in what was widely seen as retaliation for his activism against apartheid, of which his advocacy of the sporting boycott was most visible. A local minister claimed rather grandiloquently that the playing of the match would "go down as one of the blackest Tuesdays in American history." [44]

Meanwhile, confirming the observations of the Springboks, the police were out in force. Albany police chief John Dale had canceled all vacation time and personal days for the day of the match and had ensured that all available police personnel were at the stadium, including lining the roof. New York state police were abundant as well. In all there were nine arrests, including of the four taken into custody in the night-time raid, mostly for possession of weapons or tear gas.

For all of Selfridge's and his supporters' claims about the First Amendment, he had no qualms in limiting the association and speech of others, including the very protesters whose presence the courts determined had justified the First Amendment challenge to begin with. Selfridge stood sentry at the only entrance to the stadium and "signal[ed] to police who could enter and who could not." Furthermore, "as a special precaution, the tickets for the game had been changed at the last moment."[45]

Dan Retief, a print journalist whose reports chronicled the entirety of the Springboks' 1981 adventures, found himself on the wrong side of Selfridge's one-man show. Since the South African press corps had not been issued tickets to the match, they had to enter through a narrow passageway after two members of their group, photographer Wessel Oosthuizen and Quintus van Rooyen, confirmed their journalist status to Selfridge, who stood guard and decided who could enter and who could not. They then were searched and passed through a metal detector.

When Retief entered it was pouring rain, so "I was huddled under the hood of my Adidas rainsuit and followed the group of spectators around to the left of the field." But he soon realized that the "press party had gone to the other side of the field." When he tried to cross over to where his press colleagues were standing, he showed two policemen his South African passport "and I was allowed to pass through their cordon." Communication was not clear among the authorities, as "the next thing, however, I was grabbed from behind by two of the cops, my arms held behind my back, and marched back to the entrance." He showed an officer his passport when he was released "and he apologized, saying the wrong person had been pointed out." So Retief "again started to walk toward where my press colleagues were seated and this time Selfridge shouted: 'He's going out!' I protested and tried to establish the reason, but a few sharp prods in the back from one of those big baseball 'bats' convinced me that discretion was the better part of valour and left." Selfridge "later told an American reporter that the reason" Retief "had been evicted was because I had been following him around all day and he was sick of it." Apparently, with Selfridge in charge, freedom of the press, a vital component of the First Amendment that Selfridge and the other American supporters of the Springbok tour claimed to so value, was tossed out of the stadium because Selfridge "was sick of it."[46] Selfridge also had an American reporter ejected, causing Retief to write in the *Rand Daily Mail*, "This, mind you, from the same man who invoked the American constitution and the rights of individuals to have a match played. Talk of a hypocrite."[47] In a somewhat more charitable view Retief reflected, "The rainsuit I was wearing was bright red. Perhaps that's why he didn't want me near the Springbok reserves on the other side of the field."[48] This does not explain his being thrown from the stadium rather than asked to remove his raincoat, nor does it counter Selfridge's own explanation.

Similar to what happened in Racine, the preparations for the match "were like something out of a detective movie," according to Claassen. The team changed at the hotel and did their warm-up routine in a hotel function room rather than at the stadium. "We then put on street clothes over our Springbok gear, boarded the micro-buses and were quickly driven to the stadium," which they entered "on the side opposite the main entrance behind the posts and immediately ran onto the field where our opponents were already waiting." The reserve players and other members of the party were sent "to a certain spot and were not allowed to leave." The entire team was instructed "that if any trouble started we should look for a guy wearing a red raincoat and waving a flag and go to him."[49] That figure was Tom Selfridge.

Despite the soggy conditions and the protests, the Springboks crushed their overmatched foes 41–0. Rob Louw later wrote, "We were constantly reminded of the farcical nature of our American visit. A good example was that," like in Racine, "the goalposts for this match were actually behind the dead ball line."[50] The ERU Colonials, representing a dozen unions across a massive swath of the United States from Louisiana across to Florida and up the eastern seaboard through New England, played conservatively, and had kept the Springboks off the scoreboard for fifteen minutes or so. It was only 8–0 at the half, but eventually talent, physicality, skill, and experience overwhelmed the Americans. The Springbok pack "splashed through pools of water and clouds of steam hovered like mist over the scrums, but at the end of it" the visitors "were so totally in command they were walking the Colonials backwards whenever they felt like it." The Springboks ran in seven tries despite the wet conditions, and while "they were playing under lights with a ball as slippery as a soap cake covered with grease" they still "turned on a demolition job that smashed the Colonials into total submission." The pack provided a dominant platform for the backs, and "there were some incredibly good movements in patches, but generally the foulness of the weather ruined any hope of the match becoming the spectacle American fans had hoped for." Colonials captain Mike Sherlock said after the match that he had never seen a better pack of forwards, and the evidence was clear given that five of the tries came from the forwards, including two from Hennie Bekker and one each from Div Visser, Burger Geldenhuys, and the skipper, Wynand Claassen. Wing Gerrie Germishuys and center, Colin Beck rounded out the try scoring, and in the wet, slippery conditions, Naas Botha hit two of his conversions plus a penalty goal and a drop goal. Fullback Johan Heunis also slotted a penalty kick. One South African match report did have a point of praise for the hosts albeit one couched in criticism: "The Colonials, like most American sides it seems, were strong on tackling, but lacking in other techniques."[51]

According to Sherlock, "These guys gave us a lesson and we were happy to learn it. In America we need more games against quality opposition like this."[52] Gary Lambert, who found himself in a scuffle late in the game and who emerged from the match bloodied, said, "This was the hardest international game I ever played in, the most physical. I was cheap hit a minimum of 15 times." Springbok captain Claassen responded, "All over the world rugby is a rough game. The French are rough. New Zealand is rough. South Africa is rough." After the game, Selfridge acknowledged that elite rugby games like those the Springboks regularly played "have a whole other level of pace that has to be maintained. The Eastern Rugby Union pace varies. It's quick and aggressive early on, then as the game goes on, they lose it." This level of competition was, of course, the driving force for inviting the Springboks. "It's something you can only learn with games of this caliber. Every guy out there learned a lesson tonight, and every man will be a better rugby player."[53]

The Albany *Times-Union* described a "good old-fashioned butt kicking the Springboks administered to a willing but outclassed Eastern Rugby Union side (team) in the most controversy-marred athletic event ever played in the Capital District." Some of the American players did not even know the score of the match when all was said and done, and Tom Selfridge's early prediction that the ERU might pull off "the biggest upset in the history of rugby" proved mere bluster.[54] Worse, the Americans by-and-large were either clueless about the protests or did not understand why everyone was so worked up about a rugby tour. ERU player Tim Moser from Concord, New Hampshire, noted that they had barely met the Springbok players, only shaking their hands, and that there was "no animosity" between them and the Springboks, so "I can't see where the protesting comes in." Gary Lloyd, described as a "diminutive inside center from Tallahassee," was "totally unaware of any protest" but enjoyed the attention. "Rugby players get so little recognition . . . there's no pay, no TV. We play for the love of the game. Now we get this kind of exposure. . . . Everyone's kind of excited to be in the limelight for a brief, little period of time." Lloyd said he had heard none of the noises of the protests going on in the vicinity. "I was totally unaware of any protest." Moser had heard the noise and thus realized this was no ordinary game, but, he said, "I felt I was playing a club rugby game, except of the high intensity. I'm not used to TV and the chanting, but once the whistle blew, it was rugby." He did notice that the Springboks had been secreted into the venue. Neither player really grasped the protests. According to Lloyd, "To me, it's another excuse for them to protest. It's an excuse for a lot of people to express their frustrations. I honestly believe a lot of people didn't have any idea what is happening in South Africa." Moser asserted, "It's almost idiotic," though he stated his opposition to apartheid, noting, "Obviously I don't agree with what's going on in South Africa, and I still don't agree after playing the match."[55]

Selfridge "was pleased" with how the event turned out. "Inside the stadium sportsmen could do what they want to do and outside they did what they wanted to," he boasted.[56] But for all his veneration of the First Amendment and the right to gather that Selfridge had hidden behind in recent weeks, he explicitly had forbidden the protesters from doing what they wanted to do inside the stadium.

Selfridge became something of a celebrity in local and South African circles as a result of his swashbuckling defense of the tour. The ejected journalist Dan Retief "was impressed to see Tom Selfridge giving the people selling programs and t-shirts (one of which I bought) a pep talk.

I was amazed he found time for such a task with all the other cares on his shoulders."[57] South African rugby journalists Edward Griffiths and Stephen Nell have described Selfridge as "the larger-than-life chairman of the Eastern Rugby Union and the hero of this particular adventure" who served as a "one-man security system" and who represented what was "certainly a fresh style of rugby officialdom."[58]

The players did not stick around on the pitch for the usual post-match camaraderie. "The moment the game was over," Wynand Claassen recalled a few years later, "we ran straight to the buses without pausing to shake hands with our opponents."[59] The buses were on the opposite side from where the protesters had amassed and the players "were whisked away" rather than risk confrontation.[60] But later that evening, players from both sides did ultimately gather in the grand old tradition of rugby the world over. They had a banquet at the hotel that was hosting the Springboks. The Colonials' captain, Mike Sherlock, said that facing the Springboks had been an "exhilarating experience and the chance of a lifetime." Wynand Claassen wryly notes, "We felt the same, but for different reasons."[61]

The postmatch festivities led to some internal controversy within the Springboks, who still had a test match to play. The Colonials game had taken place on a Tuesday, as matches against provincial sides and the like almost always take place midweek. On the Wednesday after the match, coach Nelie Smith announced that a number of regular Springboks would not be allowed to play in the test match still scheduled for Saturday. Even against a side like the lowly Americans, receiving a cap for playing for the national side was a tremendous honor, especially in an era where teams played far less than they do in the modern era, and so Smith's initial decision met with confusion, frustration, and anger among the players. Following the evening match against the Colonials in Albany, there was a hotel dinner with the expected drinks. According to Wynand Claassen, "The dinner at our Hotel ended quite late as the ladies bar was due to close we ordered some beers and went to one of the rooms to watch American football. Though we stayed up late, it wasn't a very noisy party." But at one point late in the night, Springbok lock Louis Moolman "bumped into Smith in the passage" and the coach "told Moolman to tell us to go to sleep." The next morning, when the selectors met to determine the final composition of the test squad, "Smith told Prof Claassen that certain players had had a party until the early hours of the morning and that if this was their attitude they should not be considered for the test (this on Tuesday night with the test due on the Saturday!)" Wynand Claassen, who had seen the team through weeks of controversy, was not happy. "I confronted him then and asked him to stop making insinuations about the players. I pointed out that it was still early in the week and there had never been any reason to doubt the players' ability to behave themselves." He reminded his coach, "It had been a long and strenuous tour, the players had always given their best, and they had a right to enjoy themselves." The coach "was clearly angry and he tried to stare me down, but I refused to back down and eventually got my way."[62]

The test match, scheduled to take place just days later, would arguably be the weirdest rugby match in history. And not just for the match on the pitch.

7

ALBANY II

The Test Match

AMATEUR HOUR: PREPPING FOR THE TEST MATCH

The bizarre Springbok tour culminated in a bizarre test match played under bizarre conditions in tiny Glenville, a town so remote that, as one South African put it, "even local residents have difficulty in telling you exactly where it is."[1] Although the plans for the match had been kept under wraps, the game was initially scheduled for Bleecker Stadium and was only moved the thirty miles or so into the countryside to try to remain a step ahead of the growing protest movement.

On Friday morning, September 25, hours before the Springboks were to face off against the US Eagles in Upstate New York (and three days after the bombing in Schenectady), two explosions and a fire gutted the headquarters of Evansville, Indiana's rugby club. The week before, the All Whites (so named for the color of their uniforms) had voted unanimously to seek a match against the Springboks. Three of the All Whites were black. Local officials could not find a suitable location for the game. The Evansville Black Coalition opposed the proposed contest in letters to local officials as well as to reporters, but Bobby Ogburn, an official for the organization, only said, "I don't know who's responsible" for the bombing. Evansville's mayor, Michael Vandeveer, who was in Indianapolis for a convention on the day of the explosion, had heard "no reports of trouble brewing," and there had been no threats to the club before the detonation of the explosives. One club member had been staying at the headquarters but had moved out just a day or so before the incident. According to Doug Bartholome, another team member, "We told him after" the bombing in Schenectady "that he'd better get out in case something happened." Bernie Bartholome, Doug's brother, was the president of the Evansville Rugby Club, and he said the club building, which was destroyed in the blast, was worth "over $100,000." He also reported that a club member owned a house next door that was also destroyed.[2]

Meanwhile, after the match against the ERU all-stars, the Springbok party changed hotels and "continued to move about experiencing the American way of life." They also saw themselves in the news media, though the "demonstrations and minor displays of violence" were "nothing like those in New Zealand," at least until the Evansville bombing. "This was the one thing that really scared the Springboks," according to Wynand Claassen. "Demonstrators you can at least see, but a bomb or an assassin (there was talk of one of us being shot) was a different story." It was also at this point that money had changed hands—the $50,000 from the South African Rugby Board to the ERU to "defray costs" and the $25,000 "gift" from Louis Luyt. "This was quite an embarrassing incident for us," Claassen recalled, "because it left the impression that our visit had been 'bought'; more so because we had no knowledge of the donation to the ERU."[3]

The Glenville game was accorded full test match status according to the South African Rugby Board "in accordance with an (International Rugby Board) resolution," but, in the words of a South African account of the Springboks' 1980 and 1981 travels, the test "was turned into a farce, as in fact was their two-week stay in America."[4] The very status of the match as a test is an anomaly. Test matches in that era went on the global rugby test and tour calendar that was maintained by the International Rugby Football Board (IRFB) years in advance. The IRFB met in Cardiff from March 11 to 13, 1981. Those minutes contained a detailed list of season-long tours, other tours, and scheduled tests from the preceding 1979–1980 period through to the tentative and still-developing 1982/1983 season. For 1981, as of March, the official IRFB schedule included the South Africa tour to New Zealand as a "season-long tour." It included Ireland to South Africa under "other tours." It included approximately ten other global tours for 1980 and 1981/1982.

Just six months prior to the Springbok arrival in the United States, a tour of or test match in the United States was not on the IRFB radar, a radar that extended for many years, that was incredibly thorough, and that served as the official word of the sport's global governing body. At minimum, the granting of the test represented an exceedingly rare example. Most likely it was the result of special pleading by South African rugby that may have been a pariah in the global sporting community but that nevertheless had leverage at the highest levels of rugby's elite global hierarchies.[5]

In light of escalating protests that the Springboks faced, organizers upped the ante on secrecy. When the Springboks left their hotel early on Friday, journalists grew suspicious. Those suspicions were well placed. Only those Springbok players involved in the test match were told, "Get dressed, you're going to play it right now," and they headed to Owl Creek Polo Field in Glenville.[6]

There was yet another indignity to come for the Springboks, who had been shuttled to participate in the match to face the Americans. When international teams compete, they have a special jersey prepared for each match. During the amateur era, those preparations would include jerseys for the midweek matches against various clubs, select sides, and the like. This would give players the opportunity to keep their jersey or to trade it for one of their opponent's. Yet by the tail end of the exhausting New Zealand tour, it had become clear that the support staff had not prepared sufficient jerseys. It was especially perplexing for the players because two of the matches in New Zealand had been canceled, meaning that there ought to have been Springbok jerseys to spare. Instead, those who had played in Albany were told that they had to keep their jerseys, and, in some cases, share them with teammates. It would turn out that some players who would be substituted in the test at Owl Creek would appear in a teammate's game-worn jersey with a starter's number and at least one would appear in a numberless jersey. In the words of Springbok captain Wynand Claassen, embarrassed by the amateurism embodied in the jersey fiasco, "What an advertisement for South African rugby!"[7]

Making matters worse for the players, Springbok management decided to "name a whole squad of players for the final test to," in the words of Claassen, "keep the players out of mischief! What a ridiculous way to treat a group of grown men." Furthermore, there was a real selection controversy even after Nelie Smith and company chose the actual gameday squad in that they chose two scrumhalves, to be finalized depending on whether conditions were wet or dry. Finally, they were still scrambling for jerseys and no one knew where and under what conditions the match would be played.[8]

The selection debacles rankled several players. Rob Louw was one of those left behind for the Glenville test, a foreshadowing of selection issues he would face in the future and that many believed were tied to his liberal politics. Louw had been told that he would be one of the gameday nineteen, likely as a starter either at flank or as eighth man, but if not, certainly as one of the reserves. Meanwhile the scrumhalf decision was really starting to grate some of the squad. The announcement had been made that if conditions were dry, Divan Serfointein would get the start, and if they were wet, Barry Wolmarans would get the nod. Rob Louw was flabbergasted by the decision. "Divan had been one of the big successes in the rain and slush of New Zealand. In fact, he had played the best rugby of his career in New Zealand, and unlike Barry, was accustomed to wet conditions in Cape Town. This was mind-boggling."[9] Perhaps this was just grousing, remembering the end of a long and exhausting tour a few years after its completion, but it seems clear that discontent had begun to set in by the time the end of the tour was approaching.

THE TEST MATCH

Because Mayor Ed Koch had banned the match from New York City, Tom Selfridge "had become a one-man army against the politicians as he assumed full responsibility for the day-to-day running of the tour." The Friday morning before the scheduled Saturday test match Professor Johan Claassen and Nelie Smith met with Selfridge where they made yet another decision that would help define the match as at best unorthodox and more accurately as ridiculous. They chose to play the match, an international test match, that day rather than on the Saturday when it had been scheduled and shoehorned into the international calendar. Wynand Claassen recognized this as another mistake on the part of the organizers, including Selfridge, as he believed they ought to have informed "certain administrators," American fans, "many of whom had traveled miles to be at the test"; and even possibly the media, some of whom had accompanied the Springboks across America. [10]

Those players not joining the squad that day went on a sightseeing jaunt that also provided a decoy. Rob Louw remembered that they had been "taken by coach to a sort of museum" that "specialized in the history of baseball." Naas Botha confirmed later that the trip Louw remembered brought them to Cooperstown, home of the Baseball Hall of Fame, which is just under seventy-five miles from Albany. "Being a keen tourist and always being interested in lifestyles that were foreign to me, I initially found the trip fascinating. After all, it was all about sport, and I love sport, all types." But "eventually it got rather boring walking around looking at all the exhibits" and he was relieved to be heading back to the hotel for what he presumed would be extended rest and mental preparation for the next day's test. [11]

Those players who were going to suit up (assuming jerseys could be secured) had yet another adventure geared toward throwing protesters off the scent. The players who were to serve as decoys dressed in full Bok kit, complete with medical equipment and water bottles. The players chosen for the test would wear street clothes and be shuttled in minivans (known as "kombis" in South Africa) departing at random intervals and driving around for long enough that police could be sure that they were not being followed before heading to Tom Selfridge's house. They practiced this drill for an hour or so the morning of the test.

During this down period, which was more tense than restful, future Springbok captain Theuns Stofberg decided to have a bit of fun with teammate Gysie Pienaar, a fullback. Stofberg called his teammate and "said in a deep, husky voice: 'Hello. Are you one of the Springboks?'" Pienaar was flustered, ultimately made up a fake name that he thought sounded American but in fact sounded very Afrikaans (Peete von der Vyfer) and simply hung up the phone. [12] It was a rare moment of levity, at least for Stofberg, on a day that was consistently tense if occasionally absurd.

The Springboks slated for the test were eventually shuttled to Selfridge's house, which was near the field where the match would be played. "In true Hollywood style, we waited at Selfridge's house while he opened the double garage from the inside." Once they were granted admission, they went downstairs to the basement to get taped and rubbed down, to change into their game gear, and to pull on plain tracksuits to mask their green-and-gold Springbok kit. From there, according to Claassen, they "sneaked back up the stairs, into the little busses, and off to the field, trying to be as inconspicuous as possible." Selfridge's house was about fifteen minutes away from Owl Creek, through "farm houses and fields, trees turning into autumn colors, and with each mile the scenery became more and more rural" until they got to the dirt road "winding through trees." They were brought to the paddock where the busses parked and went inside to warm up, "taking care not to step in any horse dung!" Claassen recalled "a beautiful autumn day with a bright sun bringing out the reds and yellows in the changing leaves of the trees." These also meant that Divan Serfontein had been chosen to play scrumhalf for the Boks, as he was determined to be a better player in those conditions. "It was almost like a fantasy, a weird dream, with the Springbok jerseys looking hopelessly out of place." Springbok hooker Robert Cockrell, who would earn his last of fourteen test caps against the Americans, "said that he just could not believe that the Springboks, having warmed up in a paddock, were about to play a test match on a polo field."[13] Star center Danie Gerber was more succinct about the set-up: "It was a disgrace."[14]

Naturally, the polo field was not set up for a rugby match. When the Springboks arrived, there were no goalposts set up. Several of the US Eagles reserves were helping to get them in place, and Springbok reserve Thys Burger joined them "to add some weight to the ropes." While the posts were erected, Claassen took the opportunity to inspect the field. He was less than impressed: "It was very muddy, there was a strong smell of horse dung but more significantly I noticed that the ground sloped sharply, almost three metres from tryline to tryline. On top of this the breeze was also blowing downhill." As a result, when he won the coin toss, he decided to have his team running uphill in the first half in order to benefit from the downslope in the second.[15]

The Springboks wore their customary green jerseys, and the Eagles dressed in red tops. Although the match had been rescheduled at the last minute to a different date, time, and location, organizers had managed to put together modest programs with a cover depicting an illustration of a number eight trying to break free from a mustachioed tackler. The program advertised "International Rugby" with "USA Springboks Tour" and the classic image of the Springbok logo next to the illustration. The backside of the little program had been updated to include the referee and had the two teams' starting lineups. The Springboks were, of course, a who's who of international stars from the country's elite provincial rugby unions. Northern Transvaal, in Pretoria, contributed seven of the starters; Western Province, based in Cape Town, provided three; Transvaal two; and Eastern Province, South West Districts, and Natal, one each. The US Eagles team, meanwhile, would have been known only to American rugby diehards, and even then, most would have been obscure. None qualified as stars. Their regions (Pacific, Midwest, and Eastern) were listed rather than a club affiliation.

Despite the bizarre and distracting conditions, the Boks ran away from the overmatched US Eagles on Friday afternoon, September 25, in a match that started fifteen minutes late, at 3:15 p.m., emerging with another easy win on American soil, 38–7. Because of the "distinct slope," with the Boks facing the uphill burden in the first half, the visitors only led 6–4 at the halftime break. But when the teams switched sides, South Africa cruised. Eagles captain Skip Niebauer said after the game, "It became too much for us to chase them up the hill all the time in the second half." The American plight was made worse by the fact that the Springbok match was their first of the season and at least a few of the players had only prepared for the game by following coach Ray Cornbill's mailed instructions. The Springboks were, of course, mentally and physically exhausted after weeks of touring marked by political tumult. But Bok wing Ray Mordt made history when he became the first (and only) Springbok player—and only the second player in the history of international test rugby—to score a hat trick (three tries) in two successive test matches; he had also scored a more impressive three tries in the third and final test at Eden Park against New Zealand.[16] The lone American try was scored by African American wing Lin Walton, who would go on to have a distinguished career in the United States Navy and would become a high-ranking official in USA Rugby.

Claassen could not deny the effort of both teams. "Though the conditions might have given the impression of a relaxed Sunday afternoon social game, the test was played with a lot of guts and determination, like any other international." Both the Eagles and the Springboks "went at it as hard as in any other game I've ever played, uphill and downhill, slipping and sliding, scrumming and mauling through the mud and manure." He noted that "the Eagles played courageously, and their tackling was especially hard and competitive, something which was probably a throw-back to their days as grid-iron players."[17] Danie Gerber observed, "Despite the scoreline it was not an easy test against the Eagles. They were very physical in their approach and played the game hard—probably a legacy of their 'hit' approach from the gridiron. But they lacked finesse and subtle skills and that's where they came short."[18] Div Visser was "impressed with their standard" and felt, given that the US "did not play against big sides," the Springbok victory margin was not especially big.[19]

To give a hint of just how obscure rugby was in the United States, *New York Times* identified the American national rugby team as "a team of amateur players"—a description that applied to the Springboks as well—and "a team called the Eagles."[20]

Ed Hagerty, of the American *Rugby* magazine would later write, "Despite the lack of spectators the game was as intense as if it were played before a packed house and the action was spectacular. It was a shame, however, that more people didn't see the game, and it was eerie to have the game's sparkling play greeted with silence."[21] The advertisement for rugby that Selfridge and other supporters had hoped would come from the Springbok visit had failed.

But the rushed and conspiratorial context and nonregulation field conditions only begin to capture the peculiarity of the world event. Only a small handful of people witnessed this match, including a few dozen state troopers, a tiny group of spectators ("mostly friends of the owner of the polo field," according to one account), reporter Albert Stevens, and a television crew that had followed the Boks to the field. In the words of Quintus van Rooyen, the editor of the *SA Rugby Annual*, the attendance consisted of "35 spectators, twenty policemen, one television crew, one reporter, and no demonstrators."[22] Wynand Claassen estimated "about 75 NY State Troopers" whose "unmarked squad cars" were "hidden among the trees." Beyond the players, Claassen believed "the only other spectators . . . were about 30 locals who did not have a clue about rugby."[23] In the end, the official tally would be that 29 spectators watched the match, still the record low attendance for a rugby test match.

The president of USA Rugby, David Chambers, was not among the spectators. He had traveled from Texas to see the match, but no one told him of the change in time and venue and he was shocked afterward to discover that the teams had played. He and other USA rugby officials were furious, and Selfridge would later be called to the carpet to answer for his increasingly authoritarian leadership.

Wynand Claassen had thought that not telling Chambers about the change in the secret Friday meeting was especially problematic. The official match referee, another Texan, John Reardon, was not in his room when officials called on him, and so a local man, Dr. John Morrison, was deputized to oversee the international test match. Morrison had been awoken at four in the morning, much to his dismay, but he immediately knew that he was being summoned to referee the test. He lived 150 miles from Albany and would only learn details when he arrived at Owl Creek. Much like the players, Morrison was part of some subterfuge to get to the match, with various stop-off checkpoints, including a McDonald's restaurant, Tom Selfridge's business office, and then Selfridge's home. Morrison had to make a couple of decisions before the teams even took to the pitch, including determining whether the Springbok boots were legal because they had a front-toe stud that he concluded that the International Rugby Board had outlawed, but that the Springboks had worn throughout New Zealand. He chose not to make the Boks change their studs and simply informed both teams of his decision.[24]

Springbok flank Thys Burger, had arguably the strangest day in the history of international rugby. The Bok, who was slated to be a reserve, helped set up the goalposts and officiated as a touch judge, roles that would never be fulfilled by team support staff, never mind a player, in a legitimate test match. Burger had not appeared in any of the tests in New Zealand, but selectors had chosen him in place of Rob Louw, who was among the players not even at Owl Creek that day. Burger would end up replacing Theuns Stofberg, earning a cap and even scoring a try.

Because South African journalist Herman Le Roux, the rugby writer who was covering the tour for his country's *Nasionale Pers*, was also "kept in the dark" about the fixture, he decided to ask his fellow Free Stater, the Bok Edrich Krantz to write a match report. Krantz, a medical doctor and Bok reserve in an era when even the world's most elite rugby players were amateurs, had been dispatched to buy gifts for the Americans the morning of the Friday match. When he returned, the team was about to depart. Although he was not on the roster for that day, he ended up as the only Springbok not involved in the game to attend the match. This nearly got Le Roux in trouble with Alex Kellerman, secretary of the South African Rugby Board, who was worried about the propriety of a player writing a match report, but Le Roux convinced Kellerman that Krantz had received no payment for his work (which if he had may well have violated the strict amateurism rules still in effect at the time) and Kellerman let the issue go.[25]

THE DIRTIEST OF DIRTY TRICKS: A SENSE OF BETRAYAL

Wynand Claassen sympathized with "the shock and annoyance of the South African press party when it was discovered the match had been played, and what I found most unacceptable was the fact that our fellow Springboks who had not been selected were denied the chance to be with us for the final game of the tour." Among those excluded were Errol Tobias, who had been used as a human shield by so many supporters of the tour, including Selfridge and other apologists. "Considering everything that we had been through," Claassen reflected just a few years later, "and the fact that our motto was 'all for one, and one for all,' I was browned off that the players had not been consulted when the decision was taken that the rest of the team would not be a part of the test." He understood the need "to throw protesters off the scent," but still believed that "this group of Springboks, who acted as a decoy, could at least have been given instructions on how to get to the game once they had made sure they had not been followed." Making matters worse, the decision may not have been as impromptu as it initially appeared, as Ed Hegerty, editor of *Rugby* magazine (a niche publication if ever one existed) in the United States, would later report that he had been told as far back as that Tuesday by Ed Watkins, the Eagles' manager, "to be on hand on the Friday morning," meaning "the decision to play the test on Friday was taken before the Friday morning meeting with our management."[26]

By the time the reserves had gotten back to the hotel from their tourist gallivanting, they were ready to relax. "After all, a test match was to be played the next day and I wanted to start preparing myself mentally for it," wrote Rob Louw a few years later, channeling the mentality that he would not only be playing but quite possibly starting. He and

Errol Tobias, his teammate, best friend on the squad, and roommate, lounged in their beds and switched on the television, only to see the news that the test match had been played that afternoon. "We couldn't believe it. The dirtiest of dirty tricks had been played on us. Our management had simply betrayed us." They were official Springboks and found out via an Albany area television station that their teammates had played a test match while they were being used unknowingly as decoys. "Errol and I just looked at each other. Nothing made sense any more." There was little solace that American rugby officials had been similarly betrayed. Johan Claassen, Nelie Smith, and Tom Selfridge "had failed us completely."[27]

Dan Retief was among the South African journalists shocked to discover on Friday that the match had already been played. "They say the best stories break in the pub," Retief wrote as an aside in Claassen's rugby memoir, which he helped write, "and that's exactly how it happened that Friday in Albany." He was drinking Budweisers with some of his journalistic cohort and several American officials when someone affiliated with USA Rugby approached them and said, "You're not going to believe this, but the test's been played." Retief ran to a phone, called the Springbok hotel and reached Prof. Johan Claassen to confirm the story and to try to get enough detail to file a story for the late editions of the *Rand Daily Mail*. On his way back to the pub, he ran into try scorers Thys Burger and Colin Beck, which allowed him to "rush upstairs again and pad out my story." That was not quite the end of Retief's American tale. "What really got my goat was the fact that an American reporter, who had been told the test was about to be played while it was kept secret from us, was on another phone trying to sell the story of the test to my paper."[28] Retief's story in the *Cape Times* September 26 issue carried the simple title, "Boks win on polo field." John Ryan's story in the same paper declared that "Secrecy surrounds Boks to the end."[29]

Reflecting just a handful of years later, Wynand Claassen assessed the match and its larger implications. "In a way the match showed that all we wanted to do was just play our game, no matter what the politicians thought or did." Claassen quotes *Rugby* magazine's Ed Hagerty who wrote, "In the final analysis, of course, rugby is for the players; not the administrators, not the coaches, not the spectators and most of all, not the politicians. The Springboks were invited to tour so that American players could test themselves against the world's best."[30] This naivety was at least earnest—South African sport (or music, or theater, or any other aspect of life) could not be separated from politics. Rugby certainly could not. The supporters of the Irish in South Africa, the South Africans in New Zealand, and the South Africans in America never quite grasped the connections between sport, politics, and daily life in apartheid South Africa.

After the match was over, the players "swopped jerseys" and would only see the Eagles players the next day. "We boarded our buses, full of mud and reeking to high heaven of you know what."[31] When they got to the hotel, they "arrived in a jovial mood. They were happy to have won." But Rob Louw and the rest of the players who had been left behind "felt very, very out. We were not part of the team. We were very upset." They were told that they were used for "pulling demonstrators away from the match. But no-one had told us. They couldn't trust us. It was absolutely pathetic." Making matters worse were even more of the selection decisions that Louw only discovered after the fact. Theuns Stofberg had been injured in New Zealand and was not fully recovered. He was included and even started the match but had to leave the field early, to be replaced by Thys Burger. While Burger had done it all that day on and off the pitch, "he had been one of the few flops in New Zealand." Louw never could accept that "the team that played in the test against the American Eagles was chosen on merit." As a result of these circumstances, "This was the lowest point in my career as a rugby Springbok."[32]

The long tour had come to the strangest of possible ends in the unlikely setting of the United States. "What a tour it had been!" Claassen later wrote. "It was almost Shakespearean in its breadth, drama, tears, laughs, joy and sadness, defeats and victories." He wondered, "could there ever be another tour such as this one?" On the ride back to Albany, he reflected on the previous few months. "I found myself sliding into a mood of introspection. The feeling I had at that moment I'll never forget, nor can I describe it in words. In a way, I suppose, it was a kind of sadness that it had all come to an end so abruptly."[33]

It is perhaps ironic that the match was played on a polo field in wet and muddy conditions. For the athletes who tend to exert themselves the most on a polo field are of the equine variety for whom relieving themselves as necessary does not bring about false modesty. But as this waste product merged with the mud and the rainy conditions of recent days, a perfect metaphor emerged. The authorities emerged squeaky clean and proud of having stayed one step ahead of the protesters, who had been left behind as a result of the legerdemain. The players, the targets of so much of the wrath of those protests, came off the pitch soaked, muddy, and covered in shit. In the words of Rob Louw, "Literally as well as figuratively, the Springbok jersey had been dragged through the manure."[34]

AFTERMATH: PUNCH DRUNK OR A DRUNK PUNCH?

Because of the fears of protests, the traditional post-test affair between the two teams was held the next night. The night after the game, therefore, the Springboks debauched amongst themselves. A few went out, but the bulk stayed together in the hotel. Eben Jansen, a flank who made his sole career test cap for the Springboks in the first test in Christchurch, helped make the night memorable by wrestling with his captain, Claassen. They gathered in the room of Louis Moolman, the team's giant, bearded lock, where "the refreshment bill hit a record high," a potential problem except for the presence of Abe Williams, who was "around to solve this problem for us with his signing powers."[35]

Rob Louw had a far less jocular version of the night's events. "Those who had been misled were now expected to celebrate with the players who had won the test. We couldn't celebrate—we just felt like complete outsiders." And Louw remembered not a jocular wrestling match. "Eventually the inevitable happened. A blow was struck." One of the members of the team had punched another. "Fortunately, it was only one blow, but it was one too many."[36]

The next night the teams gathered "at the beautiful old Gideon Putnam Hotel in the fabulous racing town of Saratoga." Claassen praised the ERU for its victories in court and told the gathered group that "the fact that the matches had gone on were a victory for rugby and sport in general." He further continued with the hoary old cliché "that sportsmen should always strive to keep sport out of the realms of politics" and he "assured them that we would always be available to compete against them."[37] The night ended with a spirit of drunken comradeship and friendship—that dynamic that rugby is so well known for.

ACID TEST

The drama was not quite over, however. The Springbok touring party was "set to quit the US in secret," but that did not quite happen. A "secrecy shroud" covered the team's plan to depart the United States but the by now commonplace subterfuge went into effect as rumors began circulating that they would depart from La Guardia airport rather than from JFK.[38]

The Saturday after the test match, two days before the Springboks departed, a group of protesters had gathered at John F. Kennedy International Airport, believing the South Africans were to depart that day. At least four anti-apartheid protesters broke away from the larger protest and aggressively confronted port authority police. One tossed a liquid containing battery acid and ammonia into the face of Evan Goodstein, one of the police officers at the epicenter of the clash. The thirty-five-year-old Goodstein was blinded. Another guard received twenty stitches after being knocked to the pavement and cutting his leg on the shards of glass from one of the jars containing the acid. The editors of the *Chicago Sun-Times* commented, "of course there should have been protests wherever the Springboks appeared—orderly, peaceful, dignified. The Rev. Martin Luther King Jr. showed how to do it." Peaceful protest "would have let the South Africans and their pro-government sponsors know how decent people feel about their repulsive regime. But now they can regale the folks back home with the antics of American terrorists."[39]

And in keeping with the absurd nature of the tour, the protesters were not even at the airport on the same day as the Springboks. The "Anti-Springbok Five," as they came to be known, were Tim Blank, Donna Borup, Mary Patten, Margot Pelletier, and Eve Rosahn, and their defenders pointed out that they had been beaten, arrested, and held without bail for multiple felonies, but the acid-throwing incident severely undermined any sympathy they might have gotten had they merely been vocal but peaceful protesters. Their efforts to lump the port authority police at JFK in with "the police who violently protected the Springboks throughout the tour" also rightfully gained little traction.[40] The five were associated with the Black Liberation Army, which had claimed credit for the bombing in Schenectady and were central to the Anti-Springbok 5 Defense Committee. Four of the "self-styled revolutionaries" would be sentenced to between seven and thirteen months in jail for the events at JFK. Donna Borup, accused of having thrown the acid, failed to show up for trial in May 1982 and went on the run. Borup remains at large and is on the FBI's most wanted list.

As the American Committee on Africa noted in its report on the 1981 tour, the bombings in Schenectady and Evansville "were used by police and press to smear all rugby protesters."[41] Stop the Apartheid Rugby Tour (SART) embraced a "consistent adherence to a clearly defined and announced position of organizing only non-violent demonstrations." SART opposed such actions because they served to divert attention from the issues at stake and to generate some sympathy for the Springboks which they could not have created for themselves."[42] Nonetheless, SART embraced the legal protection of the four accused.

Meanwhile, it turns out that the bombing at the Evansville club had not represented a random target after all, but not for the reasons that critics of tour protests had surmised. Tour advocates had conjured up images of radical terrorists afoot prepared to destroy lives and property because of their obsession with the Springboks. So it was strange, but perhaps not surprising, when the real story emerged, receiving almost none of the coverage that the alleged bombing and arson received. The president of the All Whites, Bernie Bartholome, who had told reporters at the time of the bombing that the building was worth "over $100,000," would later be charged with arson. His motivation was not at all political. He just hoped to collect the insurance money.[43]

The Springboks departed from Kennedy airport on Monday, September 28 and arrived home at Jan Smuts International Airport on Thursday, October 1. Claassen led them to the international arrivals hall where a large crowd was there to meet them. In the words of South African journalists Edward Griffiths and Stephen Nell, "With no barbed wire, no demonstrators and no Welsh referees in sight, they relaxed. Their adventure was over."[44] At about the same time, the city comptroller's office of Albany admitted that the Springbok visit had cost the city $45,000 for police and other security measures.

ASSESSMENTS

The 1981 Springbok tour to the United States is an event nearly lost in the transom of time that nonetheless had significant implications. It occurred at a time when the American anti-apartheid movement, which lagged far behind that in the United Kingdom and other parts of the world, was beginning to awaken. The tour and protests surrounding it arguably helped to prod that awakening. It took place on the cusp of radical changes in South Africa, which would enter a period of unimaginably ugly years even as the regime attempted to chip away at the edifice of apartheid.

Almost no one at the time really understood the reason for the tour. Rob Louw, the liberal Springbok loose forward, Errol Tobias' best friend on the Springboks, and quite likely a man who had his Springbok career cut short because of his progressive politics, argued that "If the New Zealand tour had been a diplomatic disaster" the US leg "was doubly so" and personally "was without a doubt the worst experience" he "ever had as a Springbok rugby player." In terms of pure rugby "it appeared to serve little purpose." "However," he offered, "it may well have been arranged to take some of the international heat off of New Zealand. This is the only justification I can think of for sending us off to America."[45]

Louw is an insightful and thoughtful observer of the politics of sport in South Africa and so much more, but taking the heat off of the New Zealanders was almost certainly low on the list of priorities for South African rugby officialdom. Their scheming was actually far simpler— the Springboks needed allies, and the United States, both in rugby terms and politically, had proven to be such an ally. Once the lines of communication opened up between the Americans and the South Africans, the South Africans leapt, certainly not taking into account the actual players themselves, and clearly not anticipating that rugby would become the political flashpoint that it did in America.

Supporters of the Springbok tour regularly raised a talking point that the South African government did not sponsor the Springboks, that they were a private interest, and that therefore they were not at all tied to their country's racial politics. For example, in justifying the Racine game, Eric Olson, an official for the Racine–Kenosha Rugby Club, argued, "The Springboks are not sponsored by the South African

government. The government doesn't control them, just as our government doesn't control us." Olson and David Kirk, the president of the
club, called the anti-Springbok opposition "naïve." And yet the level of
naïveté required to believe that the Springboks did not represent South
Africa was shocking and born of either willfulness or transcendent ignorance. The Springboks are the national rugby team of South Africa.
They are and were recognized as such by the International Rugby
Board. They were subject to the laws of South Africa, the mandates of
the South African Ministry of Sport and Recreation, and all the laws of
apartheid that had long kept sport segregated despite the occasional
fissure in the dam of white supremacy. Furthermore, given the central-
ity of the Springboks to Afrikaner nationalism and the realities of athletic competition on the ground in South Africa, it beggars belief to assert
that the Springboks existed independent of the policies of the South
Africa they so embodied.

Yet none of this meant that there was nothing to the First Amendment argument made by so many tour supporters, players, fans, journalists, politicians, and even Supreme Court justice Thurgood Marshall.
In American constitutional law, the American rugby hierarchy and the
clubs within it had the right to invite the Springboks and to play them,
though one wonders if that meant they could play any place at any time
and that any municipality had to host them. It also was true that protesters should have had the right to protest, to picket, to challenge—a right
that those who claimed to hold the First Amendment so dear did so
much to deny them. But why? If they were not ashamed of what they
were doing, why did tour organizers go to such lengths of secrecy, of
legerdemain, of bait-and-switch, of hiding in the shadows, of duplicity?
Why did they change schedules and forbid fans and remove journalists
and send those who did not know secret passwords on wild goose
chases? If what they were doing was so right, why did they act so
wrong? The answer is that the protesters may have had it right all along
and by doing so much to try to fool, dissuade, exclude, and misdirect
the protesters, American rugby officials knew it: They were playing with
apartheid. Theirs was perhaps a living embodiment of "constructive
engagement," but engagement it was.

William Simon, a former secretary of the treasury in the Nixon and
Ford administrations, was the newly minted president of the United
States Olympic Committee (USOC) when the Springboks toured in

September 1981. The tour immediately put Simon on the defensive. He argued that if only the other countries in the Olympic movement better understood the United States, they would then better appreciate the USOC position on the Springbok situation, which was effectively not to have a position. "It's a non-issue; it is much ado about nothing," Simon argued. "We successfully submerged the whole tour. People used this as an excuse to land all over us for something we had nothing to do with. Ours is a free country and it is not up to the U.S.O.C. to deny entrance to anyone. Ours is not a foreign policy organization, and this has been blown completely out of proportion."[46]

Simon somewhat condescendingly addressed the prospect of an African boycott of the 1984 Olympics, asserting that if only the Africans had "strived to better understand" the USOC position, they would have rejected the idea of a boycott. Simon seemed to not take into account that the Africans were not discussing the United States Olympic Committee. They were talking about boycotting sporting events with the United States, full stop, as a protest against American policies allowing the Springboks to tour the United States to begin with. When someone asked Simon about the propriety of the Moscow Olympic boycott, he justified it as "a matter of national security" and therefore every American had a "responsibility" to support it.[47] Irrespective of the merits of the 1980 boycott, Simon's rhetorical tap dancing revealed that politics and sport may well be strange bedfellows, but they were, and always have been, bedfellows, nonetheless. The Olympic Games are, after all, organized along the ultimate political dividing line, the nation state.

Only two African teams boycotted the 1984 Summer Olympics in Los Angeles: Ethiopia and Angola. Their decision was based on Cold War–geopolitical questions and not on apartheid. But the possibility of a boycott in the wake of the 1981 Springbok tour had nonetheless been very real until superpower politics obviated any smaller boycotts amidst the Soviet Bloc's tit-for-tat boycott of the Los Angeles games.

Meanwhile, the Springboks were back in South Africa. Little did they know they were about to spend a number of years in the rugby wilderness.

CONCLUSION

The Long Tail of Post-1981 South African Rugby

THE END OF TOURS?

Doc Craven was among many involved in South African rugby who believed that the Springboks might never tour again after 1981, though he was determined for it to happen.[1] The editors of the *Rand Daily Mail* acknowledged, "At the end of the 1981 Springbok rugby tour one thing is clear: this abnormal society cannot expect to play normal international sport, at least not if 'normal' means the old-fashioned business of playing games for the fun of it."[2] Wynand Claassen, too, believed that the Springboks might not tour again any time soon because of the country's political situation. "We cannot contemplate any rugby tours in the foreseeable future unless further and important changes are made in South Africa."[3] Dan Retief, who had accompanied the Springboks through New Zealand and the United States, and who had faced Tom Selfridge's wrath in upstate New York, was even more definitive: "The curtain is almost certain to come down today on the last Springbok rugby tour overseas for a good few years," he wrote in the *Cape Times* as the Springboks prepared to depart New Zealand (a statement whose timing also revealed just what an afterthought the US leg of the 1981 tour was).[4] These prognostications proved correct, as Springbok rugby would continue to play, but only as hosts, and with one exception, against "rebel teams" and not against national sides.

Meanwhile, even as the American government claimed that the South African national rugby team had an absolute right to travel and play in the United States, that same government was trying to have poet, writer, scholar, and anti-apartheid activist Dennis Brutus deported. Officially, they were trying to deny Brutus permanent residency and hinged their argument on a lapsed visa, despite Brutus having spent a decade in the United States. Adding to the irony was the fact that Brutus was certainly most famous for his stalwart work in opposing apartheid sport, opposing tours like the Springbok tours to New Zealand and to the United States. But to deny permanent residency was to effectively call for deportation, and to subject Brutus to very real threats of retaliation from the South African government, including assassination, a tool that would increasingly become part of the security force arsenal in the brutal 1980s. As the Dennis Brutus Defense Committee pointed out, "the notorious rugby team from South Africa" included "four members of the South African military and two members of the police force" who "tour[ed] the United States as privileged guests" even as "the INS is steadfastly forcing Dennis Brutus, a distinguished scholar of impeccable credentials to expose himself to assassination attempts by the feared and racist secret police of South Africa," in no small part as a result of his leadership in SANROC.[5] Brutus would eventually be allowed to seek asylum, but his fight would take nearly two years to resolve, and stood in stark contrast to the support that the Springboks received from the same government that had seriously fought to deport Brutus. This was a pretty good example of the realities of constructive engagement.

DAYS IN THE WILDERNESS: 1982–1991

In great understatement, the editor of the 1982 S.A. Rugby Writers Toyota Annual wrote "at the end of 1981 the future of Springbok rugby looked less secure that [sic] at the beginning of the year. A couple of difficult years loom ahead."[6] In the period from the end of the American leg of the 1981 tour and the Springbok return from isolation in 1992, the Springboks played just twelve times, but only two of which came against actual official national teams. The rest of the time the

Springboks got by playing "select" sides in what amounted to rebel tours.

Incidentally, England's national rugby team toured North America in 1982. Apparently, the Springbok visit a few months earlier did not exactly temper the Americans for world-class rugby, as the visitors humiliated various American teams in six matches. These included a 58–9 pasting of the Midwestern RFU, a 41–0 whitewashing of the Eastern RFU, and a humiliating 59–0 mauling of the USA Eagles in addition to easy wins over three other American sides and two in Canada, including the national team. American boosters would try to sell the argument that the tour was a good building block for American rugby, as Selfridge and others had done in the wake of the South African visit, but if it did serve such a purpose the impact was very much indirect.

NASTY (COWBOY) BOOT

Naas Botha used his time in the United States as a springboard to pursue options away from South African rugby and away from the restrictions of amateurism. Botha played at a time when national teams played relatively few test matches. Yet by the end of an international career that spanned just a few years (and a total of twenty-eight tests) Botha held every significant scoring record in Springbok history. Indeed, he already held those marks when he took what appeared to be a retirement from the game, at least at the international level, in 1982. In his time in the wilderness, Botha took an "ill-advised decision to seek a career in gridiron."[7]

Hendrik Egnatius "Naas" Botha, who bore several nicknames, one of which was "Nasty Boot" because of his excellence in the all-important kicking game in rugby union, did not choose to try out for just any gridiron team. In 1983, he tried out for the Dallas Cowboys, the team that had, in true monomaniacal Texas fashion, declared themselves to be "America's Team." This caused consternation in anti-apartheid circles, including SAN-ROC, on whose behalf the American-based Dennis Brutus proposed "to launch a vigorous campaign of protest on this matter."[8] And while there were smatterings of complaints and protest, most of Botha's experience was quiet; if anything, he was a novelty. He showed glimpses as a punter and was surprised when he was told he did not make the team for those duties but was being kept on as a place-kicker. Nonetheless, the Cowboys had a quality kicker in Rafael Septien, and Botha found he was not needed in Dallas. He had an offer to sign with the San Antonio Gunslingers of the ill-fated United States Football League, but he rejected that offer as well, instead sticking around Dallas to play golf and to star for the Dallas Harlequins, an amateur rugby club with at least ten internationals on it that went on to win the US rugby club championship. The next summer, he signed a contract with the New England Patriots, but they, too, had a kicker, and Botha found that his heart was no longer in it.

But part of Botha's interest in American football was based on the fact that he had actually found himself on the outs in South African rugby. He was disenchanted with Northern Transvaal, and he found himself on the outside looking in with the Springboks. Football was a game for which his skill set was only partially suited, and where, as a punter or placekicker, he would have been on the fringe after having been a central figure in a game where kicking was merely part of a well-rounded rugby portfolio (though ironically, in some rugby circles, Botha was unfairly seen as one dimensional—as basically just a kicker). When Botha moved on to try his hand in the NFL, he found himself on the bad side of rugby's strict amateurism laws, as going professional in any sport was enough to revoke his amateur status in rugby. But as soon as rugby authorities in South Africa relented, Botha was prepared to return to South Africa and resume his career as a rugby star rather than try his hand as a fringe specialist in the alien game of American football. Into 1992, Botha continued to play rugby for the Italian club Rovigo, leading them to several championships. A suspicious number of international players had descended on the otherwise second-tier rugby nation of Italy to play for its clubs, leading to speculation that they were being paid on the side. Nonetheless, the issue of whether Botha was being compensated was never cleared up, and he continued to play provincial rugby for Northern Transvaal and when possible for the Springboks.

In 1984, the Springboks hosted England, the last and only national team to play South Africa between the end of the American tour in 1981 and the Springbok return to international play in 1992. Indeed, this was only the second time England had ever traveled to South Africa. They had played and beaten the Springboks at Ellis Park in 1972, in a test that, even at the time, was controversial in England. South Africa, captained by Theuns Stofberg, who had also served as captain for the Boks in the match against the Midwest XV in Racine, won both games comfortably, with the most noteworthy aspects being that in the tests at Boet Erasmus Park in Port Elizabeth on June 2 and at Ellis Park in Johannesburg on June 9, Errol Tobias played and shined. At Ellis Park he scored a try, his only one in a test match, and kicked a conversion. The South Africans defeated England by the largest margin the Brits had ever suffered. Tobias would later identify that match as the greatest game he ever played. Perhaps equally noteworthy, Avril Williams, a coloured wing from the Western Cape and the Federation tradition that was the source of so much controversy, became the second black Springbok, playing in both matches with Tobias. Williams had a nephew, Chester, who would go on to become the third black Springbok, starring for the legendary 1995 World Cup squad.

If it was even possible to imagine South Africa reentering the global sporting community, the latter months of 1984 made clear that no rapprochement was coming any time soon. In early September 1984, the National Party government had engaged in a series of what it touted as constitutional reforms. Among those reforms was the establishment of a "Tri-Cameral Parliament"—one house for whites, one for coloureds, and one for Indians, with the African majority noticeably absent even from these tepid reforms—that would allow limited self-oversight to the coloured and Indian communities. The response to the September opening of the parliaments was an uprising in the Vaal Triangle that spread to the rest of the country, thus beginning maybe the most intense years of opposition to apartheid, which in turn led to some of the most oppressive years in an already oppressive country. The years 1984–1987 in particular would be characterized by campaigns from organizations like the United Democratic Front (UDF—operating in the vacuum created by the banned ANC) to "Make South Africa Ungovernable," which led to the government's "Total Strategy" of increased security police and military force in the face of what they wrongly but cynically declared to be a "Total Onslaught" from communists, a strategy that was meant to appeal as much to Cold War Washington and London as to white South Africa. In the wake of these events, a return to the sporting world seemed more distant than ever as South Africa became ever more a pariah state.

Even as the country descended further into chaos, another cobbled-together squad, this time consisting of South Americans and a smattering of players from rugby minnows Spain visited South Africa for a two-test series. The Springboks won both matches with Divan "DJ" Serfontein, a scrumhalf who had played in the American matches, including the absurd Glenville test, serving as captain for the only time in his career.

The events of the period after 1984 meant that prospective tours to South Africa were increasingly scrutinized. Unchastened by the epochal events of 1981 and subsequent crises in South Africa, the New Zealand RFU had been set to send the All Blacks to South Africa in 1986. Saner heads finally prevailed as the result of a decision in New Zealand's high court in July 1985, prohibiting the All Blacks from representing the NZRFU. The decision did not prevent a team chock full of All Blacks—twenty-eight of the thirty players chosen to represent the national team for the 1985 tour were part of the 1986 rebels appropriately named Cavaliers—from touring and playing that year. Only David Kirk and John Kirwin refused to tour alongside their All Black teammates. The Cavaliers prepared for the South Africa trip over the objections of increasing numbers of people, including stalwarts such as Dennis Brutus, who wrote David Lange, whose Labour Party had defeated Robert Muldoon in a landslide in 1984, making Lange the country's youngest-ever prime minister at forty-one. Almost a year before the Cavaliers' departed for South Africa, Brutus wrote on behalf of SAN-ROC, "We urgently entreat you to take all possible further steps to halt, even at this late hour, the proposed tour of racist South Africa by a representative rugby union team."[9]

These protests and those over the next eleven months proved futile, and the Cavaliers played twelve times in South Africa, including four matches against the Springboks in Cape Town, Durban, Pretoria, and Johannesburg. The Springboks won three of these matches, losing one narrowly. But New Zealand found itself increasingly under fire and withdrew all support for engagements with South African rugby in the future. The rebel Cavaliers were a creation that existed only for the obfuscatory purposes of the 1986 tour. The selected players did not leave as a group, but rather slinked off to South Africa in dribs and drabs, some working the trip into other official international business. Otherwise, the Cavaliers very much represented the elites of New Zealand rugby. Rumors have always circulated that someone in South Africa—many believe it to be Danie Craven, others pointed to Japanese auto manufacturer (and Springbok rugby sposors) Toyota—had arranged for handsome payments to the rebels. The tour once again revived the fissures of 1981 in New Zealand, albeit with far less intensity because the matches were being played in South Africa. However, the New Zealand government and rugby officials met with widespread sympathy at home and abroad given that both had tried to prevent the tour. Nonetheless, it was clear that playing with apartheid was still viable to too many in New Zealand, the country most important to South Africa's status in world rugby.

1997 saw the International Rugby Board's inaugural World Cup, from which South Africa was excluded. For a while, Danie Craven tried to make plans to hold its own international tournament to challenge the IRB event, but to no avail. The first World Cup, cohosted by Australia and New Zealand and won by the All Blacks, went off with South Africa being missed as an opponent, perhaps, but not lamented. The United States did participate, finishing third in their four-team pool, behind Australia and England, who defeated the Eagles by a combined sixty-four points, but ahead of Japan, whom the Americans beat 21–18 in Brisbane. On the pitch, it surely would have been a better and more competitive tournament had the Springboks played. The finals might even have seen the Springboks and All Blacks meet for the official world championships after so many de facto clashes for that honorific, but the rugby world had finally cast South Africa out for good, at least for any rugby that mattered.

There was another quiet American engagement with apartheid rugby in 1988 when the West Coast Grizzlies visited South Africa in what had become part of the trend of "rebel tours," tours in contravention to the spirit of the anti-apartheid boycotts. Just a few years after American rugby officials gave their stamp of approval to the Springbok tour of the United States, the USA Rugby Football Union expressed its concern about the trip, though it had in fact been approved by the USARFU board a year earlier. Nonetheless, in 1988 American rugby authorities proved to be far more sensitive to international will, if for no other reason than that there were fears of American involvement prompting yet another wave of Olympic boycotts and that rugby, already a minor sport in America, might alienate any minor sponsorships that it had mustered as it continued to struggle to grow in the United States. At the last minute, the USARFU tried to stop the Grizzlies from going to South Africa, but it was far too late. The tour received almost no attention in the media, though a letter from rugby player Mark Scott to the *Los Angeles Times*, which had given the tour and its controversy a tiny bit of coverage, argued, "claims by rugby officials that the" Pacific Coast Rugby Football Union (PCRFU) "tour of South Africa is *only* in the interest of promoting the sport are short-sighted and self-serving." Scott believed that "rugby is probably the least racist sport I know of, at any level, but we must look beyond the game itself. Continued tours of South Africa surely cannot help the world's perception of the game and its players." He speculated, "Perhaps the day will come when we can tour South Africa with pride in the fact that we were part of the solution. Until then, we are part of the problem." [10]

The PCRFU stubbornly insisted on going ahead with the tour, playing seven matches in South Africa that were sponsored by the First National Bank of South Africa, which a year earlier had sponsored a rebel tour of the South Sea Barbarians, made up of players from the rugby-mad Pacific islands. The American team included three native-born South Africans, a Scot-turned-American who had played for the Eagles, and several players from the Eagles team from the inaugural rugby World Cup in 1987, including five who had played in the win against Japan. Soon after the Americans finished their first game, a bomb hidden in a car exploded at Ellis Park shortly after the Transvaal–Orange Free State match, killing two and injuring thirty-five, a reminder of the political stakes within the country the Americans had so cavalierly entered to play rugby.

On the pitch, the Americans rarely humiliated themselves, though they usually lost handily, sometimes against teams including provincial players and even Springboks. They did pull off an impressive win against the Orange Free State. Following that victory, the Americans, per pretour agreements, played a "non-white" team, the Anglo-Freegold XV based in the mining town of Welkom, the second largest city in the Orange Free State. The Welkom "project" for the development of nonracial rugby had begun in 1980. In the words of historian Hendrik Snyders, "this meant that the Grizzlies unwittingly became part of the attempt to build a multi-racial rugby tradition in which the scores" of matches were secondary. Nonetheless, led by talented black players including Welcome Ndumo and Patrick Mdudo, the South Africans pasted the Americans 31–9 in a match that "was not a contest."[11] The Grizzlies would go on to defeat a Natal side in a big upset victory that saw a young player, Joel Stransky, appear for the South African side. Stransky would kick his way to fame with the winning drop goal in the famous 1995 rugby World Cup finals victory against New Zealand. The Americans would also win a match in Cape Town during a time when anti-apartheid activists had won a case in court to allow for public political events, including a celebration of Nelson Mandela's seventieth birthday. The Americans enjoyed the fruits of being white rugby players in apartheid South Africa while acquitting themselves well on the pitch, but they also seem to have learned few lessons about apartheid and what it still meant in South Africa in 1988.

The Grizzlies did so well that there were rumors that some Americans might be included in the World XV "select" team that would play the Springboks in South Africa in 1989. Not surprisingly, the World XV team got caught up in the political maelstrom as well. France, Wales, and England made clear that their players should not participate, with the possible sanction of banning from the sport on the table. A longstanding South African rugby ally, New Zealand, wavered briefly before doing the same. The International Rugby Board stated its opposition to the tour and many suggested that South Africa should withdraw from the body. Nonetheless players from France, Wales, England, Scotland, and Australia gathered in South Africa in August 1989.

Yet by 1988, the ANC had already recognized that "rugby diplomacy" might represent a way to win the hearts and minds of white South Africans, especially Afrikaners, while at the same time pushing the government to change not only its sports policies, but also its national politics. In October 1988, members of the ANC met with Danie Craven and other rugby officials in Harare, Zimbabwe, to forge an agreement that appeared "to have set a precedent which could transform all South African sport." The negotiations were geared toward developing truly nonracial sports policies, and after two days the parties had emerged with an agreement to develop national nonracial sports bodies with the centerpiece being the development of a nonracial rugby board that would become the official board for South African rugby, including the Springboks. Among those representing the ANC and the nonracial

South African Rugby Union were future South African president Thabo Mbeki, and future minister of sport (and one-time rugby player), Steve Tshwete. The "Joint Statement of the South African Rugby Board, the South African Rugby Union, and the African National Congress" issued on October 16, 1988, affirmed the formation of a single governing board "organized according to non-racial principles," "called on all people of goodwill inside and outside South Africa to support this process," emphasized that "the accomplishment of the goals stated here is a necessity for South African rugby to take its rightful place in world rugby," and asserted that the parties that participated in the Harare meeting were "ready to meet at all times and shall meet any other parties or groups that may also play such a role." The brief statement closed by revealing that the ANC were central power brokers then and going forward. "The ANC accepted the good faith and sincerity of the rugby administrators at the meeting and undertook to use good offices to ensure that non-racial South African rugby takes the rightful place in African and world rugby."[12]

The deal was seen in the eyes of many white rugby supporters, including Craven, as a path forward for the Springboks to return to proper international play, even as it blindsided many members of the National Party government, including then-minister-of-education and soon-to-be president F. W. de Klerk. One comment from the government-sponsored South African Broadcasting Corporation asserted that the "terrorist" ANC was flailing and needed the Harare meeting for positive publicity.[13] At the same time, many in the anti-apartheid movement felt betrayed by the secret meeting. Nonetheless, the Harare indaba was an important but small step on the way to ending sporting isolation, even as ANC policy continued to strongly advocate keeping South African sport isolated.

Perhaps tellingly, in 1991, before South Africa had been allowed back into the global rugby fraternity in 1992, Tom Selfridge had invited the Springboks back to the United States for a three-match tour that he hoped would take place in May 1992. In the words of Snyders, "Given the SARB's commitment to achieving rugby unity, it politely declined the invitation and gave an undertaking that the matter would be revisited after the establishment of a single and non-racial rugby body."[14] Selfridge, meanwhile, said at around the same time, "The next time the Springboks come to the United States, apartheid will be gone. And the game will occur and maybe the score will be down next to the high school scores."[15]

A ROUGH RETURN: 1992–1995

By 1990, there were many who believed that with the release of Nelson Mandela South African sport should be able to recommence immediately with no prejudice and no restrictions. But the African National Congress and other factions in the liberation struggle and much of the world of sport wanted to hold off, to see real change in South Africa, and to see if the release of Mandela and the loosening of apartheid restrictions also led to the true end of apartheid and ultimately, to actual democratic elections. Ironically, as sporting codes returned to the global fold, many global anti-apartheid bodies, including the British Anti-Apartheid Movement, were furious and took their ire out not on the sporting codes but on an ANC they saw as acquiescing far too quickly to National Party sporting aspirations.

In quick succession (but not without controversy, especially within the ANC and other liberation organizations), South Africa was allowed back into the Olympic movement (without a flag for the Barcelona games), and the national cricket team toured the West Indies, an interesting choice given the West Indies' rebel tour of South Africa just a few years earlier. But rugby fans and administrators, in particular, were antsy and ready to return to a world of rugby it had barely left.

In June of 1992, even as the ANC, National Party, and other interested parties worked through the Convention for a Democratic South Africa (CODESA) on negotiations that would lead to the end of apartheid and National Party rule and would result in the elections that would bring Nelson Mandela and the ANC to power in 1994, there was a massacre at a workers' hostel outside of the township of Boipatong in the Witwatersrand. Members of the Inkatha Freedom Party attacked the hostel and its largely ANC-supporting body in what was initially sold as so-called "black-on-black" political violence. But such violence always carried some of the fingerprints of the state that had created such tensions to begin with, and the murder of forty-five people and wounding of many more at Boipatong was no exception, as the fomenting of violence between the ANC and Inkatha was in part a feature of the "dirty tricks" of the apartheid state. In the wake of Boipatong, the CODESA talks broke down, as Mandela and the ANC insisted they could not negotiate in good faith when the National Party's security apparatus continued to operate in the shadows unchecked. Only when F. W. de Klerk promised to rein in the police did negotiations resume.

It was against this backdrop that the Springboks hosted New Zealand at Ellis Park Stadium on August 15, 1992, in what was called "The Return Match." The competition was a close one that New Zealand won 27–24, but the importance of the match was not in what took place on the pitch. The ANC had laid out a series of expectations to the South African Rugby Football Union (SARFU), at the head of which sat Louis Luyt, to give its stamp of approval for the match: to hold a moment of silence for the victims of the Boipatong Massacre, not to wave the old South African flag, which had been abandoned but not yet replaced, and not to play or sing *"Die Stem van Suid-Afrika,"* the apartheid national anthem. The ANC also requested that visiting teams visit Boipatong, but when SARFU officials (and possibly the visiting teams themselves) demurred, the ANC did not push this last request.

All three promises were broken. The far-right Conservative Party, which opposed negotiations and the ending of apartheid, handed out the old South African flag and leaflets endorsing the singing of *"Die Stem van Suid-Afrika."* During the moment of silence, thousands of whites in the crowd made noise, including loudly and aggressively singing the old anthem. Before the All Blacks did their traditional haka war dance, Luyt explicitly broke the agreement by playing an instrumental version of the old anthem, and, again, the crowd and a number of the Springbok players joined in. The crowd also waved the old flag defiantly throughout the game. All week the country's overwhelmingly right-wing Afrikaans-language press had encouraged the politics of resistance with rugby as the backdrop. In the wake of that boorishness manifesting itself, Johannesburg's *Star* newspaper wrote, "For that moment inside the concrete bowl, it seemed like a besieged tribe had gathered to take strength in their numbers and to send, from the protected citadel, a message of defiance to their perceived persecutors."[16] Louis Luyt was defiant as ever, growling, "I will not be threatened by anybody, and I don't care if certain people, not having rugby at heart, feel upset about my decision."[17]

Luyt could snarl and gnash all he wanted, but the power dynamic had changed. The ANC, while not yet officially in power, nonetheless held sway in what was becoming a new dispensation in which they would control the levers of South African rugby's fate. They threatened not to support the next match a week later against visiting Australia. For safety reasons alone, that almost certainly meant the match would have been canceled, but then the Australians, who had completely shut out South African rugby after 1970, made it clear that they would not play without the ANC's approval. Furthermore, national rugby officials emphasized "its dissatisfaction" and promised to "instruct" the Transvaal Rugby Football Union, the organization that Luyt headed, "to ensure that rugby unity is preserved and that the cause of non-racial rugby is enhanced at all times."[18] Furthermore, South Africa had been awarded hosting duties for the 1995 IRB World Cup in April, and that honor could be rescinded. Luyt, who would "not be threatened by anybody," backed off.

The Australia match was played, the fans and officials behaved themselves, and the Wallabies crushed the Springboks 26–3 at Cape Town's Newlands Stadium. Prior to another moment of silence for "all victims of violence in South Africa," the announcer at Newlands Stadium "pointedly reminded the crowd that the eyes of the rugby world" (not to mention the ANC) were upon them and "for 17 seconds, the stadium fell about as silent as one could expect." Once again, conservative politicians and journalists wanted to rouse the rabble, hoping that they would sing *"Die Stem van Suid-Afrika"* again. This time, however, the ANC had indicated that the crowd could do so as long as it was not officially sanctioned within the stadium. But to avoid any such impromptu performances from getting into the listening ears of radio and television audiences at home and abroad, the stadium staff immediately played loud music that would drown out any such performances. Many fans were disappointed, even feeling "betrayed" both by acquiescent white rugby officials but also by the ANC. As one man said, "We're getting fed up with the ANC that is bringing it down our throats— you're not allowed to show the flag but you must stop and obey the moment of silence." Yet as ANC spokesman Saki Makisoma argued, "That is an anthem which celebrates the conquest of black people in this country, and I have never felt a sense of loyalty and that national anthem seeks to negate what I am and what I feel." Even before the transition to democracy, white rugby fans had begun complaining about an ANC "dictatorship," a concern that would have been deeply ironic had it not been so profoundly stupid.[19]

Indeed, the rest of 1992 would be a bit of a disaster for the newly emergent Springboks who believed they would come back from isolation dominant, as they always had been, only to discover that the rugby world had caught up and surpassed them during their absence. They split a test series in France in October in which France looked much the better side and, in November of that year, England handled them easily at Twickenham. This lack of success vexed South African rugby fans even more than the political questions.

MADIBA MAGIC

The prospect of South Africa hosting the 1995 World Cup was one factor that influenced how South African rugby officials and fans were learning to behave themselves. This would be the third in that event's history after the first two tournaments in 1987 and 1991, but there was no way that was going to happen without the imprimatur of the ANC, without an assurance that the world's television cameras and journalists would not show racist ugliness from South Africans, and without the prospect of a redemption narrative to spin to the world.

The 1995 Springboks are arguably the most famous rugby team in the history of the sport. They certainly are the team best known to the world outside of rugby's elite nations, largely as the result of the Clint Eastwood film, *Invictus*, which was based on John Carlin's bestselling book, *Playing the Enemy*. The 1995 *Invictus* myth goes as follows: Nelson Mandela savvily embraced the 1995 Springboks, who had been chosen to host the 1995 World Cup, and he reached out, in particular, to Springbok captain Francois Pienaar, who embraced Mandela's vision because Mandela's vision embraced the Springboks. Indeed, his intervention helped to save the Springbok logo and the country's traditional green and gold colors, which most in the ANC and other liberation organizations desperately wanted to toss into the dustbin of history. In so doing, the 1995 Springboks had helped to save a vulnerable new country.

And there is no question—the 1995 Springbok victory, with sole black player Chester Williams, the third black Springbok and the first since his uncle Avril in 1984, was inspiring and fraught with symbolism. Mandela embraced the team, making them more palatable to a country swept up in "Madiba Magic," the enchantment cast by the inspirational leader who had been imprisoned for twenty-seven years but who came out in a spirit of reconciliation. The script practically wrote itself: Mandela wore Pienaar's #6 jersey during the celebration of the 15–12 Springbok victory—naturally, over the heavily favored All Blacks. Pienaar rose to the occasion. SABC's David van der Sandt addressed the captain, "Francois, fantastic support from 63,000 South Africans today?" Pienaar responded "We didn't have the support of 63,000 South Africans today. We had the support of 42 million South Africans."[20] But despite Carlin's assertion that the Springbok victory "made a nation," such treacle overstates the importance of a rugby match, of how much work had already been done to make the new South Africa, but also how very much remained and indeed remains to this day. The 1995 World Cup victory is symbolically important—and symbols matter, sometimes significantly—but it has become a bit too easy to overstate the case, especially since it was in seemingly everyone's interest to perpetrate the myth.[21]

LOWS, HIGHS , AND UNBEARABLE LUYTNESS

Rugby in South Africa continued to intersect with politics in South Africa because in South Africa everything ends up being about politics, especially that which at first glance might seem not to. Politics in South Africa are inseparable from race. At the same time, after the 1995 World Cup, rugby made the leap to professionalism. It was the last major global team sport to do so, and something many thought would never happen to the game that more than any other had embraced the amateur ideal.

Louis Luyt, the former rugby player, fertilizer salesman, founder of the propaganda organ *The Citizen*, rugby potentate, and ultimate purveyor of the old school values in South African rugby and society, the man who had helped sponsor the 1981 tour, who had defiantly played *"Die Stem van Suid-Afrika"* and encouraged the waving of the old flag, continued to serve in positions of authority in South African rugby through the 1990s, including for years as head of the South African Rugby Union. Always divisive, rarely repentant, Luyt at one point refused to testify before the high court on issues related to racism in South African rugby and then managed to maneuver to humiliate Nelson Mandela by getting a right-wing judge to summon Mandela to testify in court, an unprecedented moment for a head of state, though the gambit backfired. Long accused of racism himself, and then of corruption, Luyt finally stepped down as president of SARU in 1998, only to enter right-wing South African politics, serving in parliament for a number of years. Luyt died in 2013. He was eighty years old.

Racial incidents would continue to scar South African rugby. In 1997, a newly hired Springbok coach, Andre Maarkgraaff, was caught on tape referring to "kaffirs," South Africa's n-word on steroids. He lost his job. In 2003, a white Afrikaner player, Geo Cronje, was unwilling to room with or even use the same bathroom, toilet, or shower as Quinton Davids, another black Springbok from the country's coloured community. Cronje lost his Springbok place. There have been constant allegations of racism in South African rugby in the boardroom, the broadcast studio, and the bars. And, of course, there are the ongoing allegations that the Springboks are too white. There are also counteraccusations that Springbok rugby selects players based on politics, not on merit, an accusation noticeably silent when white players are chosen seemingly based on the fact that their parents were Springboks, or serve as rugby administrators, or as prominent coaches, or that they look the part, or any other permutation where accusations of the meritocracy crumbling cannot be attributed to racial grievance. The pace of racial "transformation," a South African buzzword for racial progress, has been slow, the excuses many.[22]

But there have also been highlights. The 2007 Springboks, who were captained by the inspirational John Smit, and were also led by Bryan Habana, defeated England 15–6 to win the World Cup in France. Habana was South Africa's first true black global superstar, a coloured wing who could fly, sometimes metaphorically, as one of the fastest players in the world, but also almost literally, as some of the most famous images of Habana involve him joyously diving across the tryline, his mouthguard exacerbating his ebullient grin, to score another try. And score tries he did, finishing his career tied with the legendary New

Zealand wing, Jonah Lomu, for most tries in the history of the World Cup, with fifteen, and the most tries in one World Cup in 2007, with eight. Habana scored the second most tries in the history of test rugby (and the most among those nations in the first tier) with sixty-seven, second only to Japanese legend Daisuke Osata. Habana was 2007 IRB Player of the Year and by any measure goes down as one of the greatest players in the history of rugby union. By 2007, it was almost unnecessary to point out how much Habana smashed to bits the age-old lie in South African rugby circles that "blacks are not rugby people."

In 2008, the Springboks hired Peter de Villiers as head coach, the first nonwhite coach in the history of the South African national team, with officials doing him no favors by making clear that race had been a deciding factor among the finalists.[23] De Villiers' record was not out of pace with that of other post-isolation Springbok coaches, and in some ways, he was more successful—there have been twelve coaches who have coached at least one test match since 1992 (as of May 2021 Jacques Nienaber, hired to replace Rassie Erasmus, had not coached a match). De Villiers' winning percentage among those coaches ranks sixth, and he is one of only four Springbok coaches to have won the Tri-Nations/Rugby Championship. De Villiers coached the second most test matches of any coach since the end of isolation, and by most standards he did so well, though he did not win a World Cup. De Villiers was often pilloried within the rugby establishment, and his tendencies toward being frankly spoken, especially about racial issues, coupled with an inclination toward malapropisms (in English, his second language) earned him far more scorn than less accomplished coaches. Since his firing from the Springboks in 2011, he has not received anywhere near the kinds of high-profile job offers that have been standard for even those far less accomplished as Springbok coaches. Perhaps this is mere coincidence. I do not think it is, and neither does he.[24]

Indeed, the position of Springbok coach in the post-isolation era has been described as a "poisoned chalice," a "potentially untenable position" in the words of another outspoken former Bok coach and rugby commentator, Nick Mallett, because of both "the pressures of the job and the structural weaknesses of South African rugby."[25]

Allister Coetzee, who followed de Villiers' successor (Heyneke Meyer) as Springbok coach, certainly found the contents of the chalice to be bitter. As only the second black coach in Springbok history, he would have been right to worry that the poison had been applied by the rugby hierarchy in his country. He was hired relatively late after several months of speculation, he was basically left to deal with a deeply politicized environment in which all his decisions ran the risk of appearing to be informed by a mandate for quotas, and his teams were decidedly not good, among the weakest of the post-isolation period, losing more than they won and, oftentimes, not looking good even when they emerged victorious. Coetzee had a strong record on transformation when he was head man at Stormers, yet he seemed tentative, perhaps too sensitive to accusations of acting politically. By the time he was fired in 2018, it was almost an inevitability in rugby circles.

"WE CAN PULL TOGETHER": SIYA KOLISI AND THE 2019 SPRINGBOKS

And then there is the 2019 team: the defending world champions as I write this conclusion in the Second Year of Our Coronavirus 2021, when rugby, like every institution major and minor, has been disrupted and the Springboks thoroughly grounded. Siya Kolisi, the inspirational captain, led the 2019 Boks, a truly multiracial team with stars representing the entirety of Desmond Tutu's "Rainbow Nation of God," who in the finals defeated England in a walk, 32–12. Coach Rassie Erasmus, the architect of the 2019 squad, had appointed Kolisi the first black Springbok captain in 2018, and the gamble (if it was that, as Kolisi had been a successful leader at all levels, including as captain of the Stormers Super Rugby side in Cape Town) paid off handsomely. Kolisi became the figure touted in advertisements, with the idea of the Rainbow Nation always as much text as subtext, and with his beautiful multiracial family front and center. In some ways it was, perhaps, an improbable victory—the Springboks had been at a nadir in the period from 2016 to 2018, and among other historic elements of their triumph was the fact that they became the first team to win the World Cup despite losing a pool match, as they had fallen, naturally, to their ancient foes, the All Blacks, in the first game of the tournament. This was after having just edged out the All Blacks for the Rugby Championship—the Southern Hemisphere tournament involving South Africa, New Zealand, Australia, and Argentina—weeks earlier. Kolisi showed why he was such a powerful figure for South African rugby in the immediate aftermath of the finals when he gave a quick speech that resonated deeply:

> We have so many problems in our country, but to have a team like this—we come from different backgrounds, different races, and we came together with one goal. I really hope we have done that for South Africa—to show that we can pull together if we want to achieve something.[26]

It was enough to bring a tear to the eye and a catch to the throat of even the most cynical fan, journalist, or historian.

And yet.

In the weeks before the World Cup, South African rugby was hit by yet another alleged racial incident involving popular and formidable lock Eben Etzebeth (who, after his debut as Springbok captain, where he led the Boks to a 35–12 win over France at Ellis Park in June 2017, walked into the press room and said, "Welcome to the best day of my life!"). In August 2019, Etzebeth was accused of having been involved in a racial incident at a bar in Langebaan in the Western Cape. Etzebeth's elevation to captain under Coetzee was already seen in some circles as a peculiar choice. After all, Etzebeth played alongside Siya Kolisi for the Stormers in Super Rugby and served as Kolisi's vice captain. Coetzee had a solid record of transformation as a coach, and as the second black Springbok coach, he was expected to build upon that record for the national team. Etzebeth had a reputation as a hard man, an enforcer, a hothead, something that can make one a great teammate but perhaps not the greatest captain, a position that requires poise and leadership by example. As for what happened in Langebaan, we may never know. An investigation went nowhere. Someone in Etzebeth's party—it may or may not have been the big man himself—is alleged to have called another man a racial slur. There may have been a scuffle. Etzebeth does not have a reputation for racism, and indeed, his black teammates by and large came to his defense. Still, yet another incident involving the Springboks served as a reminder of how far rugby had to go in a country where the sport had always served as a thermometer of the country's racial temperature. As I wrote soon after the alleged incident, " The reality is that racism still swirls around some circles of the 'ruffians' game played by gentlemen.' And, that will be the case in spite of whatever decisions are made regarding Eben Etzebeth, who once, not so long ago, experienced the best day of his life."[27]

South African rugby has come a long way since 1981. Especially at the elite national level, where it turns out, winning conquers most all excuses. Yet the country still lags at the developmental levels—the grassroots, where rugby pitches in townships tend to be rare and dilapidated. At the schools, the game is dominated by the elite prep schools that maintain some of the whiff of apartheid—overwhelmingly white and upper- or middle-class bastions of privilege where there are none more privileged than the boys who play for the First XV—even if they have sincerely tried to be more inclusive.

USA RUGBY: WHERE EAGLES . . . SOAR?

In the wake of the tour to the United States, Wynand Claassen argued, "The tour had brought an important dimension into SA/USA rugby relations with the playing of the first official test match. I told the teams we had played against, to forget about the scores and continue to compete against as many top teams as possible."[28] And by any measure, American rugby is worlds ahead of where it was in 1981. The team successfully competes in The Americas Rugby Championship, an admittedly watered-down affair since Argentina's Pumas play in the Rugby Championship every year, with the South Americans sending an Argentina XV—effectively a developmental squad—to the Americas tournament. The Eagles have won the competition twice, in 2017 and 2018, with the Argentina XV winning the others. The US Eagles also qualify regularly for the rugby World Cup (only missing the 1995 edition in South Africa), and while they have never made the knockout stages, they acquit themselves well on the international stage, continuing to be a team always becoming the rising giant of the future, if a minnow in the present. The US national team gained at least one long-term fan in 1981: Springbok player Div Visser. Visser noted, "Now when I watch the world cup matches I support the USA side. Maybe [because] of the invisible bond that was formed then when we toured the US and played the US Eagles."[29] American players increasingly compete in international professional leagues, most notably in Europe, and in North America's Major League Rugby (MLR), which began play in 2018 and is increasing in quality, and may well prove to be something of a retirement destination for international stars. Indeed, Tendai "Beast" Mtawarira, the Springbok legend, one of the stars of the 2019 World Cup, became MLR's most splashy international signing when he joined Old Glory DC in 2020. As it did to so much in that year, COVID-19 scuttled his debut.

The Springboks have played the US Eagles rugby team four times since 1981. They defeated the Americans handily each time. The two teams played a test match in Houston in 2001, the Springboks' first return to the United States two decades after 1981, and won by a comfortable 43–20 margin. In 2007, the Springboks swamped the American Eagles 64–15 in Montpelier, France, in the World Cup on the way to their second world championship. In a 2015 World Cup group match, the Springboks obliterated the USA 64–0 in London. It is possible that in the professional era, the gap between the teams is actually growing, even as American rugby improves.

But these were just games. The improbable and absurd 1981 Springbok tour of the United States was about much, much more.

NOTES

PREFACE

1. Tony Collins, *The Oval World: A Global History of Rugby* (London: Bloomsbury, 2015), p. 3.

2. For Kaunda Ntunja's commentary as Kolisi walked onto the pitch, see: https://www.youtube.com/watch?v=dCe2WZHa6W4

INTRODUCTION

1. See Rob Nixon, *Homelands, Harlem and Hollywood: South African Culture and the World Beyond* (New York and London: Routledge, 1994) and Lacy Molina, "You Can't Buy Me I Don't Care What You Pay: Music, Musicians, and the Cultural Boycott of South Africa," MA Thesis, University of Texas Permian Basin, 2020.

2. Allister Sparks, *The Sword and the Pen: Six Decades on the Political Frontier* (Johannesburg & Cape Town: Jonathan Ball Publishers, 2016), p. 158.

3. Quoted in South African Institute of Race Relations, *A Survey of Race Relations in South Africa 1975* (Johannesburg: SAIRR, January 1976), p. 279.

4. SAIRR *A Survey of Race Relations in South Africa 1977*, p. 557.

5. SAIRR, *A Survey of Race Relations in South Africa 1977*, p. 564.

6. See, for example, SAIRR, *A Survey of Race Relations in South Africa 1981*, pp. 418–19.

7. See Harry Edwards, *The Revolt of the Black Athlete: 50th Anniversary Edition* (Urbana: University of Illinois Press, 2017) and Douglas Hartman,

Race, Culture, and the Revolt of the Black Athlete (Chicago: University of Chicago Press, 2003).

1. THE ACCIDENTAL TOURISTS

1. Phone memo from Douglas Reid to SARB, July 15, 1980. South Africa Rugby Archives, Stellenbosch, "Groot toere," VIII, 1.37 B, 1981. The original Afrikaans parenthetical: (*asof ons nie genoeg het nie*).

2. Alex Kellermann SARB Memorandum, July 1980. South Africa Rugby Archives, Stellenbosch, "Groot toere," VIII, 1.37 B, 1981.

3. Edmund W. Lee letter to Alex Kellermann, August 3, 1980. South Africa Rugby Archives, Stellenbosch, "Groot toere," VIII, 1.37 B, 1981.

4. Edmund W. Lee letter to Alex Kellermann, August 3, 1980. South Africa Rugby Archives, Stellenbosch, "Groot toere," VIII, 1.37 B, 1981.

5. Doug Reid to Alex Kellermann, December 5, 1980. South Africa Rugby Archives, Stellenbosch, "Groot toere," VIII, 1.37 B, 1981.

6. Doug Reid to Alex Kellermann, December 5, 1980. South Africa Rugby Archives, Stellenbosch, "Groot toere," VIII, 1.37 B, 1981.

7. Doug Reid to Richard Nixon, July 22, 1980. South Africa Rugby Archives, Stellenbosch, "Groot toere," VIII, 1.37 B, 1981.

8. Doug Reid to Richard Nixon, July 22, 1980. South Africa Rugby Archives, Stellenbosch, "Groot toere," VIII, 1.37 B, 1981.

9. Richard Nixon to Doug Reid, August 18, 1980. South Africa Rugby Archives, Stellenbosch, "Groot toere," VIII, 1.37 B, 1981.

10. Doug Reid to Ronald Reagan, August 18, 1980. South Africa Rugby Archives, Stellenbosch, "Groot toere," VIII, 1.37 B, 1981.

11. Doug Reid to Ronald Reagan, August 18, 1980. South Africa Rugby Archives, Stellenbosch, "Groot toere," VIII, 1.37 B, 1981. Of course, it was untrue that the Carter Administration did not "recognize" South Africa.

12. Doug Reid to Ronald Reagan, August 18, 1980. South Africa Rugby Archives, Stellenbosch, "Groot toere," VIII, 1.37 B, 1981.

13. Edmund W. Lee letter to Alex Kellermann, August 3, 1980. South Africa Rugby Archives, Stellenbosch, "Groot toere," VIII, 1.37 B, 1981.

14. Edmund W. Lee letter to Alex Kellermann, August 3, 1980. South Africa Rugby Archives, Stellenbosch, "Groot toere," VIII, 1.37 B, 1981.

15. See Ron Nixon, *Selling Apartheid: South Africa's Global Propaganda War* (Auckland Park: Jacana Media, 2015).

16. Information service of South Africa, *Progress Through Separate Development: South Africa in Peaceful Transition* Fourth Edition (New York: Information Service of South Africa, 1973), p. 7. Another publisher, Johannesburg's

Afrikaanse Pers-Boekhandel, served as an adjunct to the Information Services, publishing a substantial number of books geared toward an English-speaking audience despite the clear Afrikaans origin of the press. J. E. Holloway's 1964 *Apartheid: A Challenge*, for example, asks on its back cover "Is not apartheid a reasonable and realistic approach to the handling of an ecological problem, which is unique not only in history but also in the present-day world?"

17. See Donald Woods, "Minister Mulder's Hopscotch Thesis" in Woods, *South African Dispatches: Letters to My Countrymen* (New York: Henry Holt & Company, 1986), pp. 4–6. This book consisted of columns Woods had written as editor of South Africa's *Daily Dispatch*, in the eastern Cape city of East London between 1975 and 1977, when he was banned for challenging the government's stand after the death of Woods' friend Steve Biko.

18. On the Information Scandal/Muldergate and the investment in Western Media, see Mervyn Rees and Chris Day, *Muldergate: The Story of the Info Scandal* (Johannesburg: Macmillan South Africa, 1980); Nixon, *Selling Apartheid*, chapter 5, pp. 91–100; Dan O'Meara, *Forty Lost Years: The Apartheid State and the Politics of the National Party, 1948–1994* (Randburg: Ravan Press, 1996), Chapter 12, pp. 229–49; Eschel Rhoodie, *The REAL Information Scandal* (Pretoria: Orbis, 1983); Chris Patterson and Vanessa Malila, "Beyond the Information Scandal: When South Africa Bought into Global News," *Ecquid Novi: African Journalism Studies*, Vol. 34, #2, 2013, pp. 1–14.

19. See Allister Sparks' "On the Trail of Info Scandal's 'Deep Throat'," *Sunday Times*, March 6, 2016, which is an excerpt from his memoir, *The Sword and the Pen: Six Decades on the Political Frontier* (Johannesburg and Cape Town, Jonathan Ball, 2016).

20. For this argument, I owe an intellectual debt to O'Meara, who best articulates it in *Forty Lost Years*. See especially p. 231.

21. Les de Villiers, *South Africa: A Skunk Among Nations* (London: Tandem, 1975). The chapter on sport, "Et Tu Brutus?" covers pp. 120–48; quotation from p. 148.

22. Les de Villiers to Ed Hagerty, 19 November 1980. South Africa Rugby Archives, Stellenbosch, "Groot toere," VIII, 1.37 B, 1981.

23. Les de Villiers to Ed Hagerty, 19 November 1980. South Africa Rugby Archives, Stellenbosch, "Groot toere," VIII, 1.37 B, 1981.

24. Danie Craven testimonial for Louis Luyt, November 1980. South Africa Rugby Archives, Stellenbosch, "Groot toere," VIII, 1.37 B, 1981.

25. Edmund W. Lee to Alex Kellermann, November 24, 1980. South Africa Rugby Archives, Stellenbosch, "Groot toere," VIII, 1.37 B, 1981.

26. Alex Kellermann letter to Edmund Lee, December 17, 1980. South Africa Rugby Archives, Stellenbosch, "Groot toere," VIII, 1.37 B, 1981.

27. Edmund Lee to Alex Kellermann, December 31, 1980. South Africa Rugby Archives, Stellenbosch, "Groot toere," VIII, 1.37 B, 1981.

28. Tom Selfridge Telegram to Danie Craven c/o Louis Luyt, n.d. (early January, possibly January 6) 1981, South Africa Rugby Archives, Stellenbosch, "Groot toere," VIII, 1.37 B, 1981. [I have chosen not to replicate the all-capitalized format of the telegrams and have thus made decisions on which words to begin with capital letters.]

29. Ed Lee Telegram to Danie Craven, January 20, 1981. South Africa Rugby Archives, Stellenbosch, "Groot toere," VIII, 1.37 B, 1981.

30. Ed Lee Telegram to Danie Craven, likely January 22, 1981, South Africa Rugby Archives, Stellenbosch, "Groot toere," VIII, 1.37 B, 1981.

31. Alex Kellermann Telegram to Ed Lee, February 9, 1981.

32. Alex Kellermann to Tom Selfridge, February 9, 1981, South Africa Rugby Archives, Stellenbosch, "Groot toere," VIII, 1.37 B, 1981.

33. Alex Kellermann to Ed Lee, February 9, 1981, South Africa Rugby Archives, Stellenbosch, "Groot toere," VIII, 1.37 B, 1981.

34. Alex Kellermann to Ed Lee, February 9, 1981, South Africa Rugby Archives, Stellenbosch, "Groot toere," VIII, 1.37 B, 1981.

2. STARTING TO PLAY

1. Nelie Smith Obituary, *Sunday Times* (Johannesburg), May 8, 2016.

2. Louis Babrow to Louis Van Der Watt, June 6, 1995. Letter courtesy of David McLellan, Select Books, Cape Town. See also the booklet, "UCT Rugby Club Tribute to Louis Babrow," 2003.

3. Wim van der Berg, *150 Years of South African Rugby*, p. 68.

4. *Sydney Morning Herald*, July 19, 1981.

5. *Sydney Morning Herald*, July 21, 1981.

6. John Griffiths, "Ask John" column, ESPNscrum, April 26, 2010.

7. *Mail & Guardian*, October 24, 2013.

8. *Charleston News and Courier*, August 12, 1978.

9. South African Institute of Race Relations, *A Survey of Race Relations in South Africa 1976* (Johannesburg: South African Institute of Race Relations, 1977), p. 394.

10. South African Institute of Race Relations, *A Survey of Race Relations in South Africa 1976* (Johannesburg: South African Institute of Race Relations, 1977), p. 395.

11. South African Institute of Race Relations, *A Survey of Race Relations in South Africa 1977* (Johannesburg: South African Institute of Race Relations, 1978), p. 558–59.

12. South African Institute of Race Relations, *A Survey of Race Relations in South Africa 1978* (Johannesburg: South African Institute of Race Relations, 1979), p. 487–88.

13. South African Institute of Race Relations, *A Survey of Race Relations in South Africa 1978* (Johannesburg: South African Institute of Race Relations, 1979), p. 487.

14. Tom English, *No Borders: Playing Rugby for Ireland* (Edinburgh: Arena Sport, 2016), p. 86–87. On Lenihan, see *Irish Times*, January 5, May 5, 1981.

15. *Irish Times*, February 21, 1981.

16. English, *No Borders*, p. 86.

17. *Irish Times,* May 2, 1981; English, *No Borders*, p. 87.

18. *Irish Times*, January 7, 17, 1981; *Independent* (Dublin), December 15, 2013.

19. *Irish Times*, March 2, 1981.

20. The IRFU published a self-justifying full-page statement in the *Irish Times* on January 14, 1981.

21. Eamonn Sweeney, "Answering Apartheid's Call," *Independent* (Dublin), December 15, 2013.

22. Quoted in English, *No Borders*, p. 86.

23. *Independent* (Dublin), February 2, 1981.

24. See *Glasgow Herald*, March 13, 1981, and "Alone They Stood," Broadsheet, December 6, 1981.

25. Eamonn Sweeney, "Answering Apartheid's Call," *Independent* (Dublin), December 15, 2013.

26. English, *No Borders*, p. 87.

27. *Irish Times*, January 31, 1981.

28. English, *No Borders*, p. 87.

29. English, *No Borders*, pp. 87–89.

30. English, *No Borders*, p. 89.

31. *Irish Times*, March 18, 1981.

32. English, *No Borders*, p. 87.

33. English, *No Borders*, p. 90.

34. English, *No Borders*, p. 90.

35. English, *No Borders*, p. 91.

36. English, *No Borders*, p. 90–91.

37. English, *No Borders*, p. 89.

38. English, *No Borders*, p. 89.

39. *Irish Times*, February 4, May 6, 7, 1981.

40. English, *No Borders*, p. 89.

41. Reg Sweet, "Ireland to South Africa 1981" in Vivian Jenkins, ed. *Rothmans Rugby Yearbook 1982–1983* (Aylesbury: Rothmans Publications Limited, 1981–82) p. 44.

42. *Independent* (Dublin), December 15, 2013.

43. On Kader Asmal and the Irish Anti-Apartheid Movement, see *Irish Times*, January 14, 1981; Eamonn Sweeney, "Answering Apartheid's Call," *Independent*, December 15, 2013; On SARU's response, see *Irish Times*, January 29, 1981.

44. South African Rugby Board, "Ireland Rugby Football Union Team to South Africa: May/June, 1981," in "Ireland vs. South Africa, 1981 Tour Book," South African Rugby Union Archives, Parow Warehouse.

45. South African Rugby Board, "Ireland vs. South Africa, 1981 Tour Book," South African Rugby Union Archives, Parow Warehouse.

46. *Irish Times*, May 29, 1981.

47. See Derek Catsam, "Tobias' historic bok role remembered," *Weekend Post* (Port Elizabeth, South Africa), June 25, 2016. On the "surprise" nature of the start, see *Irish Times*, May 25, 1981.

48. *Independent* (Dublin), June 7, 1981.

49. English, *No Borders*, p. 93.

50. Errol Tobias, *Pure Gold* (Cape Town: Tafelberg, 2015), pp. 83–84.

51. Eamonn Sweeney, "Answering Apartheid's Call," *Independent* (Dublin), December 15, 2013.

52. See Sean Diffley, "The 1981–82 Season in Ireland," in Vivian Jenkins, ed., *Rothmans Rugby Yearbook 1982–1983* (Aylesbury: Rothmans Publications Limited, 1981–82), pp. 197–200.

3. APART HATE

1. Capital District Committee Against Apartheid, "Say 'No' to Apartheid, Stop the South African Rugby Tour," MSU African Activist Archive.

2. Capital District Committee Against Apartheid, "Say 'No' to Apartheid, Stop the South African Rugby Tour," MSU African Activist Archive.

3. Capital District Committee Against Apartheid, "Say 'No' to Apartheid, Stop the South African Rugby Tour," MSU African Activist Archive. The body of the mimeographed flyer was typed in all capital letters.

4. *New York Times*, September 18, 1981.

5. William Booth, telegram to Chester Crocker, July 9, 1981, Africa Action Archive (of the African Activist Archive), Michigan State University Libraries Special Collections.

6. Daily Report, Middle East and Africa, FBIS-MEA-81-144, Foreign Broadcast Information Service Daily Reports, Kaduna Domestic Service, July 27–28, 1981. NewsBank.

7. American Committee on Africa, "Memo: South African Rugby Tour of the United States," July 13, 1981, Africa Action Archive (of the African Activist Archive), Michigan State University Libraries Special Collections.

8. Dennis Brutus, SANROC Statement, "Tour of United States by Rugby Team from Racist South Africa," July 14, 1981, African Activist Archives, Michigan State University Libraries Special Collections.

9. "Phelps–Stokes Fund Protest Admitting South African Rugby Team to the U.S." July 15, 1981, George M. Houser Africa Collection of the African Activist Archive, Michigan State University Libraries Special Collections.

10. United Nations Press Release, "Anti-Apartheid Committee Acting Chairman Appeals to United States to Stop Proposed South African Rugby Tour," July 10, 1981, ACCESS Papers, Michigan State University Libraries Special Collections.

11. Richard Lapchick Mailgram to William Haffner, July 7, 1981, ACCESS Papers, Michigan State University Libraries Special Collections.

12. ACCESS, "ACCESS Condemns United States State Department Decision to Grant Visas to South African National Rugby Team," July 15, 1981, ACCESS Papers, Michigan State University Libraries Special Collections.

13. ACCESS, "ACCESS Calls on Governors of New York State and Illinois to Ban Use of Facilities in Their States to the South African Springbok Rugby Team," July 16, 1981, ACCESS Papers, Michigan State University Libraries Special Collections.

14. ACCESS, "ACTION ALERT—the South Africans are coming!" July 16, 1981, ACCESS Papers, Michigan State University Libraries Special Collections.

15. SART Introductory Press Release, July 1981, African Activist Archive, Michigan State University Libraries Special Collections.

16. ACOA, "Stopping the Springboks: Report on the Campaign Against the South African Rugby Tour," October 1981.

17. ACOA, "Stopping the Springboks: Report on the Campaign Against the South African Rugby Tour," October 1981.

18. *Boston Globe*, September 25, 1981.

19. Alex Kellermann letter to Keith Seaber, December 3, 1981, South Africa Rugby Archives, Stellenbosch, "Groot toere," VIII, 1.37 B, 1981.

20. Alex Kellermann Telegram to Tom Selfridge, July 3, 1981, South Africa Rugby Archives, Stellenbosch, "Groot toere," VIII, 1.37 B, 1981.

21. Alex Kellermann letter to Keith Seaber, October 19, 1981; Alex Kellermann telegram to Keith Seaber, October 19, 1981; Alex Kellermann to RJ

Watkins, December 2, 1981; all in South Africa Rugby Archives, Stellenbosch, "Groot toere," VIII, 1.37 B, 1981.

22. Alex Kellermann letter to Keith Seaber, December 3, 1981, South Africa Rugby Archives, Stellenbosch, "Groot toere," VIII, 1.37 B, 1981.

23. American Committee on Africa, "Memo: South African Rugby Tour of the United States," July 13, 1981, Africa Action Archive (of the African Activist Archive), Michigan State University Libraries Special Collections.

24. G. T. Selfridge to Citibank, June 1981, ACCESS Papers, Michigan State University Libraries Special Collections.

25. *The Cape Times*, May 18, 1981.

26. *Washington Post*, July 14, 1981.

27. See *Do Not Enter: The Visa War Against Ideas*, Richter Videos, 1986; *New York Times*, August 27, 1983, March 14, 1984, July 28, 1985.

28. ACCESS, "Developments with Apartheid Rugby Tours," Access Update, no. 4, August 6, 1981. On the message to New Zealand, see "An Open Letter to the New Zealand Government," April 13, 1981.

29. ACCESS, "Developments with Apartheid Rugby Tours," Access Update, no. 4, August 6, 1981.

30. Chris Schoeman, *Danie Gerber: Maestro of the Midfield* (Cape Town: Sable Media, 1995), p. 54. "Kaffir" is arguably the most explosive racial epithet in South Africa, a word approximately equivalent to "nigger" in tone and intent. Tobias' Afrikaans response was "Toemaar, hierdie Hotnot gaan eers oor 'n maand-en-'n-half huistoe!" ("Shut up, this Hotnot is only going home in a a month-and-a-half!").

31. Email from De Villiers Visser, April 25, 2016.

32. ACCESS, "Developments with Apartheid rugby tours," Access Update, no. 4, August 6, 1981.

33. Alex Kellermann letter to Fritz Grunebaum, July 6, 1981, South Africa Rugby Archives, Stellenbosch, "Groot toere," VIII, 1.37 B, 1981.

4. THE 1981 SPRINGBOK TOUR TO NEW ZEALAND

1. Barry Gustafson, *His Way: A Biography of Robert Muldoon* (Auckland: Auckland University Press, 2000), p. 311

2. "Rugby in South Africa: The Facts," New Zealand Rugby Museum, Palmerston North.

3. Gustafson, *His Way*, p. 311.

4. "Azania Solidarity #4, in "Organizations—Political: General," Box 9, South African Subject Collection, Hoover Institution Archives, Stanford University.

5. See Juliet Morris, *With All Our Strength: An Account of the Anti-Tour Movement in Christchurch* (Christchurch: Black Cat, 1982), pp. 61–67.

6. Graham Mourie with Ron Palenski, *Graham Mourie: Captain* (London: Arthur Barker Limited, 1983), p. 26.

7. Mourie with Palenski, *Graham Mourie: Captain*, pp. 26–27.

8. Mourie with Palenski, *Graham Mourie: Captain*, p. 27.

9. Ian Gault, *For the Record: The Allan Hewson Story* (Auckland: Rugby Press, Ltd., 1984), pp. 73–74.

10. Andy Haden, *Boots'n all!* (Auckland: Rugby Press Ltd., 1983), p. 187.

11. Wynand Claassen, *More Than Just Rugby* (Melville: Hans Strydom Publishers, 1985), p. 102.

12. Claassen, *More Than Just Rugby*, p. 115.

13. Geoff Chapple, *1981: The Tour* (Wellington: Reed, 1984), p. 75

14. Chapple, *1981: The Tour*, p. 77.

15. Claassen, *More Than Just Rugby*, p. 138.

16. Chapple, *1981: The Tour*, p. 132.

17. Tom Newnham, *By Batons and Barbed Wire: A Response to the 1981 Springbok Tour of New Zealand* (Auckland: Real Pictures, 1981), p. 39. For Newnham's memoir, see *Interesting Times: A Kiwi Chronicle* (Auckland: Graphic Publications, 2003).

18. Chapple, *1981: The Tour*, p. 137.

19. Diane Moore, "Remembering the battle of Molesworth Street," *Dominion Post*, July 29, 2011.

20. Newnham, *By Batons and Barbed Wire*, p. 39.

21. Newnham, *By Batons and Barbed Wire*, p. 41.

22. Newnham, *By Batons and Barbed Wire*, p. 43.

23. Newnham, *By Batons and Barbed Wire*, p. 43. See also Tony Eyre, *Winter of Discontent: A Story About Dunedin Opposition to the 1981 Springbok Tour* (Kindle: Bookbaby, 2013).

24. Chapple, *1981: The Tour*, p. 186.

25. Richard Shears and Isobelle Gidley, *Storm Out of Africa: The 1981 Springbok Tour of New Zealand* (Auckland: Macmillan, 1981), pp. 94–95.

26. Chapple, *1981: The Tour*, p. 188–89.

27. Cameron, *Barbed Wire Boks*, p. 179.

28. Shears and Gidley, *Storm Out of Africa*, p. 97.

29. Cameron, *Barbed Wire Boks*, p. 179.

30. Chapple, *1981: The Tour*, p. 193.

31. Cameron, *Barbed Wire Boks*, p. 184.

32. Meurant, *The Red Squad Story*, p. 79.

33. Chapple, *1981: The Tour*, pp. 231–32.

34. Richards, *Dancing on our Bones*, pp. 222–23; Chapple, *1981: The Tour*, pp. 236–37.

35. Richards, *Dancing on our Bones*, p. 223.

36. Cameron, *Barbed Wire Boks*, p. 198.

37. Gault, *For the Record*, pp. 78–79.

38. Cameron, *Barbed Wire Boks*, p. 199.

39. Cameron, *Barbed Wire Boks*, p. 204.

40. Cameron, *Barbed Wire Boks*, pp. 205–6.

41. Chapple, *1981: The Tour*, pp. 273–74.

42. Richards, *Dancing on Our Bones*, p. 224.

43. Cameron, *Barbed Wire Boks*, p. 220–22.

44. Gault, *For the Record* pp. 82.

45. Stu Wilson and Bernie Fraser with Alex Veysey, *Ebony & Ivory: The Stu Wilson, Bernie Fraser Story* (Auckland: MOA Publications Ltd., 1984) p. 158.

46. Claassen, *More Than Just Rugby*, p. 188.

47. Griffiths, *Naas*, p. 94; *Cape Times*, September 14, 1981.

48. Mexted, *Pieces of Eight*, p. 115.

49. Griffiths and Nell, *The Springbok Captains*, p 304.

50. Gault, *For the Record*, pp. 72–73.

51. Haden, *Boots'n All!*, p. 205.

52. Claassen, *More Than Just Rugby*, pp. 191–92.

53. Newnham, *By Batons and Barbed Wire*, p. 86.

54. Gault, *For the Record*, p. 82.

55. Haden, *Boots'n All!*, p. 194.

56. Shears and Gidley, *Storm Out of Africa!*, p. 152.

57. Barry Gustafson, *His Way: A Biography of Robert Muldoon* (Auckland: Auckland University Press, 2000), p. 312.

58. Mary Baker, "From a Letter to a Friend Overseas," in Margaret Freeman and Rosemary Hopkins, *Arms Linked: Women Against the Tour* (Auckland: Published by the editors, 1982), pp. 30–31.

59. Haden, *Boots'n All!*, p. 205.

60. Richards, *Dancing on Our Bones*, p. 225.

5. CLOAKS, DAGGERS, AND RUGBY

1. *Cape Times*, September 14, 1981.

2. Wynand Claassen, *More Than Just Rugby*, p. 234.

3. *Cape Times*, September 14, 1981. On Lapchick, see Lapchick, *Broken Promises: Racism in American Sports* (New York: St. Martin's/Marek, 1984), p. 103.

4. *Chicago Tribune*, September 11, 1981.

5. *Chicago Tribune*, September 11, 1981.

6. On this remarkable sporting pioneering ferment at UCLA, see James W. Johnson, *The Black Bruins: The Remarkable Lives of UCLA's Jackie Robinson, Woody Strode, Tom Bradley, Kenny Washington, and Ray Bartlett* (Lincoln: University of Nebraska Press, 2017). On Bradley's career, see especially chapter 25, pp. 211–19.

7. Mayor Tom Bradley to Alexander Haig, September 9, 1981, Mayor Tom Bradley Administrative Papers, Box 1409 "Administrative," Folder 3, "South African Rugby Team 1981," University of California at Los Angeles Special Collections, Charles E. Young Research Library.

8. See the letters to Tom Bradley in Mayor Tom Bradley Administrative Papers, Box 1409 "Administrative," Folder 3, "South African Rugby Team 1981," University of California at Los Angeles Special Collections, Charles E. Young Research Library.

9. Clive Gammon, "A Game They May Remember," *Sports Illustrated*, September 28, 1981, p. 36.

10. Transcript quoted in *Rugby Magazine*, April 10, 1995.

11. *Sports Illustrated*, September 28, 1981.

12. Congressman Jerry Patterson to Tom Bradley, September 23 1981; Congressman Mervyn M. Dymmaly to Tom Bradley, September 24, 1981; Text of Dymmely's remarks to Congress, n.d.; all in Mayor Tom Bradley Administrative Papers, Box 1409 "Administrative," Folder 3, "South African Rugby Team 1981," University of California at Los Angeles Special Collections, Charles E. Young Research Library.

13. Edward Marks to Tom Bradley, October 20, 1981, Mayor Tom Bradley Administrative Papers, Box 1409 "Administrative," Folder 3, "South African Rugby Team 1981," University of California at Los Angeles Special Collections, Charles E. Young Research Library.

14. *Chicago Tribune*, September 4, 1981.

15. *Chicago Sun-Times*, September 4, 1981.

16. Claassen, *More Than Just Rugby*, p. 234.

17. *Cape Times*, September 15, 1981.

18. Rob Louw, *For the Love of Rugby* (Melville: Hans Strydom Publishers, 1987), pp. 82, 85–86, and 139.

19. *Cape Times*, September 15, 1981; *Chicago Sun-Times*, September 15, 1981.

20. *Rapport*, September 13, 1981; *Cape Times*, September 17, 1981.

21. *Cape Times*, September 15, 1981.

22. *Cape Times*, September 17, 1981.

23. Claassen, *More Than Just Rugby*, p. 235.

24. Claassen, *More Than Just Rugby*, p. 235.

25. Claassen, *More Than Just Rugby*, p. 235. See also Dan Retief's article in the *Cape Times* on September 17, 1981.

26. *Cape Times*, September 15, 1981.

27. Claassen, *More Than Just Rugby*, p. 236.

28. Claassen, *More Than Just Rugby*, p. 234.

29. *Cape Times*, September 15, 1981.

30. *Cape Times*, September 16, 1981.

31. *Chicago Tribune*, September 13, 1981.

32. Claassen, *More Than Just Rugby*, p. 235.

33. *Cape Times*, September 17, 1981.

34. *Cape Times*, September 17, 1981.

35. *New York Times*, September 19, 1981.

36. Louw, *For the Love of Rugby*, pp. 139–140.

37. *Chicago Sun-Times*, September 17, 1981.

38. Racine *Journal Times*, September 16, 17, 18, 19, 1981.

39. Gammon, "A Game They May Remember," p. 37.

40. Quotation in Racine *Journal Times*, September 17, 1981. On the racial dynamic in Chicago, see *New York Times*, September 20, 1981.

41. *Cape Times*, September 19, 1981.

42. *New York Times*, September 20, 1981.

43. *Cape Times*, September 19, 1981; Louw, *For the Love of Rugby*, p. 139.

44. *Cape Times*, September 15, 1981.

45. Racine *Journal Times*, September 18, 1981.

46. *New York Times*, September 18, 1981.

47. Robert Buchanan, email to author, August 15, 2016.

48. Robert Buchanan, email to author, August 16, 2016.

49. "Wee Bob" Jefferies, "The Wisconsin Rugby Club in the 1980s," in "Detailed History of the Wisconsin Rugby Club," pp. 4–5, download available athttp://www.wisconsinrugbyclub.com/rugbyweb/about-wrc/wrc-history/

50. Racine *Journal Times*, September 19, 1981.

51. Racine *Journal Times*, September 20, 1981.

52. Gammon, "A Game They May Remember," p. 37.

53. Racine *Journal Times*, September 20, 1981.

54. Robert Buchanan, email to author, August 15, 2016.

55. *The New York Times*, September 20, 1981.

56. Racine *Journal Times*, September 20, 1981.

57. *Cape Times*, September 21, 1981.

58. Claassen, *More Than Just Rugby*, p. 237.

59. Stu Pippel, email to author, October 6, 2016.

60. Joseph Sauer, email to author, October 6, 2016.

61. Joe Sauer, "Exciting '81 for the Wisconsin Rugby Union . . . Much Due to the Milwaukee RFC," 1982 MRFC Program, courtesy of Robert Buchanan and the Madison Rugby Collection.

62. Stu Pippel, email to author, October 6, 2016.

63. Robert "Buck" Buchanan, email to author, August 16, 2016.

64. *Cape Times*, September 21, 1981. See Joe Sauer, "Exciting '81 for the Wisconsin Rugby Union . . . Much Due to the Milwaukee RFC," 1982 MRFC Program, courtesy of Robert Buchanan and the Madison Rugby Collection.

65. Gammon, "A Game They May Remember," p. 36.

66. Gammon, "A Game They May Remember," p. 36.

67. *Cape Times*, September 21, 1981.

68. Claassen, *More Than Just Rugby*, p. 237.

69. *Cape Times*, September 21, 1981.

70. Stu Pippel, email to author, October 6, 2016.

71. *New York Times*, September 20, 1981.

72. Stu Pippel, email to author, October 6, 2016.

73. Claassen, *More Than Just Rugby*, p. 237; Louw, *For the Love of Rugby*, p. 140; Gammon, "A Game They May Remember," p. 36.

74. Racine *Journal Times*, September 20, 1981.

75. Louw, *For the Love of Rugby*, p. 140.

76. Gammon, "A Game They May Remember," p. 36.

77. Racine *Journal Times*, September 21, 1981.

78. Bryden and Colley, *Springboks Under Siege*, p. 82.

79. Joseph Sauer, email to author, October 6, 2016.

80. Stu Pippel, email to author, October 6, 2016.

81. Claassen, *More Than Just Rugby*, p. 237.

82. *Cape Times*, September 21, 1981.

83. Claassen, *More Than Just Rugby*, p. 237.

84. Stu Pippel, email to author, October 6, 2016.

85. Racine *Journal Times*, September 20, 1981.

86. Racine *Journal Times*, September 20, 1981.

87. Racine *Journal Times*, September 20, 1981.

88. Racine *Journal Times*, September 20, 1981.

89. Racine *Journal Times*, September 20, 1981.

90. Racine *Journal Times*, September 21, 1981.

91. Racine *Journal Times*, September 20, 1981.

92. Racine *Journal Times*, September 21, 1981.

93. Racine *Journal Times*, September 21, 1981.

94. Racine *Journal Times*, September 30, 1981.

95. Racine *Journal Times*, September 27, 1981.

96. Racine *Journal Times*, September 27, 1981.

97. Racine *Journal Times*, September 27, 1981.

98. Gammon, "A Game They May Remember," *Sports Illustrated*, September 28, 1981, p. 37.

6. ALBANY I

1. Bryden and Colley, *Springboks Under Siege*, p. 82.

2. *Rugby Magazine*, April 10, 1995.

3. A. W. Scott, "The Show Went On—But at What Cost?" *Rugby World*, December 1981, p. 57.

4. *New York Times*, August 2, 1981.

5. *New York Times*, August 2, 1981.

6. Email from Richard Lapchick to author, September 30, 2015.

7. *New York Times*, August 2, 1981.

8. Div Visser, email to author, March 21, 2016.

9. *New York Times*, August 2, 1981.

10. *New York Times*, August 23, 1981.

11. *New York Times*, August 30, 1981.

12. *New York Times*, September 18, 1981. George Kilpatrick of Auckland, New Zealand, compiled a clippings file of the 1981 tour to New Zealand that also includes a number of New Zealand press clippings on the US tour, available at the SARU Rugby Archives-Parow Warehouse.

13. *New York Times*, September 18, 1981.

14. *New York Times*, September 18, 1981; *New York Recorder*, August 15, 1981.

15. American Committee on Africa, "Stopping the Springboks: Report on Campaign Against the South African Rugby Team," October 1981, South African Subject Collection, Box 21, "International Support: South African Rugby Tour," Hoover Institution Archives, Stanford University.

16. *New York Times*, September 20, 1981.

17. *New York Times*, September 18, 1981.

18. *New York Times*, September 22, 1981.

19. *New York Times*, September 22, 1981.

20. *New York Times*, September 22, 1981.

21. *New York Times*, September 22, 1981. See also *Schad v. Borough of Mt. Ephraim*, 452 U.S. 61 (1981).

22. *New York Times*, September 22, 1981.

23. *New York Times*, September 22, 1981.

24. *Terminiello v. City of Chicago*, 337 U.S. 1 (1949).

25. *The New York Times*, September 22, 1981.

26. *Selfridge v. Carey*, 660 F.2d 516 (2d Cir. 1981); *New York Times*, September 22, 1981.

27. *Selfridge v. Carey*, 660 F.2d 516 (2d Cir. 1981); *New York Times*, September 22, 1981.

28. *New York Times*, September 27, 1981.

29. Edward Griffiths, *Naas*, p. 96.

30. Louw, *For the Love of Rugby*, p. 141.

31. *Rand Daily Mail*, September 22, 1981.

32. Claassen, *More than just Rugby*, pp. 237–38.

33. *Rugby Magazine*, April 10, 1995.

34. *Rand Daily Mail*, September 23, 1981.

35. Anti-Springbok 5 Defense Committee, "Victory to African Liberation World-wide: Anti-Springbok 5 On Trial," May 1982, South Africa Subject Collection, "South Africa Rugby Tour," Box 21, Hoover Institution Library, Stanford University.

36. SART press release, September 26, 1981, and two "Coalition to defend Albany 9" flyers, n. d. Fall 1981, all in African Activist Archive, Michigan State University.

37. See Campaign to Oppose Bank Loans to South Africa, "Statement by Organizations Sponsoring the September 22 Demonstration," September 22, 1981; African Activist Archive, Michigan State University.

38. American Committee on Africa, "STOPPING THE SPRINGBOKS: Report on Campaign Against the South African Rugby Team," October 1981, South African Subject Collection, Box 21, "International Support: South African Rugby Tour," Hoover Institution Archives, Stanford University.

39. *New York Times*, September 27, 1981.

40. *New York Times*, September 23, 1981.

41. Bryden and Colley, *Springboks Under Siege*, p. 83.

42. Claassen, *More than Just Rugby*, p. 238.

43. Louw, *For the Love of Rugby*, p. 141.

44. *New York Times*, September 23, 1981.

45. Bryden and Colley, *Springboks Under Siege*, p. 83.

46. Claassen, *More than Just Rugby*, pp. 239–40.

47. *Rand Daily Mail*, September 24, 1981.

48. Claassen, *More than Just Rugby*, p. 240.

49. Claassen, *More than Just Rugby*, p. 238.

50. Louw, *For the Love of Rugby*, p. 141.

51. *Cape Times*, September 24, 1981.

52. *Cape Times*, September 24, 1981.

53. Albany *Times-Union*, September 23, 1981.

54. Albany *Times-Union*, September 23, 1981.

55. Albany *Times-Union*, September 23, 1981.

56. *New York Times*, September 23, 1981.

57. Claassen, *More than Just Rugby*, pp. 239–40.

58. Griffiths and Nell, *The Springbok Captains*, p. 305.

59. Claassen, *More than Just Rugby*, p. 238.

60. Bryden and Colley, *Springboks Under Siege*, p. 83.

61. Claassen, *More than Just Rugby*, p. 238.

62. Claassen, *More Than Just Rugby*, p. 113.

7. ALBANY II

1. Bryden and Colley, *Springboks Under Siege*, p. 82.

2. *The New York Times*, September 26, 2013.

3. Claassen, *More Than Just Rugby*, p. 240.

4. Bryden and Colley, *Springboks Under Siege*, p. 82.

5. "Minutes of the International Rugby Board, March 1981," in "Minutes of the Meetings of the International Rugby Football Board 1980–1985," pp. 1052, 1098–99, The Trunkers Library, Rugby Football Union, Twickenham Stadium, UK.

6. Bryden and Colley, *Springboks Under Siege*, p. 82 and 86; and Grieb & Farmer, *Springbok Miscellany*, p. 94.

7. Claassen, *More Than Just Rugby*, pp. 113–14 (quotation on 114).

8. Claassen, *More Than Just Rugby*, pp. 240–41.

9. Louw, *For the Love of Rugby*, p. 141.

10. Claassen, *More Than Just Rugby*, p. 241.

11. Louw, *For the Love of Rugby*, p. 141–42. See also Griffiths, *Naas*, p. 96.

12. Stofberg, *Stories From the Touchline*, pp. 109–10.

13. Claassen, *More Than Just Rugby*, p. 242.

14. Schoeman, *Gerber: Maestro of the Midfield*, p. 70.

15. Claassen, *More Than Just Rugby*, p. 244.

16. Bryden and Colley, *Springboks Under Siege*, p. 86; Grieb & Farmer, *Springbok Miscellany*, p. 112; S. A. Rugby Writers, *Toyota Jaarboek 1982 Annual*, p. 6.

17. Claassen, *More Than Just Rugby*, p. 244.

18. Schoeman, *Gerber*, p. 71.

19. Div Visser, email to author, April 7, 2016.

20. *New York Times*, September 26, 1981.

21. Ed Hagerty, *Rugby*, October 19, 1981; quoted in Claassen, *More Than Just Rugby*, p. 244.

22. Grieb & Farmer, *Springbok Miscellany*, p. 94.

23. Claassen, *More Than Just Rugby*, p. 242.

24. "Don Morrison—Dramatic Referee," SA Rugby Referees, January 25, 2012, https://sareferees.co.za/News/don-morrison--dramatic-referee/2829557/

25. Grieb & Farmer, *Springbok Miscellany*, p. 94.

26. Claassen, *More Than Just Rugby*, pp. 241–42.

27. Louw, *For the Love of Rugby*, p. 142; Wyngaard, *Bursting Through the Half-Gap*, p. 199.

28. Retief in Claassen, *More Than Just Rugby*, p. 241.

29. *Cape Times*, September 26, 1981.

30. Claassen, *More Than Just Rugby*, p. 244.

31. Claassen, *More Than Just Rugby*, p. 244.

32. Louw, *For the Love of Rugby*, p. 142-43.

33. Claassen, *More Than Just Rugby*, pp. 244–45.

34. Louw, *For the Love of Rugby*, p. 143.

35. Claassen, *More than Just Rugby*, p. 245.

36. Louw, *For the Love of Rugby*, p. 143.

37. Claassen, *For the Love of Rugby*, p. 245.

38. *Rand Daily Mail*, September 28, 1981.

39. Chicago *Sun-Times*, September 30, 1981.

40. The Anti-Springbok-5 Defense Committee, "Victory to African Liberation Worldwide: Free the Anti-Springbok 5," n.d., South Africa Subject Collection, "South Africa Rugby Tour," Box 21, Hoover Institution Library, Stanford University.

41. American Committee on Africa report, "Stopping the Springboks: Report on the Campaign Against the South African Rugby Tour," October 1981, South Africa Subject Collection, "South Africa Rugby Tour," Box 21, Hoover Institution Library, Stanford University.

42. "Stopping the Springboks: Report on the Campaign Against the South African Rugby Tour," ACOA, New York, October 1981, African Activist Archives, Michigan State University Special Collections.

43. See UPI wire reports, December 11 and 19, 1981. See also Chuck Miller, "Rugby in the National Spotlight: The 1981 USA Tour of the Springboks," *Rugby* magazine, April 10, 1995.

44. Griffiths & Nell, *The Springbok Captains*, p. 306.

45. Louw, *For the Love of Rugby*, p. 139.

46. *The New York Times*, September 27, 1981.

47. *The New York Times*, September 27, 1981.

CONCLUSION

1. Dobson, *Doc*, p. 170; *Rand Daily Mail*, September 30, 1981.

2. *Rand Daily Mail*, September 26, 1981.

3. *Rugby World*, November, 1981, p. 9.

4. *Cape Times*, September 12, 1981.

5. Dennis Brutus Defense Committee Press Release, September 25, 1981, Dennis Brutus Papers, 1960–1977 & Addition 1960–1985, Series 35/17, Box 30, "Sports Correspondence, 1978–1982, n.d." Northwestern University Archives.

6. Quintus van Rooyen, "The Internasionale Scene," van Rooyen, Ed., S. A. Rugby Writers *1982 Toyota Jaarboek/Annual*, p. 27.

7. Dan Retief, "Naas Botha: Did we miss his best?" in *Springboks vs. England* Official Souvenir Game program, June 9, 1984, in author's possession.

8. Dennis Brutus SAN-ROC mailing, April 24, 1983, George M. Houser (Africa Collection), African Activist Archive, Michigan State University Libraries Special Collections.

9. Dennis Brutus telegram to David Lange, June 11, 1985, Collection SPC.0001, Dennis Brutus Collection: Worcester State College Papers, Folder: "SAN-ROC: US," Archives and Special Collections Library, Worcester State University.

10. *Los Angeles Times*, July 16, 1988.

11. Snyders, *Cold Wars and Hot Scrums*, pp. 52–53.

12. "Joint Statement of the South African Rugby Board, the South African Rugby Union and the African National Congress," Harare, October 16, 1988, in Gail M. Gerhart and Clive L. Glaser, *From Protest to Challenge: A Documentary History of African Politics in South Africa, 1882–1990: Volume 6: Challenge and Victory, 1980–1990* (Bloomington & Indianapolis: Indiana University Press, 2010), p. 661

13. SABC Comment, "The ANC and the Rugby Board," transcript, October 18, 1988, South African Subject Collection, Box 3, Folder "General: South African Broadcasting, 1988," Hoover Institution Archives, Stanford University.

14. See Snyders, *Cold Wars and Hot Scrums*, p. 58.

15. Miller, "Rugby in the National Spotlight."

16. *The Star*, August 17, 1992.

17. *Washington Post*, August 18, 1992.

18. Reuters News Reports, AP Datastream International News Wire Reports, Agence France-Presse International News (via Newsnet) releases, August 16–23, 1992, all in Leroy T. Walker Africa News Service Archives, Africa: Countries, Box 157, Folder: "SA Sports 1991–," Duke University Libraries:

Archives and Manuscripts. See also *The Guardian*, August 17, 1992; August 18, 1992.

19. See transcript, "All Things Considered," National Public Radio, August 23, 1992, Leroy T. Walker Africa News Service Archives, Africa: Countries, Box 157, Folder: "SA Sports 1991–," Duke University Libraries: Archives and Manuscripts.

20. See Pienaar's biography, *Rainbow Warrior* (Jeppestown: Jonathan Ball, 1999). For his stadium speech, see p. 182.

21. Derek Catsam, "Go Amabokoboko! Rugby, Race, Madiba and the *Invictus* Creation Myth of a New South Africa," in Nigel Eltringham, *Framing Africa: Portrayals of a Continent in Contemporary Mainstream Cinema,* (Oxford: Berghahn, 2013), pp. 156–74.

22. On the excuses that endure for South African rugby's still pernicious race woes, see Derek Catsam, "Rugby Transformation as Alibi: Thoughts on Craven and Coetzee," in Todd Cleveland, Tarminder Kaur, & Gerard Akindes, Eds., *Sports in Africa Past and Present* (Athens: Ohio University Press, 2020), pp. 233–48.

23. *The Times* (London), February 4, 2008.

24. I spent an afternoon with de Villiers in July 2019 that was a combination of an interview and an informal visit and he was quite adamant that his outspokenness on matters of race has consigned him to irrelevancy among many within the top tier of rugby.

25. See Gavin Rich, *The Poisoned Chalice: The Rise and Fall of the Post-Isolation Springbok Coaches* (Cape Town: Zebra Press, 2013), and Ron van der Valk with Andy Colquhuon, *Nick & I: An Adventure in Rugby* (Cape Town: Don Nelson, 2002). Quotation on p. 203.

26. Jeremy Daniel, *Siya Kolisi: Against All Odds* Johannesburg: Jonathan Ball, 2020), 232.

27. Derek Catsam, "South African Rugby's Race Problems," August 2019, https://africasacountry.com/2019/09/south-african-rugbys-race-problems.

28. Claassen, *More Than Just Rugby*, p. 245.

29. Div Visser, email to author, April 7, 2016.

WORKS CITED/BIBLIOGRAPHY

ARCHIVES/LIBRARIES

Australia

Melbourne Cricket Club Library

England

World Rugby Museum Library, Twickenham Stadium
Webb Ellis Rugby Museum (Rugby, Warwickshire)

Ireland

James Joyce Library, University College Dublin

New Zealand

Macmillan Brown Library Archives and Special Collections, University of Canterbury
New Zealand Rugby Museum Library and Archive, Palmerston North
University of Auckland Manuscripts and Archives
University of Waikato Library Special Collections

South Africa

African Studies Centre Library, University of Cape Town
Cory Library for Historical Research, Rhodes University
South African National Archives, Pretoria
South African National Library, Cape Town
South Africa Rugby Archives, Stellenbosch
South African Rugby Union Archives, Parow Warehouse
WITS Historical Papers Research Archive, Williams Cullen Brown
 Library, University of Witwatersrand

United States

Archives and Special Collections Library, Worcester State University
The Crawford Family U.S. Olympic Archives, Colorado Springs
Duke University Libraries: Archives and Manuscripts
Hoover Institution Library, Stanford University
Michigan State University Libraries Special Collections (African Activist Archive, accessed online, available at https://africanactivist.msu.edu/)
Northwestern University Archives
University of California, Los Angeles, Special Collections Library

BOOKS

Akers, Clive, Geoff Miller, and Adrian Hill, eds. *2018 Rugby Almanack*. Auckland: Mower, 2018.
Akers, Clive, Geoff Miller and Adrian Hill, eds. *2016 Rugby Almanack*. Auckland: Mower, 2018.
Alegi, Peter. *Laduma!: Soccer, Politics and Society in South Africa, from its Origins to 2010*. Scottsville: University of KwaZulu-Natal Press, 2010.
Alfred, Luke. *When the Lions Came to Town: The 1974 Rugby Tour to South Africa*. Cape Town: Zebra Press, 2014.
Allen, Dean. *Empire, War & Cricket in South Africa: Logan of Matjiesfontein*. Cape Town: Zebra Press, 2015.
Anderson, Carol. *Eyes off the Prize: The United Nations and the African American Struggle for Human Rights*. Cambridge, UK: Cambridge University Press, 2003.
Andrew, Susannah and Jolisa Gracewood, eds., *Tell You What: Great New Zealand Nonfiction 2016*. Auckland: Auckland University Press, 2015.
Archer, Robert, and Antoine Bouillon. *The South African Game: Sport and Racism*. London: Zed Press, 1982.

Ashe, Arthur R., Jr. *A Hard Road to Glory: A History of the African American Athlete, 1915–1945*. New York: Warner Books, 1988.

Ashe, Arthur R., Jr. *A Hard Road to Glory: A History of the African-American Athlete Since 1946*. New York: Warner Books, 1988.

Bale, John, and Mike Cronin, eds. *Sport and Postcolonialism*. Oxford: Berg, 2003.

Barrow, Graeme. *All Blacks Versus Springboks: A Century of Rugby Rivalry*. Auckland: Reed Books, 1992.

Bass, Amy, ed. *In the Game: Race, Identity, and Sports in the Twentieth Century*. New York: Palgrave Macmillan, 2005.

Beckles, Hilary McD, ed. *A Spirit of Dominance: Cricket and Nationalism in the West Indies*. Kingston: Canoe Press, 1998.

Berkeley, Bill. *The Graves Are Not Yet Full: Race, Tribe and Power in the Heart of Africa*. New York: Basic Books, 2001.

Bills, Peter, and Heindrich Weingaard. *Rugby Changed My World: The Ashwin Willemse Story*. Johannesburg: GreenSmile Consulting, 2015.

Black, David, and John Nauright. *Rugby and the South African Nation: Sport, Culture, Politics and Power in the Old and New South Africa* (International Studies in the History of Sport). Manchester, UK: Manchester University Press, 1998.

Blain, Keisha N. *Set the World on Fire: Black Nationalist Women and the Global Struggle for Freedom*. Philadelphia: University of Pennsylvania Press, 2018.

Boelstelmann, Thomas. *Apartheid's Reluctant Uncle: The United States and Southern Africa in the Early Cold War*. New York: Oxford University Press, 1993.

Boestelmann, Thomas. *The Cold War and the Color Line: American Race Relations in the Global Arena*. Cambridge, MA: Harvard University Press, 2001.

Booth, Douglas. *The Race Game: Sport and Politics in South Africa*. London: Frank Cass, 1998.

Boykoff, Jules. *Power Games: A Political History of the Olympics*. London: Verso, 2016.

Bray, Gordon, ed. *The Australian Rugby Companion: "The Game They Play in Heaven."* Camberwell, Australia: Viking, 2002.

Brewer, John. *Black and Blue: Policing in South Africa*. Oxford: Clarendon Press, 1994.

Brickhill, Joan. *South Africa's "Multi-national" Sport Fraud*. London: International Defense & Aid Fund, 1976.

Brown, Geoff, and Christian Hogsbjerg. *Apartheid is Not a Game: Remembering the Stop the Seventy Tour Campaign*. London: Redwords, 2020.

Brown, Matthew, Patrick Guthrie, and Greg Growden. *Rugby for Dummies* (Second Edition). Mississauga, Canada: John Wiley & Sons, Canada, Ltd., 2007.

Bryant, Howard. *Full Dissidence: Notes from an Uneven Playing Field*. Boston: Beacon Press, 2020.

Bryant, Howard. *The Heritage: Black Athletes, A Divided America, and the Politics of Patriotism*. Boston: Beacon Press, 2018.

Bryden, Colin, and Mark Colley, eds. *Springboks Under Siege: The New Zealand Tour/ Pioneering in America/Irish in South Africa/Beaumont's Lions: An Illustrated History of Springbok Rugby in 1980 and 81*. Hillbrow, South Africa: Now Publications, 1981.

Burnard, Lloyd. *Miracle Men: How Rassie's Springboks Won the World Cup*. Johannesburg: Jonathan Ball, 2020.

Cameron, Don. *Barbed Wire Boks*. Auckland: Rugby Press, 1981.

Carlin, John. *Playing the Enemy: Nelson Mandela and the Game That Made a Nation*. New York: Penguin, 2009.

Carman, Arthur H., ed., *Rugby Almanac of New Zealand, 1982*. Auckland: Sporting Publications, 1982.

Chandler, Timothy J. L., and John Nauright, eds. *Making the Rugby World: Race, Gender, Commerce*. London: Frank Cass, 1999.

Chapple, Geoff. *1981: The Tour*. Wellington: Reed, 1984.

Chester, R. H., and A. C. McMillan. *Centenary: 100 Years of All Black Rugby*. Poole, UK: Blandford Press, 1984.

Chester, R. H., and A. C. McMillan. *The Visitors: The History of International Rugby Teams in New Zealand*. Auckland: Moa Publications, 1990.

Chester, R. H., and A. C. McMillan. *The History of New Zealand Rugby Football*, 4 Volumes. Auckland: Moa Publications, 1992.

Chester, R. H., and A. C. McMillan. *Men in Black: Complete Edition 1903–1993*. Auckland: Moa Beckett, 1994.

Claassen, Wynand. *More Than Just Rugby*. Johannesburg: Hans Strydom Publishers, 1985.

Cleveland, Todd, Tarminder Kaur, and Gerard Akindes, eds. *Sports in Africa Past and Present*. Athens: Ohio University Press, 2020.

Collins, Sheila D. *Ubuntu: George M. Houser and the Struggle for Peace and Freedom on Two Continents*. Athens: Ohio University Press, 2020.

Collins, Tony. *How Football Began: A Global History of How the World's Football Codes Were Born*. Abingdon/New York: Routledge, 2019.

Collins, Tony. *The Oval World: A Global History of Rugby*. London: Bloomsbury, 2015.

Collins, Tony. *Rugby's Great Split: Class, Culture and the Origins of Rugby League Football*. London: Frank Cass, 2003.

Connor, Jeff, and Martin Hannan. *Once Were Lions: The Players' Stories: Inside the World's Most Famous Rugby Team*. London: Herper Sport, 2009.

Crocker, Chester. *High Noon in Southern Africa: Making Peace in a Rough Neighborhood*. New York: W. W. Norton, 1992.

Cronin, Mike, Mark Duncan, and Paul Rouse. *The GAA: A People's History*. London: Collins, 2009.

Crowley, Brian. *Cricket's Exiles: The Saga of South African Cricket*. London: Angus & Robertson Publishers, 1983.

Culverson, Donald R. *Contesting Apartheid: U. S. Activism, 1960–1987*. Boulder, CO: Westview Press, 1999.

Daniel, Jeremy. *Siya Kolisi: Against All Odds*. Johannesburg: Jonathan Ball, 2020.

David, G. R. *Rugby and Be Damned: All Blacks Tour of South Africa 1970*. Wellington: Hicks, Smith & Sons, Ltd., 1970.

Davies, Rhodri. *Undefeated: The Story of the 1974 Lions*. Talybont, Aberystwyth Wales: Ylolfa, 2014.

Davis, J. E. *Constructive Engagement? Chester Crocker & American Policy in South Africa, Namibia & Angola*. Oxford/Johannesburg/Athens: James Currey/Jacana Media/Ohio University Press, 2007.

Villiers, Peter de with Gavin Rich. *Politically Incorrect: The Autobiography*. Cape Town: Zebra, 2012.

Dine, Philip. *French Rugby Football: A Cultural History*. Oxford: Berg, 2001.

Dobson, Paul. *Rugby's Greatest Rivalry: South Africa vs New Zealand*. Cape Town: Human & Rousseau, 1996.

D'Oliviera, Basil. *Time to Declare: An Autobiography*. Johannesburg: Macmillan, South Africa, 1980.

Dudziak, Mary L. *Cold War Civil Rights: Race and the Image of American Democracy*. Princeton, NJ: Princeton University Press, 2000.

Dunning, Eric, and Kenneth Sheard. *Barbarians, Gentlemen and Players: A Sociological Study of the Development of Rugby Football*. London and New York: Routledge, 2005.

Edgar, Robert E., ed. *Sanctioning Apartheid*. Trenton: Africa World Press, 1990.

Edwards, Harry. *The Revolt of the Black Athlete* 50th Anniversary Edition. Urbana: University of Illinois Press, 2017.

Eltringham, Nigel. *Framing Africa: Portrayals of a Continent in Contemporary Mainstream Cinema*. Oxford: Berghahn, 2013.

English, Tom. *No Borders: Playing Rugby for Ireland*. Edinburgh: Arena Sport, 2016.

Eyre, Tony. *Winter of Discontent: A Story About Dunedin Opposition to the 1981 Springbok Tour*. Kindle: Bookbaby, 2013.

Fieldhouse, Roger. *Anti-apartheid: A History of the Movement in Britain: A Study in Pressure Group Politics*. London: Merlin Press, Ltd., 2005.

Freeman, Margaret, and Rosemary Hopkins. *Arms Linked: Women Against the Tour.* Auckland: Published by the editors, 1982.

Gallagher, Brendan. *The Rugby World Cup: The Definitive Photographic History.* London: Bloomsbury, 2015.

Gault, Ian. *For the Record: The Allan Hewson Story.* Auckland: Rugby Press, Ltd., 1984.

Gemmell, Jon. *The Politics of South African Cricket.* London: Routledge, 2004.

Gent, D. R. *The Classic Guide to Rugby.* Gloucestershire: Amberley Publishing, 2014.

Gail M. Gerhart, Gail M. & Glaser, Clive L. *From Protest to Challenge: A Documentary History of African Politics in South Africa, 1882–1990: Volume 6: Challenge and Victory, 1980–1990,* Bloomington: Indiana University Press, 2010.

Glasspool, Barry. *One in the Eye: The 1976 All Blacks in South Africa.* Cape Town: Howard Timmins, 1976.

Goldblatt, David. *The Games: A Global History of the Olympics.* New York: W. W. Norton and Company, 2016.

Grant, Jack. *Jack Grant's Story: Educator, Cricketer, Missionary.* Guildford: Lutterworth Press, 1980.

Grant, Nicholas. *Winning Our Freedoms Together: African Americans & Apartheid.* Chapel Hill: University of North Carolina Press, 2017.

Gray, Ashley. *The Unforgiven: Mercenaries or Missionaries?* Sussex, UK: Pitch Publishing, 2020.

Grieb, Eddie, and Stuart Farmer. *Springbok Miscellany: From the Earliest Days to the Modern Era.* Johannesburg & Cape Town: Jonathan Ball, 2009.

Griffiths, Edward. *Naas.* Pretoria: Leo Publishers, 1989.

Griffiths, Edward, and Stephen Nell. *The Springbok Captains: The Men Who Shaped South African Rugby, Revised & Updated Edition.* Johannesburg & Cape Town: Jonathan Ball Publishers, 2015.

Grubbs, Larry. *Secular Missionaries: Americans and African Development in the 1960s.* Amherst: University of Massachusetts Press, 2009.

Gruesser, John Cullen. *Black on Black: Twentieth Century African American Writing about Africa.* Lexington: University Press of Kentucky, 2000.

Grundlingh, Albert. *Potent Pastimes: Sport and Leisure Practices in Modern Afrikaner History.* Pretoria: Protea Book House, 2013.

Grundlingh, Albert, André Odendaal, and Burridge Spies. *Beyond the Tryline: Rugby and South African Society.* Johannesburg: Ravan Press, 1995.

Gustafson, Barry. *His Way: A Biography of Robert Muldoon.* Auckland: Auckland University Press, 2000.

Haden, Andy. *Boots'n all!* Auckland: Rugby Press Ltd., 1983.

Hain, Peter. *Don't Play with Apartheid: The Background to the Stop the Seventy Tour Campaign.* London: George Allen & Unwin, Ltd., 1971.

Hain, Peter. *Outside In.* London: Biteback Publishing, 1912.

Hain, Peter, and Andre Odendaal. *Pitch Battles: Sport, Racism, and Resistance.* Lanham, MD: Rowman & Littlefield, 2021.

Harris, Stewart. *Political Football: The Springbok Tour of Australia, 1971.* Melbourne: Gold Star Publications, 1972.

Harte, Chris. *Two Tours and Pollock: The Australian Cricketers in South Africa 1985–1987.* Adelaide: Sports Marketing, 1988.

Hartman, Douglas. *Race, Culture, and the Revolt of the Black Athlete.* Chicago: University of Chicago Press, 2003.

Hathaway, Adam. *The Greatest Springbok Teams: Past to Present.* Cape Town: Zebra Press, 2015.

Heath, Duane, Eddie Grieb, and Smit, Kobus, eds. *South African Rugby Annual 2019.* Cape Town: South African Rugby Union, 2018.

Heath, Duane, and Eddie Grieb, eds. *South African Rugby Annual 2018.* Cape Town: South African Rugby Union, 2018.

Heath, Duane, and Eddie Grieb, eds. *South African Rugby Annual 2017.* Cape Town: South African Rugby Union, 2017.

Heath, Duane, and Eddie Grieb, eds. *South African Rugby Annual 2016*. Cape Town: South African Rugby Union, 2016.

Heath, Duane and Eddie Grieb, eds. *South African Rugby Annual 2015*. Cape Town: South African Rugby Union, 2015.

Henderson, Simon. *Sidelined: How American Sports Challenged the Black Freedom Struggle*. Lexington: University Press of Kentucky, 2013.

Hero, Alfred O. Jr., and John Barratt, eds. *The American People and South Africa*. Cape Town: David Philip, 1981.

Holloway, J. E. *Apartheid: A Challenge*. Johannesburg: Afrikaanse Pers-Boekhandel, 1964.

Hopkins, John. *British Lions 1980*. Kingswood, Surrey, UK: World's Work, 1980.

Horrell, Muriel. *Action, Reaction and Counter-reaction*. Johannesburg: South African Institute of Race Relations, 1971.

Hostetter, David L. *Movement Matters: American Antiapartheid Activism and the Rise of Multicultural Politics*. New York/Abingdon: Routledge, 2006.

Houser, George M. *No One Can Stop the Rain: Glimpses of Africa's Liberation Struggle*. New York: Pilgrim Press, 1989.

Howitt, Bob. *The Roar of the Crowd: New Zealand Rugby's Greatest Players, Magical Games and Memorable Moments*. Auckland: Penguin, 2000.

Howitt, Bob, and Dianne Haworth. *All Black Magic: 100 Years of New Zealand Test Rugby*. Auckland: Harper Sports, 2003.

Hughes, Thomas. *Tom Brown's Schooldays*. Oxford: Oxford University Press, 2008.

Hutchins, Graham. *A Score to Settle: A Celebration of All Black-Springbok Rugby, 1921–1996*. Wellington: Grantham House, 1997.

Information Service of South Africa, *Progress Through Separate Development: South Africa in Peaceful Transition* (Fourth Edition). New York: Information Service of South Africa, 1973.

Irwin, Ryan M. *Gordian Knot: Apartheid and the Unmaking of the Liberal World Order*. Oxford: Oxford University Press, 2012.

James, Carwyn, and Chris Rea. *Injured Pride: The Lions in South Africa*. London: Arthur Barker Limited, 1980.

Jarvie, Grant. *Class, Race and Sport in South Africa's Political Economy*. London: Routledge & Kegan Paul, 1985.

Jenkins, Vivian, ed. *Rothmans Rugby Yearbook 1982–83*. Aylesbury, UK: Rothmans Publications Limited,1982.

Keohane, Mark. *Chester: A Biography of Courage*. Cape Town: Don Nelson 2002.

Keohane, Mark. *Springbok Rugby Uncovered*. Cape Town: Zebra Press, 2004.

King, Michael, ed. *Pakeha: The Quest for Identity in New Zealand*. Auckland: Penguin, 1991.

King, Michael. *The Penguin History of New Zealand*. Auckland: Penguin, 2003.

Kirwin, Alison. *Thirty Bullies: The History of the Rugby World Cup*. London: Pocket Books, 2009.

Labuschagne, Fred. *All Black-ed Out*. Cape Town: Howard Timmins, 1970.

Labuschagne, Fred. *Goodbye Newlands, Farewell Eden Park*. Cape Town: Howard Timmins, 1974.

Landsberg, Christopher. *The Quiet Diplomacy of Liberation: International Politics and South Africa's Transition*. Johannesburg: Jacana, 2004.

Lapchick, Richard. *Broken Promises: Racism in American Sports*. New York: St. Martin's/Marek, 1984.

Lapchick, Richard E. *The Politics of Race and International Sport: The Case of South Africa*. Westport, CT: Greenwood Press, 1975.

Layton, Azza Salama. *International Politics and Civil Rights Policies in the United States, 1941–1960*. Cambridge: Cambridge University Press, 2000.

Lentz, Richard, and Karla K. Gower. *The Opinions of Mankind: Racial Issues, Press, and Propaganda in the Cold War*. Columbia: University of Missouri Press, 2010.

Levinson, Brian, ed. *Rugby: An Anthology: The Brave the Bruised and the Brilliant*. London: Robinson, 2015.

Lewis, George. *The White South and the Red Menace: Segregationists, Anticommunism, and Massive Resistance, 1945–1965.* Gainesville: University Press of Florida, 2004.

Lister, Simon. *Fire in Babylon: How the West Indies Cricket Team Brought a People to Its Feet.* London: Yellow Jersey Press, 2015.

Love, Janice. *The U. S. Anti-Apartheid Movement: Local Activism in Global Politics.* New York: Praeger, 1985.

Louw, Rob. *For the Love of Rugby.* Melville, South Africa: Hans Strydom Publishing, 1987.

Lyman, Princeton M., *Partner to History: The U.S. Role in South Africa's Transition to Democracy.* Washington, DC: United States Institute of Peace Press, 2002.

Manley, Michael. *A History of West Indies Cricket.* London: André Deutsch, 1988.

Marquard, Leo. *The Peoples and Policies of South Africa.* Fourth edition. London: Oxford Uniersity Press, 1969.

Martin, Charles H. *Benching Jim Crow: The Rise and Fall of the Color Line in Southern College Sports, 1890–1980.* Urbana: University of Illinois Press, 2010.

Massie, Robert Kinloch. *Loosing the Bonds: The United States and South Africa in the Apartheid Years.* New York: Nan A. Talese, 1997.

May, Peter. *The Rebel Tours: Cricket's Crisis of Confidence.* Cheltenham, UK: SportsBooks, Limited, 2009.

McConnell, Robin. *Inside the All Blacks: Behind the Scenes with the World's Most Famous Rugby Team.* London: CollinsWillow, 1999.

McLean, T. P. *The All Blacks.* London: Sidgwick & Jackson, 1991.

McLean, Terry. *Goodbye to Glory: The 1976 All Black Tour of South Africa.* London: Pelham Books, 1977.

McKinney, Stewart. *Voices from The Back of the Bus: Tall Tales and Hoary Stories From Rugby's Real Heroes.* Edinburgh and London: Mainstream Publishing, 2010.

McMahon, Robert J., ed. *The Cold War in the Third World.* Oxford: Oxford University Press, 2013.

McRae, Donald. *Winter Colours: Changing Seasons in World Rugby.* Edinburgh: Mainstream Publishing, 1998.

Meriwether, James H. *Proudly We Can Be Africans: Black Americans and Africa, 1935–1961* Chapel Hill: University of North Carolina Press, 2002.

Merrett, Christopher. *Sport, Space and Segregation: Politics and Society in Pietermaritzburg.* Scottsville, South Africa: University of KwaZulu-Natal Press, 2009.

Messick, Kurt. *Thatcher & Apartheid: A Case Study in Conflict.* Lubeck, Maine: Land's End Press, 2018.

Meurant, Ross. *The Red Squad Story . . .* Cape Town: Don Nelson, 1982.

Mexted, Murray, with Alex Veysey. *Pieces of Eight.* Auckland: Rugby Press Ltd. 1986.

Miller, Geoff. *All Blacks Supreme: The Ultimate Guide to the Ultimate Team.* Auckland: Hodder Moa, 2012.

Miller, John J. *The Big Scrum: How Teddy Roosevelt Saved Football.* New York: Harper Perennial, 2011.

Mjikeliso, Sibusiso. *Being a Black Springbok: The Thando Manana Story.* Johannesburg: Pan-Macmillan South Africa, 2017.

Moore, Louis. *We Will Win the Day: The Civil Rights Movement, the Black Athlete, and the Quest for Equality.* Santa Barbara: Praeger, 2017.

Morris, Juliet. *With All Our Strength: An Account of the Anti-Tour Movement in Christchurch.* Christchurch: Black Cat, 1982.

Mourie, Graham, with Ron Palenski. *Graham Mourie: Captain.* London: Arthur Barker Limited, 1983.

Muehlenbeck, Philip L. *Betting on the Africans: John F. Kennedy's Courting of African Nationalist Leaders.* Oxford: Oxford University Press, 2012.

Murray, Bruce, and Christopher Merrett. *Caught Behind: Race and Politics in Springbok Cricket.* Johannesburg and Scottsville: Wits University Press/University of KwaZulu-Natal Press, 2004.

Murray, Bruce, and Goolam Vahed, eds. *Empire & Cricket: The South African Experience 1884–1914.* Pretoria: UNISA Press, 2009.

Murtagh, Andrew. *Sundial in the Shade: The Story of Barry Richards: The Genius Lost to Test Cricket.* Cape Town: Don Nelson, 2015.

Nauright, John. *Long Run to Freedom: Sport, Cultures and Identities in South Africa.* Morgantown: FIT, 2010.

Nauright, John, ed. *Sport, Power and Society in New Zealand: Historical and Contemporary Perspectives.* Sydney: Australian Society for Sports History, 1995.

Nauright, John, and Mahmoud Amara. *Sport in the African World* London: Routledge, 2018.

Nauright, John, and Tony Collins, eds. *The Rugby World in the Professional Era.* New York: Routledge, 2017.

Nepia, George, and Terry McLean. *I, George Nepia: The Autobiography of a Rugby Legend.* London: London League Publications, 2002.

Nesbitt, Francis Njubi. *Race for Sanctions: African Americans Against Apartheid, 1946–1994.* Bloomington: Indiana University Press, 2004.

Newnham, Thomas Oliver. *By Batons and Barbed Wire: A Response to the 1981 Springbok Tour of New Zealand.* Auckland: Real Pictures, 1981.

Newnham, Thomas Oliver. *Interesting Times: A Kiwi Chronicle.* Auckland: Graphic Publications, 2003.

Nicholson, Chris, and Mike Hickson. *The Level Playing Field: How the Aurora Cricket Club Stumped Apartheid.* Durban: Kwa-Zulu Natal Cricket Union/Cricket South Africa, 2015.

Nixon, Rob. *Homelands, Harlem and Hollywood: South African Culture and the World Beyond.* New York and London: Routledge, 1994.

Nixon, Ron. *Selling Apartheid: South Africa's Global Propaganda War.* Auckland Park: Jacana Media, 2015.

Noer, Thomas J. *Cold War and Black Liberation: The United States and White Rule in Africa, 1948–1968.* Columbia: University of Missouri Press, 1985.

Nolan, Melanie, ed. *Revolution: The 1913 Great Strike in New Zealand.* Christchurch: Canterbury University Press with the Trade Union History Project, 2005.

Oborne, Peter. *Basil D'Oliviera: Cricket and Conspiracy: The Untold Story.* London: Time Warner Books, 2005.

Odendaal, Andre, ed. *God's Forgotten Cricketers: Profiles of Leading South African Players.* Cape Town: South African Cricketer, 1976.

Odendaal, Andre, Krish Reddy, Christopher Merrett, and Jonty Winch. *Cricket & Conquest: The History of South African Cricket Retold, 1795–1914.* Cape Town: Best Red, 2016.

Odendaal, Andre, Krish Reddy, and Christopher Merrett. *Divided Country: The History of South African Cricket Retold, 1914–1950s.* Cape Town: Best Red, 2018.

O'Reily, Titus. *A Thoroughly Unhelpful History of Australian Sport.* Melbourne: Penguin Michael Joseph, 2017.

O'Meara, Dan. *Forty Lost Years: The Apartheid State and the Politics of the National Party, 1948–1994.* Randburg: Ravan Press, 1996.

Omond, Roger. *The Apartheid Handbook: A Guide to South Africa's Everyday Racial Policies.* Harmondsworth, Middlesex, UK: Penguin, 1985.

Palenski, Ron. *Rugby: A New Zealand History.* Auckland: Auckland University Press, 2015.

Parker, A. C. *The All Blacks Juggernaut in South Africa.* Christchurch: Witcombe and Tombs, 1960.

Parker, A. C. *Now is the Hour: The 1965 'Boks in Australia and New Zealand.* Christchurch: Witcombe and Tombs, 1965.

Phillips, Jock. *A Man's Country?: The Image of the Pakeha Male: A History.* Auckland: Penguin, 1987.

Pienaar, Francois. *Rainbow Warrior.* Jeppestown: Jonathan Ball, 1999.

Plummer, Linda Gayle. *In Search of Power: African Americans in the Era of Decolonization, 1956–1974.* Cambridge: Cambridge University Press, 2013.

Plummer, Brenda Gayle. *Rising Wind: Black Americans and U. S. Foreign Affairs, 1935–1960.* Chapel Hill: University of North Carolina Press, 1996.

Plummer, Brenda Gayle, ed. *Window on Freedom: Race, Civil Rights, and Foreign Affairs 1945–1988.* Chapel Hill: University of North Carolina Press, 2003.

Powers, Angus, Karl Schoemaker, and Emil Papp. *African Bomber: The True Story of Siya Kolisi.* Sable Network, 2020. Available at: https://www.google.com/url?sa=t&rct=j&q=& esrc=s&source=web&cd=&ved=2ahUKEwjLo7Lc44jtAhXs1FkKHaoe AGwQFjABegQIBhAC&url=http%3A%2F%2Fwww.sablenetwork. com%2Fresources%2Fsiya-kolisi-true-story.pdf&usg= AOvVaw17JW3YO1TM5e5QUKf87no8

Price, Maxwell. *Springboks at Bay!* Cape Town: Longman's, Green and Co., 1956.

Procter, Mike. *South Africa: The Years of Isolation and the Return to International Cricket.* Durban: Bok Books International, 1994.

Ramsamy, Sam. *Apartheid: The Real Hurdle: Sport in South Africa & The International Boycott.* London: International Defence and Aid Fund for Southern Africa, 1982.

Ray, David. *From Webb Ellis to World Cup Rugby.* Rugby, UK: Webb Ellis Ltd., 2015.

Reason, John. *Backs to the Wall: The 1980 British Lions Tour of South Africa.* London: Rugby Football Books, Ltd., 1980.

Reason, John, and Carwyn James. *The World of Rugby: A History of Rugby Union Football.* London: British Broadcasting Corporation, 1979.

Rees, Mervyn, and Chris Day. *Muldergate: The Story of the Info Scandal.* Johannesburg: Macmillan South Africa, 1980.

Retief, Dan. *The Springboks and the Holy Grail: Behind the Scenes at the Rugby World Cup, 1995–2007.* Cape Town: Zebra Press, 2011.

Reyburn, Wallace. *A History of Rugby.* London: Arthur Barker Limited, 1971.

Reyburn, Wallace. *There Was Also Some Rugby: The Sixth Springboks in Britain.* London: Stanley Paul, 1970.

Reynolds, Jonathan T. *Sovereignty and Struggle: Africa and Africans in the Era of the Cold War, 1945–1994.* Oxford: Oxford University Press, 2015.

Reysine, Dave. *The Opening Kickoff: The Tumultuous Birth of a Football Nation.* Guilford, CT: Globe Pequot, 2014.

Rhoodie, Eschel. *The REAL Information Scandal.* Pretoria: Orbis, 1983.

Rice, Geoffrey, ed. *The Oxford History of New Zealand.* Auckland: Oxford University Press, 1996.

Rich, Gavin. *The Poisoned Chalice: The Rise and Fall of the Post-Isolation Springbok Coaches.* Cape Town: Zebra Press, 2013.

Richards, Huw. *A Game for Hooligans.* Edinburgh and London: Mainstream Publishing, 2007.

Richards, Trevor. *Dancing on our Bones: New Zealand, South Africa, Rugby and Racism.* Wellington: Bridget Williams Books, 1999.

Richardson, Paddy. *Cross Fingers.* Auckland: Hachette, New Zealand, 2013.

Roberts, Cheryl, ed., *Challenges Facing South African Sport.* Cape Town: Township Publishing Collective, 1990.

Roberts, Cheryl. *No Normal Sport in an Abnormal Society: Struggle for Non-Racial Sport in South Africa: From Apartheid to Sports Unity.* Cape Town: Havana Media, 2011.

Roberts, Cheryl, ed. *Sport and Transformation: Contemporary Debates on South Africa Sport.* Cape Town: Township Publishing Cooperative, 1989.

Robolin, Stéphane. *Grounds of Engagement: Apartheid-Era African American and South African Writing.* Urbana: University of Illinois Press, 2015.

Roger, Warwick. *Old Heroes: The 1956 Springbok Tour and the Lives Beyond.* Auckland: Hodder & Stoughton, 1991.

Rouse, Paul. *Sport & Ireland: A History.* Oxford: Oxford University Press, 2015.

Rowley, Christopher. *The Shared Origins of Football, Rugby, and Soccer.* Lanham, MD: Rowman & Littlefield, 2015.

Rooyen, Quintus van., ed. *S. A. Rugby Writers Toyota 1982 Annual.* Verwoerdberg: S. A. Rugby Writers Society, 1982.

Ryan, Greg, ed. *Tackling Rugby Myths: Rugby and New Zealand Society 1854–2004.* Dunedin: University of Otago Press, 2015.

Ryan, Greg, and Geoff Watson. *Sport and the New Zealanders: A History.* Auckland: Auckland University Press, 2018.

Ryan, Mark. *For the Glory: Two Olympics, Two Wars, Two Heroes.* London: JP Books, 2009.

Ryan, Mark. *Try for the Gold: America's Olympic Rugby Medals.* White Plains, NY: American International Media, 2009.

Samuel, John. *Follow the 1976 All Blacks.* Muizenberg: John Samuel, 1976.

S. A. Rugby Year Book. *All Blacks Tour 1976.* National Souvenir Program. Woodstock, S. A.: Playfair Sports Company, 1976.

Van Rooyen, Quintus, ed. *S. A. Rugby Writers, Toyota Jaarboek/1982 Annual.* Pretoria: S. A. Rugby Writers' Society, 1982

Saul, John S. *On Building a Social Movement: The North American Campaign for Southern African Liberation Revisited.* Trenton: Africa World Press, 2017.

Scherer, Jay, and Steven Jackson. *The Contested Terrain of the New Zealand All Blacks: Rugby, Commerce, and Cultural Politics in the Age of Globalization.* Oxford: Peter Lang, 2013.

Schoeman, Chris. *Danie Gerber: Maestro of the Midfield.* Cape Town: Sable Media, 1995.

Schrader, Peter J. *United States Policy Toward Africa: Incrementalism, Crisis and Change.* Cambridge: Cambridge University Press, 1994.

Scott, David. *Return to Rugby Land: Expatriate Reflections on the Rugby World Cup 2011, Sport, Society and New Zealand.* Colombo, Sri Lanka: Bay Owl Press, 2019.

Sengupta, Arunabha. *Apartheid: A Point to Cover: South African Cricket 1948–1970 and the Stop the Seventy Tour Campaign.* Amstelveen, Netherlands: CricketMASH, 2020.

Shears, Richard, and Isobelle Gidley. *Storm Out of Africa: The 1981 Springbok Tour of New Zealand.* Auckland: Macmillan, 1981.

Sinclair, Keith. *A History of New Zealand.* Auckland: Penguin, 2000.

Sinitiere, Phillip Luke. *Citizen of the World: The Late Career and Legacy of W. E. B. Du Bois.* Evanston: Northwestern University Press, 2019.

Skinner, Rob. *The Foundations of Anti-Apartheid: Liberal Humanitarians and Transnational Activists in Britain and the United States, c. 1919–64.* Hampshire: Palgrave Macmillan, 2010.

Slatter, Gordon. *On the Ball: The Centennial Book of New Zealand Rugby.* Christchurch: Witcombe & Tombs, 1970.

Smit, Kobus. *The Complete Book of Springbok Rugby Records.* Cape Town: Don Nelson, 2007.

Smith, Sean. *The Union Game: A Rugby History.* London: BBC Worldwide, 1999.

South African Institute of Race Relations. *A Survey of Race Relations in South Africa 1975.* Johannesburg: SAIRR, January 1976.

South African Institute of Race Relations. *A Survey of Race Relations in South Africa 1976.* Johannesburg: South African Institute of Race Relations, 1977.

South African Institute of Race Relations. *A Survey of Race Relations in South Africa 1977.* Johannesburg: South African Institute of Race Relations, 1978.

South African Institute of Race Relations. *A Survey of Race Relations in South Africa 1978.* Johannesburg: South African Institute of Race Relations, 1979.

South African Institute of Race Relations. *A Survey of Race Relations for 1979.* Johannesburg: South African Institute of Race Relations, 1980.

South African Institute of Race Relations. *A Survey of Race Relations for 1980.* Johannesburg: South African Institute of Race Relations, 1981.

South African Institute of Race Relations. *A Survey of Race Relations for 1981.* Johannesburg: South African Institute of Race Relations, 1982.

South African Institute of Race Relations. *A Survey of Race Relations for 1982.* Johannesburg: South African Institute of Race Relations, 1983.

Sparks, Allister. *The Sword and the Pen: Six Decades on the Political Frontier.* Johannesburg & Cape Town: Jonathan Ball, 2016.

Stofberg, Theuns. *Stories from the Touchline.* Cape Town: Zebra Press, 2016.

Study Commission on U.S. Policy Toward Southern Africa. *South Africa: Time Running Out.* Berkeley: University of California Press, 1986.

Sustar, Lee, and Aisha Karim. *Poetry & Protest: A Dennis Brutus Reader.* Chicago: Haymarket Books, 2006.

Swindall, Lindsey R. *The Path to the Greater, Freer, Truer World: Southern Civil Rights and Anticolonialism, 1937–1955*. Gainesville: University Press of Florida, 2014.

Talton, Benjamin. *In This Land of Plenty: Mickey Leland and Africa in American Politics*. Philadelphia: University of Pennsylvania Press, 2019.

Templeton, Malcolm. *Human Rights and Sporting Contacts: New Zealand Attitudes to Race Relations in South Africa 1921–1994*. Auckland: Auckland University Press, 1998.

The Australian Society for Sports History, Wray Vamplew, et al., eds. *The Oxford Companion to Australian Sport* (Second Edition). Melbourne: Oxford University Press, 1994.

The Original Rules of Rugby. Oxford: Bodleian Library, 2014 Edition.

Thomas, Cornelius, ed. *Sport and Liberation in South Africa: Reflections and Suggestions*. Alice, South Africa: University of Fort Hare, 2006.

Thomas, Cornelius, ed. *Time with Dennis Brutus: Conversations, Quotations and Snapshots*. East London, South Africa: Wendy's Book Lounge, 2012.

Thompson, Richard. *Retreat from Apartheid: New Zealand's Sporting Contacts With South Africa*. Wellington: Oxford University Press, 1975.

Thörn, Håkan. *Anti-Apartheid and the Emergence of a Global Civil Society*. Basingstoke, UK: Palgrave Macmillan, 2009.

Tillery, Alvin B. Jr. *Between Homeland and Motherland: Africa, U.S. Foreign Policy, and Black Leadership in America*. Ithaca, NY: Cornell University Press, 2011.

Tobias, Errol. *Pure Gold*. Cape Town: Tafelberg, 2015.

Tossell, David. *Grovel! The Story and Legacy of the Summer of 1976, England v. West Indies*. Durrington, UK: Pitch Publishing Limited, 2012.

Turley, Alan. *Rugby: The Pioneer Years*. Auckland: Harper Collins Publishers, 2008.

van der Berg, Wim. *150 Years of South African Rugby*. Johannesburg: Bookstorm and Pan MacMillan South Africa, 2011.

Valk, Ron van der, with Andy Colquhuon. *Nick & I: An Adventure in Rugby*. Cape Town: Don Nelson, 2002.

Van Wyk, Chris. *Now Listen Here: The Life and Times of Bill Jardine*. Johannesburg: Sue Publishers, 2003.

Villiers, Les de. *In Sight of Surrender: The U. S. Sanctions Campaign against South Africa, 1946–1993*. Westport, CT: Praeger, 1995.

Villiers, Les de. *South Africa: A Skunk Among Nations*. Tandem: London, 1975.

Vinson, Robert Trent. *The Americans Are Coming!: Dreams of African American Liberation in Segregationist South Africa*. Athens: Ohio University Press, 2012.

Van Esbeck, Edmund. *Irish Rugby Scrapbook*. London: Souvenir Press, 1982.

Van Esbeck, Edmund. *Irish Rugby, 1874–1999: A History*. Dublin: Gill & Macmillan, 1999.

Van Esbeck, Edmund. *The Story of Irish Rugby*. London: Stanley Paul, 1986.

Von Eschen, Penny M.. *Race Against Empire: Black Americans and Anticolonialism, 1937–1957*. Ithaca, NY: Cornell University Press, 1997.

Walker, Ranginui. *Nga Tau Tohetohe: Years of Anger*. Auckland: Penguin, 1987.

Waters, John W. *Springbok Challenge: A Pictorial Record of the 1965 Springbok Tour of New Zealand*. Books One and Two. Palmerston North: Viscount Printing & Publishing, 1965.

Westad, Odd Arne. *The Cold War: A World History*. New York: Basic Books, 2017.

White, Steven. *The 50 Greatest Rugby Union Players of All Time*. London: Icon Books, 2015.

Wiggins, David K. *More Than a Game: A History of the African American Experience in Sport*. Lanham, MD: Rowman & Littlefield, 2018.

Wiggins, David K., ed. *Out of the Shadows: A Biographical History of African American Athletes*. Fayetteville: University of Arkansas Press, 2006.

Wigginton, Russell T. *The Strange Career of the Black Athlete: African Americans and Sports*. Westport, CT: Praeger, 2006.

Wilder, Gary. *Freedom Time: Negritude, Decolonization, and the Future of the World*. Durham: Duke University Press, 2015.

Williams, Mark, and Tim Wigmore. *The Best: How Elite Athletes Are Made*. London: Nicholas Brealey, 2020.

Wilson, Stu, Bernie Fraser, and Alex Veysey. *Ebony & Ivory: The Stu Wilson, Bernie Fraser Story.* Auckland: MOA Publications Ltd., 1984.

Woods, Donald. *South African Dispatches: Letters to My Countrymen.* New York: Henry Holt & Company, 1986.

Woods, Jeff. *Black Struggle and Red Scare: Segregation and Anti-Communism in the South, 1948–1968.* Baton Rouge: Louisiana State University Press, 2004.

Writer, Larry. *Pitched Battle: in the Frontline of the 1971 Springbok Tour of Australia.* Melbourne: Scribe, 2016.

Wyngaard, Heindrich. *Bursting Through the Half-Gap: The Story of Errol Tobias, South Africa's First Black Springbok: Trailblazer or Traitor?* Melville, South Africa: Dickie & Bugler, 2017.

Zavos, Spiro. *Winters of Revenge: The Bitter Rivalry Between the All Blacks and the Springboks* Auckland: Viking, 1997.

JOURNAL ARTICLES/BOOK CHAPTERS

Arthur, Michael, and Jennifer Scanlon. "Reading and Rereading the Game: Reflections on West Indies Cricket" in Amy Bass, ed., *In the Game: Race, Identity, and Sports in the Twentieth Century.* New York: Palgrave Macmillan, 2005: pp. 117–35.

Catsam, Derek. "Go Amabokoboko! Rugby, Race, Madiba and the *Invictus* Creation Myth of a New South Africa," in Nigel Eltringham, *Framing Africa: Portrayals of a Continent in Contemporary Mainstream Cinema.* Oxford: Berghahn, 2013, pp. 156–74.

Catsam, Derek. "Rugby Transformation as Alibi: Thoughts on Craven and Coetzee," in Todd Cleveland, Tarminder Kaur, and Gerard Akindes, eds., *Sports in Africa Past and Present.* Athens: Ohio University Press, 2020, pp. 233–48.

Catsam, Derek Charles. "The African Diaspora and Sport in the United States," in John Nauright and Mahfoud Amara, eds. *Sport in the African World.* London: Routledge, 2018, pp. 146–68.

Catsam, Derek. "The Policing Paradox: The Dilemma of Colonial Policing and Military Security in the Age of Terrorism." *Warfare in the Age of Non-State Actors: Implications for the US Army* (Proceedings of the US Army Combat Studies Institute's Military History Symposium), Fort Leavenworth, KS: Combat Studies Institute Press, 2007.

Catsam, Derek Charles. "W. E. B. Du Bois, South Africa, and *Phylon's* 'A Chronicle of Race Relations,' 1940–1944," in Phillip Luke Sinitiere, *Citizen of the World: The Late Career and Legacy of W. E. B. Du Bois.* Evanston, IL: Northwestern University Press, 2019.

Crocker, Chester A. "South Africa: Strategy for Change." *Foreign Affairs,* Winter 1980/1981.

Crocker, Chester A. "Southern Africa: Eight Years Later." *Foreign Affairs,* Fall 1989.

Downes, Aviston D. "Forging Afro-Caribbean Solidarity within the Commonwealth?: Sport and Diplomacy during the Anti-apartheid Campaign," in Heather L. Dichter and Andrew L. Johns, eds., *Diplomatic Games: Sport, Statecraft, and International Relations Since 1945.* Lexington: University Press of Kentucky, 2014.

Elkind, Jerome B., and Antony Shaw. "The Municipal Enforcement of the Prohibition Against Racial Discrimination: A Case Study on New Zealand and the 1981 Springbok Tour." *British Year Book of International Law* Vol. 55. 1984. pp. 189–248.

Freedman, Eric M. "Freedom of Information and the First Amendment in a Bureaucratic Age." *49 Brook. L. Rev.* 835. 1983, pp. 851–53.

Grundlingh, Albert. "Dressed for Success: Historicizing Nelson Mandela's Involvement in the 1995 World Cup," in John Nauright and Tony Collins, eds. *The Rugby World in the Professional Era.* New York: Routledge, 2017, pp. 175–84.

Grundlingh, Marizanne. "'When Jerseys Speak': Contested Heritage and South African Rugby," in John Nauright and Tony Collins, eds. *The Rugby World in the Professional Era.* New York: Routledge, 2017, pp. 147–60.

Grundlingh, Albert and Marizanne. "Fractured Fandom and Paradoxical Passions: Explaining Support for New Zealand All Black Rugby Teams in South Africa, 1960–2018." *International Journal of the History of Sport* 2019, pp. 1–16.

Grundlingh, Albert, Stephane Robolin, Abigail Hinsman, Lily Saint, Sharrona Pearl, and Samantha Pinto. "Roundtable on *Invictus*." *Safundi: The Journal of South African and American Studies*, Vol. 13, Nos. 1–2, January–April 2012, pp. 115–50.

Hamlin, Philip K. "The 1981 Springbok Tour of New Zealand." *Auckland University Law Review* 313, 1980–1983, pp. 313–25.

Holmes, Bob, and Chris Tau. "My Greatest Game: Errol Tobias," in Brian Levinson, ed., *Rugby: An Anthology: The Brave the Bruised and the Brilliant*. London: Robinson, 2015, pp. 171–73.

Lakier, Genevieve. "Sport as Speech." *University of Pennsylvania Journal of Constitutional Law* 1109, 2014.

Lever, Carla. "Performativity, Identities and Rugby from Field to Stage in the New South Africa," in John Nauright and Tony Collins, eds. *The Rugby World in the Professional Era*. New York: Routledge, 2017, pp. 161–74.

MacLean, Malcolm. "Making Strange the Country and Making Strange the Countryside: Spatialized Clashes in the Affective Economies of Aotearoa/New Zealand during the 1981 Springbok Rugby Tour," in John Bale and Mike Cronin, eds., *Sport and Postcolonialism*. Oxford: Berg, 2003.

Maingard, Jacqueline. "Imag(in)ing the South African Nation: Representations of Identity in the Rugby World Cup 1995." *Theatre Journal*, Vol. 49, No. 1, "Performing in South Africa," March 1997, pp. 15–28.

McDougall, Hamish. "'The Whole World is Watching': New Zealand, International Opinion, and the 1981 Springbok Rugby Tour." *Journal of Sport History*, Vol. 45, No. 2. Summer 2018, pp. 202–23.

Morgan, Eric. "His Voice Must Be Heard: Dennis Brutus, the Anti-Apartheid Movement, and the Struggle for Political Asylum in the United States." *Peace & Change*, Vol. 40, No. 3, July 2015, pp. 368–94.

Nauright, John, "'A Besieged Tribe?': Nostalgia, White Cultural Identity, and the Role of Rugby in a Changing South Africa," *International Journal of the Sociology of Sport*, 31, 1996, pp. 69–86.

Patterson, Chris, and Vanessa Malila. "Beyond the Information Scandal: When South Africa Bought into Global News." *Ecquid Novi: African Journalism Studies*, Vol. 34, No. 2, 2013, pp. 1–14.

Rankin, Elizabeth. "Banners, Batons and Barbed Wire: Anti-apartheid Images of the Springbok Rugby Tour Protests in New Zealand." *De Arte*, Vol. 76, 2007, pp. 21–32.

Roche, Michael M. "Protest, Police and Place: The 1981 Springbok Tour and the Production and Consumption of Social Space." *New Zealand Geographer* 53, no. 2, 1997, pp. 50–57.

Charles I. Schachter, *Selfridge v. Carey:* "The First Amendment's Applicability to Sporting Events," 46 ALB. L. REV. 937, 977–78, 1982.

Rooyen, Quintus van. "The Internasionale Scene." Quintus van Rooyen, ed., S. A. Rugby Writers *Toyota Jaarboek/Annual*, 1982, p. 27.

Thompson, Alex. "Incomplete Engagement: Reagan's South Africa Policy Revisited." *Journal of Modern African Studies*, Vol. 33, No. 1, 1995, pp. 83–101.

Thompson, Shona M. "Challenging Hegemony: New Zealand Women's Opposition to Rugby and the Reproduction of a Capitalist Patriarchy." *International Review for the Sociology of Sport*, Vol. 23, No. 3, 1988, pp. 205–12.

Tilden, C. L., Jr. "Winners in a Foreign Game— Rugby Football." *Games of the VII Olympiad: United States Olympic Committee Official Report, Antwerp Belgium, 1920.* (1920 USOC Olympic Report), pp. 137–40.

"U.S. Government Seeks to Expel South African Activists," *Ufahamu: A Journal of African Studies* 11, No. 1, 1981, pp. 150–51.

Watterson, John S. "The Gridiron Crisis of 1905: Was it Really a Crisis?" *Journal of Sport History*, Vol. 27, No. 2, Summer 2000, pp. 291–98.

Watterson, John S. "The Football Crisis of 1909–1910: The Response of the Eastern 'Big Three.'" *Journal of Sport History*, Vol. 8, No. 1, Spring 1981, pp. 33–49.

PERIODICALS: (NEWSPAPERS/MAGAZINES/ONLINE PUBLICATIONS)

Africa is a Country
Boston Globe
Broadsheet
Cape Times
Charleston News and Courier
Christian Science Monitor
The Dominion (Wellington, New Zealand)
Dominion Post (Wellington, New Zealand)
ESPN Scrum
Glasgow Herald
The Guardian (United Kingdom)
Independent (Dublin, Ireland)
Irish Times
Journal Times (Racine, Wisconsin, USA)
Los Angeles Times
Mail & Guardian (South Africa)
New York Recorder
New York Times
Newsweek
Observer
The Public Sphere
Pundit Arena
Rand Daily Mail
Rolling Stone
Rugby Magazine
Rugby World
SA Rugby Magazine
SA Sports Illustrated
Sports Illustrated
Sun-Times, (Chicago, Illinois, USA)
Stanford Magazine
The Star (Johannesburg, South Africa)

Sunday Times (Johannesburg, South Africa)
Sydney Morning Herald
Time
The Times (London, United Kingdom)
Times-Union, (Albany, New York, USA)
Washington Post
Weekend Post (Port Elizabeth, South Africa)

THESES AND DISSERTATIONS

Maralack, David Mark, "Transforming Sport and Identity in the post-Apartheid Nation State," Ph.D. Dissertation, University of Minnesota, 2010.

Molina, Lacy. "You Can't Buy Me I Don't Care What You Pay: Music, Musicians, and the Cultural Boycott of South Africa." MA Thesis, University of Texas Permian Basin, 2020.

Morrison, Melissa A. "The Grassroots of the 1981 Springbok Tour: An Examination of the Actions and Perspectives of Everyday New Zealanders during the 1981 Springbok Rugby Tour of New Zealand." MA Thesis, University of Canterbury, 2017.

Potgieter, Sebastian Johan Shore. "'Barbed-Wire Boks': The Long Shadow of the 1981 Springbok Tour of New Zealand and the United States of America." MA Thesis, Stellenbosch University, 2017.

Russell, Andre. "The New Zealand Rugby Football Union and the 1981 Springbok Tour." MA Thesis, Massey University, 1999.

DOCUMENTARIES/VIDEOS

A Giant Awakens: The Rise of American Rugby. DVD. Directed by Sylvain Doreau. BIN15 Productions, 2010.

A Political Game. DVD. Directed by David Crerar, TV New Zealand. Available at https://www.nzonscreen.com/title/a-political-game-2004.

Do Not Enter: The Visa War Against Ideas, Richter Videos.

Fire in Babylon. DVD. Directed by Stevan Riley. Tribeca Films, 2011.

Have You Heard from Johannesburg. DVD. (7 DVD set, but especially episode 4: "Fair Play) Clarity Films, 2010.

Invictus. DVD. Directed by Clint Eastwood. Warner Video, 2009.

Kaunda Ntunja's commentary on Siya Kolisi's debut as Springbok captain. SuperSport. Available at: https://www.youtube.com/watch?v=dCe2WZHa6W4.

Patu! Directed by Merata Mita, NZ On Screen, 1983. Available at https://www.nzonscreen.com/title/patu-1983.

The 16th Man. DVD. Directed by Clifford Bestall, ESPN 30 for 30, ESPN Films, 2010.

Try Revolution, directed by Leanne Pooley, NZ On Screen, 2006. Available at https://www.nzonscreen.com/title/try-revolution-2006.

OTHER

Schad v. Borough of Mt. Ephraim, 452 U.S. 61 (1981).

Snyders, Hendrik. *Cold Wars and Hot Scrums*. Unpublished book manuscript. In author's possession.

Vance, Cyrus. Speech Before the 58th Annual Meeting of the United States Jaycees, June 20, 1978, Department of State, Washington, D.C., Department of State Publication 8950, African Series 59, Office of Public Communications, Bureau of Public Affairs, June 1978.

INDEX

1952 Immigration and Nationality Act. *See* McCarran–Walter Act
1968 Olympics, xxviii
1970 Olympics, xxii
1976 Olympics, 55, 81
1980 Olympics, xix, 18, 81, 146
1984 Olympics, 43, 49, 81, 84, 120, 146

Abbey on Lake Geneva, 90
Aer Lingus, 35
African American, xxi, xxvii, 81, 89, 115, 135
African National Congress (ANC), xx, 8, 36, 48, 87, 151, 155, 156, 157–158, 159, 160
Afrikaans, 1, 48, 84, 133, 158
Against South Africans Playing (ASAP), 44, 119
Albany, 39, 42–44, 105, 107, 109, 111, 113, 116–117, 119–121, 124, 126, 131, 133, 137–140, 143
Albany City Hall, 111, 119
Alfred, Luke, 23
All Blacks, 23, 37, 50, 52–55, 58–60, 67–70, 73–75, 152, 153, 158, 161, 164
All Whites, 129, 143
America, xix–xxi, xxiv, xxvii, xxviii, 1–4, 6, 9–12, 14, 17, 24, 38, 40–50, 76, 80–84, 85, 85–86, 88–91, 94–97, 101, 103–104, 105, 108, 110, 112, 114, 115, 116, 119, 121, 122, 123–124, 126, 129, 130–131, 132, 133, 136, 137, 138–140, 142, 143, 144–146, 148, 148–150, 152–155, 166–167
America's Team. *See* Dallas Cowboys
American Committee on Africa (ACOA), 40–42, 119
American Coordinating Committee for Equality in Sport and Society (ACCESS), 40, 41, 43, 44, 48, 49, 108, 119
American Cougars, 2, 24, 107
American International Fixtures Secretary, 6, 45
American. *See* America
Americans. *See* America
Anglo-Free-gold XV, 154
Anti-apartheid, xix–xxii, xxii, xxiv, 15, 20, 22, 24, 27–31, 35–37, 40, 49, 52, 53–54, 56, 63, 71, 72, 81, 84, 101, 102, 109, 110, 114, 119, 142, 144, 148, 149, 153–155, 157
Anti-Springbok Five, 142
Aotearoa, 69
Apartheid, xv, xvii, xx–xxvi, xxviii, 4–8, 10, 18, 19, 21, 22, 23, 25, 26, 28–29, 30, 31, 33, 39–40, 41, 42–44, 48, 52, 54–55, 56, 57–58, 59, 60, 74, 75, 80, 82, 83, 89, 90, 91, 95, 102, 104, 107, 108, 110, 112–113, 118, 119, 121, 124, 139, 143, 144–145, 146, 151, 152, 156–158, 166

Armstrong, Dr. John, 29
Asmal, Kader, 30, 35
Athletic Park, 69
Australia, xxii, xxiv, xxv, 18, 19, 47, 54, 66, 107, 153, 155, 159, 164
Azania, 69

Babrow, Louis, 21, 22
Baker, Mary, 75
Bantustans, xxvi, 6, 8
Barbarians, 22, 23, 36, 154
Barclays Bank, 46
Bartholome, Bernie, 129
Bartholome, Doug, 129
Baseball Hall of Fame, 133
BBC, 99
Beck, Colin, 97, 123, 139
Bekker, Hennie, 68
Belfast, Northern Ireland, 35
Black Coalition Against the Rugby Tour, 88
Black Liberation Army, 117, 142
Blank, Tim, 142
Bleecker Stadium, 111
Bloemfontein, 19
Blue Squad, 57
Boet Erasmus Stadium, 21
Boipatong, 157
Boipatong Massacre, 158
Border Rugby Union Grounds, 24
Bort, Sam, 104
Borup, Donna, 142
Boston Globe, 45
Botha, Naas, 37, 68, 70, 73, 87, 116, 123, 133, 149–150
Botha, Pieter Willem "PW," 9
Bradley, Tom, 49, 81
British Irish Lions, xxiv, 17–19, 31, 32, 34
Brock, Laura, 90
Brooklyn Dodgers, xxvii
Brown, Malcolm, 23
Brutus, Dennis, xxiv, 42, 121, 148, 149, 152
Buchanan, Buck, 95, 98
Buchanan, Robert, 91, 93
Burger, Thys, 134, 137, 139, 140
Burgess, Bob, 59
Byrne, Jane, 84

Caesar's Palace, 86
Cameron, Don, 71
Campbell, Ollie, 33, 34
Cape Times, 47, 79, 85, 90, 139, 147
Cape Town, xxv, 1, 4, 21, 22, 37, 50, 97, 132, 134, 152, 154, 159, 164
Capital District Committee Against Apartheid, 39, 40, 119
Cardiff,, 130
Carey, Hugh, 111
Carisbrook, 65
Carlos, John, xxviii
Carter III, Hodding, 83
Carter, Jimmy, 3
Central High School, 112
Chambers, David, 136
Chapple, Geoff, 61, 67
Chicago, 39, 42–44, 80, 83–91, 93, 94, 96, 98, 99, 101, 109, 114, 115, 142
Chicago Athletic Association's (CAA), 85, 87
Chicago Cubs, 85
Chicago Lions, 35, 86, 93
Chicago Tribune, 80
Christchurch, New Zealand, 52, 57, 61, 65–67, 75, 141
Chung, Billy, 97
Church of Ireland, 29
The Citizen, 8, 11, 161
Citizens Against the Tour (CAT), 57
The Citizens Association for Racial Equality (CARE), 57
Citizens Opposed to the Springboks Tour (COST), 57
Claassen, Wynand, 37, 60, 62, 73, 79, 83, 86–87, 94, 97, 121, 123, 124, 126, 130, 131–139, 147, 166
Clark, B. Alporode, 30
CNN, 39
Coetzee, Allister, 163
Cold War, xx, 4, 18, 146, 151
Cole, Grant, 72
Communist Workers Party, 112
Constantine, Dorothy, 102
Cooperstown, 133
Cork, Ireland, 35
Cornbill, Ray, 135
Corning II, Erastus, 111, 113
Cotton, James, 100

COVID-19, xvi
Craven, Danie, 6, 11–13, 20, 21, 25, 31, 37, 152, 153, 155
Crawford, Thomas, 102
Crocker, Chester, xx, 41, 83
Cronje, Geo, 162
Currie Cup, 19, 23
Cushe, Morgan, 20, 23, 24

D. F. Malan Airport, 2, 50
D'Oliviera, Basil, xxiii
Dairy Flat, 72
Dale, John, 121
Dallas Cowboys, 149
Dallas Harlequins, 149
Dalton, Andy, 73
Dave Canfield, 92, 93
Davids, Quinton, 162
Davies, Gerald, 18
Davis, Danny, 87
Day of Shame, 60–62
de Klerk, F. W., 156, 157
de Villiers, Lourens Erasmus Smit "Les," 10–13
de Villiers, Peter, 163
Dennis Brutus Defense Committee, 148
Department of Defence (Ireland), 32
Detroit, Michigan, 5
Die Groot Krokodil. *See* Botha, Pieter Willem "PW"
Disneyland, 49
Douglas, William O., 115
Dr. John Bryant Center, 96
Dreyfus, Lee, 91
du Plessis, Carel, 86, 97
du Plessis, Willie, 37
Du Toit, Hempies, 97
Dublin, Ireland, 35
Duggan, Willie, 35
Duguid, Paul, 110
Dunedin, 65
Durban, South Africa, 37, 98, 152
Dymmaly, Mervyn, 82

Eastern Province, 19, 25, 134
Eastwood, Clint, 160
Eden Park, 71–73, 76, 135
Ellis Park, xv, 150, 154, 158, 165

England, xv, xxii, xxiii, xxv, 22, 149, 150, 153, 155, 160, 162, 164
Erasmus, Rassie, 163
Estis, Aaron, 118
Etzebeth, Eben, 165
Evansville Black Coalition, 129
Evansville Rugby Club, 129
Evansville, Indiana, 129

Faubus, Orval, 112
Federal Information Council, 25
Federal Plaza, 87
Ferrell, Robert, 49
Fianna Fáil, 28
First National Bank of South Africa, 154
Fischer, Bram, 22
Fitzgerald, Ciaran, 32
Flour Bomb match, 71, 72
France, 19, 32, 107, 155, 160, 162, 165, 167
Free State, 19, 137, 154
Furlong, Blair, 54

Gault, Ian, 73
Germishuys, Gerrie, 70, 123
Ghana, 108
Gideon Putnam Hotel, 141
Gisborne, 60, 61
Gleaneagles Agreement, 18, 56
Glenville, 129–132, 152
Going, Sid, 54
Gold Cup XV
Goodstein, Evan, 142
Graham, John, 59
Grahamstown, 20
Grant Park, 85
Gray, Ken, 59
Griqualand West, 19
Group Areas Act, 26, 27
Group of 77, 28
Grunther, Gerald, 114, 115
Guinness, 33
Gustafson, Barry, 75
Gutfleish, Ronald, 110

Habana, Bryan, 162
Haden, Andy, 59, 73, 76
Haffner, William, 43, 45
Haig, Alexander, 81

Hain, Peter, xxiii, 18
Hall, David, 80
Halt All Racist Tours (HART), 54, 57, 62,
    65–67, 70
Happel, Marvin, 98, 103
Harare, 155, 156
Harris, Joseph L., 98, 103
Harvard Law School, 114
Haughey, Taoiseach Charles, 28
Hawaii, 79
Hearns, Thomas "Hitman," 86
Hewson, Allan, 59, 72, 73
Hillery, Patrick, 28
Holmes, Bevan, 59
Holyoake, Keith, 53
Honolulu, 81
House Foreign Affairs Committee, 40
Houston, 167
Howa, Hassan, 27, 31
Howard Johnson's, 92, 94
Hurley, Denis, 29, 36

Independent, 29
Information Scandal, 9–10, 45
Inkatha Freedom Party, 157
International League, xxvii
International Tennis Federation, 26
Invercargill, 65
Invictus, 160
Ireland Rugby Football Union (IRFU), 28
Ireland. See Irish
Irish, xxii–xxiv, 17, 20, 28–38, 86, 130,
    139, 155
Irish Times, 29
Irwin, David, 32

Jackson, Jesse, 87–88, 90
Jan Smuts International Airport, 143
Jansen, Eben, 141
JFK airport, 48, 142
Joe Louis Arena, 5
Johannesburg, xv, 8, 14, 54, 110, 150, 152,
    158
Jones, Marx, 72
Jordan, Boji, 119
Journal Times, 90, 91, 93, 102–104

Kaduna, 41
Kahotea, Des, 69

Keane, Moss, 30, 31
Kellermann, Alex, 1, 12, 14, 46, 50
Kenosha County, 92
Kiernan, Tom, 30
King, Jr. Dr. Martin Luther, 88
Kirk, Norman, 54, 56
Knight, Gary, 72
Koch, Ed, 112, 132
Kolisi, Siya. See Kolisi, Siyamthamba
    "Siya"
Kolisi, Siyamthamba "Siya," xv, xvi, 164,
    165
Koornhof, Dr. Piet J. G., 25
Koppel, Ted, 81
Krantz, Edrich, 97, 137
Kravets, Vladimir A., 42
Ku Klux Klan, 112, 113

Labour Party (Ireland), 34
Labour Party (New Zealand), 152
Labour Party (UK), 18
Lady Diana, 63
Laidlaw, Chris, 59
Lake Michigan, 86, 90
LaMartina, Michael, 104
Lancaster Park, 67–68
Landry, Tom, 108
Lane, Dale, 117
Langebaan, 165
Lansdowne Road, 28
Lee, Edmund, 2
Lenihan, Brian, 28
Leonard, Sugar Ray, 86
Leopards, 23
Le Roux, Herman, 137
Limerick, Ireland, 34
Linwood Rugby Club, 67
Little Rock Nine, 112
Lloyd, Gary, 124
Lomu, Jonah, 162
London, United Kingdom, 24, 35, 36, 167
Los Angeles, 49, 81, 83, 84, 87, 117, 119,
    146
Louw, Rob, 37, 79, 83, 89, 97, 98, 116,
    121, 123, 132, 133, 137, 138, 140, 141,
    144
Luyt, Louis, 8, 11–12, 45, 108, 120, 130,
    158, 161

Maarkgraaf, Andre, 162
MacNeill, Hugo, 30, 32
Madiba. *See* Mandela, Nelson
Madigan, Paddy, 37
Maitai River, 68
Makisoma, Saki, 159
Mallett, Nick, 163
Manawatu, 65
Mandela, Nelson, xv, 22, 154, 157, 160, 161
Maoris, 51, 53, 54, 57, 69, 75
Margolick, David, 114
Markgraaf, Andre, 162
Marks, Edward, 82
Marquette University, 103
Márquez, Gabriel García, 47
Marshall, Thurgood, 115, 145
Mbeki, Thabo, 155
McBride, Willie John, 18
McCarran-Walter Act, 47
McDonald's, 137
McGrath, James, 117
McLaughlin, Gerry, 34
McQuarrie, Pat, 62, 72
Mdudo, Patrick, 154
Meyer, Heyneke, 163
Michaelson, Vera, 118
Midwestern RFU, 149
Milner, Buff, 54
Milwaukee, 90, 98
Milwaukee Journal, 105
Ministry of Information, 8, 9
Minto, John, 65
Molbeck, Jack, 102
Molesworth Street, 62–64
Moneymaker, Dick, 2
Mongrel Mob, 68
Montevideo, Uruguay, 19
Montpelier, 167
Montreal Royals, xxvii
Moolman, Louis, 126, 141
Mordt, Ray, 73, 135
Morgado, Robert J., 112
Morrison, John, 137
Moscow, xix, 18, 81, 146
Moser, Tim, 124
Mourie, Graham, 58, 59
Mtawarira, Tendai "The Beast," xvi, 166
Mulder, Cornelius "Connie," 8

Muldergate, 9–10
Muldoon, Robert, 42, 51, 56, 75
Munson, Howard G., 115

NAACP, 100, 115, 119, 120
Namibia, 119
Napier, 69
Nasionale Pers, 137
Natal, 134, 154
National Basketball Association, xxvii
National Football League, xxvii
National Guard, 94, 96, 112, 115
National Hockey League, xxvii
National Party, xx, xxii, xxvi, 7, 9, 25–27, 75, 76, 85, 88, 151, 156, 157
Naude, Beyers, 22
Ndumo, Welcome, 154
Nelson, 68
Nelson Bays, 68
Neo-Nazi, 80, 90
Neruda, Pablo, 47
New England Patriots, 149
New Plymouth, New Zealand, 62, 63
New York, 4, 11, 39, 40, 42–44, 48, 49, 105, 107–116, 119–121, 129, 132, 136, 147
New York Civil Liberties Union, 112, 113
New Zealand, xxii, xxiv, 11–14, 17, 18, 21, 32, 37, 41–44, 47, 48, 49, 50, 51–63, 65, 66, 67, 69, 70–76, 79–80, 83–85, 87–89, 91, 108, 110, 120, 124, 130–132, 135, 137, 139–140, 144, 147, 152–155, 158, 162, 164
Newlands Stadium, 23, 37, 97, 159
Newnham, Tom, 63
Niebauer, Skip, 135
Nienaber, Jacques, 163
Nigeria. *See* Nigerian
Nigerian, 30, 33, 41
Nixon, Richard, 4–5, 145
Noble, Johnny, 20, 23
Nollman, Tyke, 93
Norling, Clive, 72, 73
Ntunja, Kaunda, xv, xvi

O'Callahan, Mick, 59
Ó Fiaich, Cardinal Tomás, 29
O'Hare Airport, 83
O'Ree, Willie, xxvii

Oberholzer, Judex, 98
Ogburn, Bobby, 129
Old Glory DC, 166
Olsen, Stephen, 103
Oosthuizen, Okkie, 96
Orange Free State, 11, 154
Organization of African Unity
    Headquarters, 44
Osata, Daisuke, 162
Otago, 65
Owens, Corrine, 100
Owl Creek Polo Field, 131, 133, 137
Oxford, 32

Pacific Islanders, 51, 54
Palmerston North, 65
Pan Africanist Congress, 8, 119
Patel, Ebrahim, 36
Patten, Mary, 142
Patterson, Colin, 31
Pelletier, Margot, 142
People United to Save Humanity
    (PUSH), 88, 90
Peppers, Paula, 104
Pettit, Martha, 100
Phelps-Stokes Fund, 42, 45, 108
Philadelphia Phillies, 85
Pienaar, Francois, 160, 161
Pienaar, Gysie, 97, 133
Pippel, Stu, 94, 95, 98, 99
Pitcher's Pub, 93
Playboy club and hotel, 90
Playing the Enemy, 160
Port Elizabeth, xv, xvi, 21, 25, 150
Potchefstroom, 36
Potemkin Village, 36
Poverty Bay, 60
President's Trophy XV, 36
Pretoria, xx, xxv, 4, 13, 17, 36, 40, 41, 47,
    82, 87, 88, 98, 109, 134
Pretorius, J. P. "Hannes," 1, 50
Prince Charles, 63

Queen's University, Belfast, 32
Queens Students Union, 32

Racine, Wisconsin, 90, 103
Rafael Septien, 149
Rand Daily Mail, 8, 9, 122, 139, 147

Randall's Island, 44
Rapport, 84, 85
Reagan, Ronald, xx, 3, 5, 6, 13, 40–41, 44,
    47, 83, 84, 88, 103, 119, 121
Reardon, John, 137
Red Escort Group. *See* Red Squad
Red Squad, 57, 63, 68, 85
Reid, Douglas, 1–3, 108
Reservation of Separate Amenities Act, 26
Retief, Dan, 85, 87, 122, 125, 139, 147
Rhoodie, Eschel, 9
Richards, Trevor, 63, 71, 76
Rivonia, 22
Robbie, John, 33–34
Robertson, Bruce, 59
Robinson, Jackie, xxvii, 81
Robinson, William, 45
Rosahn, Eve, 142
Rotorua, 71
Rovigo, 150
Rowan, Carl, 83
Rugby Football Federation, 23
Rugby in South Africa: The Facts, 55
Rutherford Hotel, 68

S.A. Rugby Writers Toyota Annual, 148
Sacramento Star, 9
Samaranch, Juan Antonio, 81
Samuels, Dorothy J., 113
San Antonio Gunslingers, 149
Santiago, Chile, 19
Satterfield, Clara, 120
Sauer, Joseph, 94, 98
Savalas, Telly, 116
Scheitlin, Joe, 94, 96
Schenectady Trust Account, 46
Scotland, xxiv
Scott, Mark, 153
Seeger, Pete, 121
Selfridge, Tom, 13–14, 45, 46, 50,
    107–108, 117, 122–125, 132, 133,
    136–138, 147, 156
Selleck, Tom, 79
Serfointein, Divan, 132, 133, 152
Sexton Street, 34
Shannon, Ireland, 35
Shapiro, Steven R., 113
Sharma-Jensen, Greeta, 103
Sharpeville Massacre, 7, 53

Sharpeville, South Africa, 7, 53
Shaw, Alick, 63, 65
Sherlock, Mike, 123, 126
Shields, "Turkey," 20, 23
Shields, Hennie, 107
Skokie Nazi march, 80
Slattery, Fergus, 35, 37
Smit, John, 162
Smith, Cornelius "Nelie," 19, 23
Smith, Tommie, xxviii
Songwiqi, Father Eric, xvi
South Africa, xv, xvii, xix, xxi–xxvi, xxviii,
    1–11, 12–14, 17, 18–19, 20, 20–22, 23,
    24, 25, 27, 28–29, 30–32, 33, 33–36,
    37, 38, 39, 40–41, 42–44, 44–45, 46,
    47–49, 50, 51, 52, 52–54, 54–55, 56,
    57, 58, 59, 61, 62, 63, 65, 66, 67, 69,
    72, 73, 75, 76, 80, 81–83, 83, 84, 85,
    86–88, 89, 90, 94, 96, 97, 98, 100–104,
    105, 107, 108–110, 112–113, 114, 116,
    117, 119–120, 121, 122, 123–124, 125,
    129, 130, 131, 133, 135, 137, 138, 139,
    142, 143, 144, 146, 147, 148, 149, 150,
    156–166
South African Broadcasting Corporation,
    156
South African Council on Sport (SACOS),
    27
South African Davis Cup, 43
South African Defence Force (SADF), 44
South African Districts B, 36
South African Gazelles, 36
South African Institute of Race Relations,
    xxvi
South African Mining XV, 36
South African Non-Racial Olympic
    Committee (SANROC), 30, 42, 44,
    148
South African Rugby Association (SARA),
    22
South African Rugby Board (SARB), 1, 3,
    10, 11, 12, 13, 19, 21, 22, 23, 25, 27,
    45, 46, 50, 55, 60, 130, 137, 155, 156
South African Rugby Federation (SARF),
    22
South African Rugby Union (SARU), 22,
    27, 36, 155, 161
South America, 17, 19, 152, 166
South Sea Barbarians, 154

Southland, 65
Soviet Union, xix, xx, 81
Soweto Uprising of 1976, 25, 27, 54, 109
Soweto, South Africa, 34
Spearman, John, 118
Sports Illustrated, 81, 90, 97
Spring, Donal, 30, 31
Springboks, xv–xvii, xix, xxiii, xxiv, 1, 11,
    13, 14, 17–18, 19, 20–21, 23, 32, 33,
    37, 38, 39, 40, 41–43, 44, 46, 47, 48,
    49, 50, 51, 52, 53, 54, 55, 56, 57, 58,
    59, 60, 62, 65, 67, 68, 68–69, 70, 71,
    73, 73–74, 75, 76, 79–80, 81, 82, 83,
    84, 85, 86, 87, 88, 89, 90, 91, 94,
    95–96, 97, 98, 99, 101, 102, 104, 107,
    108–109, 110, 111, 112–113, 116, 118,
    119–120, 121, 122, 123, 124, 126,
    129–131, 132, 133–136, 137, 138, 139,
    141, 142–143, 144–146, 146, 147, 148,
    150, 152, 153, 154, 156, 158, 159, 160,
    162, 163–165, 167
St. Andrews College, 20
Stanford Law School, 114
State University of New York at Albany,
    120
Steinbrenner, George, 108
Stellenbosch University, 20
Stevens, Albert, 136
Stinson, George, 100
Stone, Geoffrey R., 114
Stop the Apartheid Rugby Tour (SART),
    40, 43–45, 49, 80, 88, 90, 117–119, 143
Strode, Woody, 81
Sun City, xxi
Supreme Council of Sport in Africa, 39,
    120
SW County Districts, 107
Swanson, Charles, 100
Sweeney, Eamonn, 30
Sydney Morning Herald, 23

Talboys, Brian, 56
Taylor, John, 18
Test series, xv, 17, 36, 52, 54, 67, 68, 73,
    150, 152, 160
Texas, 136, 137
Thayer, Lanney E., 113
Tobias, Errol, 20, 22, 23–24, 37, 48, 60,
    79, 89, 91, 107, 109, 138, 144, 150

Toyota, 152
Transvaal, 26, 33, 134, 150, 154
Transvaal Cricket Union, xxv
Transvaal-Orange Free State match, 154
Treurnicht, Andries, 26
Tri-Cameral Parliament, 151
Tribe, Lawrence, 114
Trinity College Dublin, 32
Tshwete, Steve, 155
Tsotsobe, Toto, 20, 23
Twickenham, 160

UCLA, 81
Ueberroth, Peter, 81
UN Special Committee against Apartheid.
    See United Nations Special
    Committee against Apartheid
United Democratic Front (UDF), 151
United Nations, 28, 42, 81, 108
United Nations Center Against Apartheid,
    43
United Nations Special Committee
    Against Apartheid, 36, 42
United States, xix, xx, xxi, xxiv, xxvii–xxviii,
    1, 3, 4, 5, 7, 10, 11, 12, 13–14, 15, 17,
    39, 40, 42–44, 47, 49, 50, 55, 76, 79,
    80, 81–82, 83, 85, 87, 88, 97, 98, 103,
    104, 107, 108, 109, 111, 115, 119, 120,
    123, 130, 135, 136, 140, 142, 144, 145,
    146, 147, 148, 149, 153, 156, 166, 167
United States Court of Appeals, 115
United States Football League, 149
United States of America Rugby Football
    Union, 1, 2, 12, 13, 45, 46, 48, 88, 153
University of Auckland, 54
University of Canterbury, 66
University of Cape Town, 21
University of Chicago Law School, 114
University of Otago, 65
USA Rugby Football Union. *See* United
    States of America Rugby Football
    Union
USA Rugby Hall of Fame, 107
USARFU. *See* United States of America
    Rugby Football Union

Vaal Triangle, 151
van der Sandt, David, 161
van Eck, George, 13

van Esbeck, Edmund, 36
Vanderbeke, Sister Lois, 101
Vandeveer, Michael, 129
Verwoerd, Hendrick, xxii, 53
Victoria University, 64
Visser, Div, 49, 79, 110, 123, 135, 166
Vorster, John, xxiii, 9, 20

Waikiki, 79
Wales, xxiv
Walker, Moses, xxvii
Walton, Lin, 135
Wanganui, 65
Ward, Tony, 30, 31, 33
Washington Post, 9, 45
Washington Star, 9
Washington, Kenny, 81
Watkins, Robert, 2
Webley, Gordon, 63
Welkom, 154
Wellington, 57, 61, 63, 64, 65, 68, 69, 75
Wellington Girls' College, 63
West Coast Grizzlies, 153
West Indies, 157
West Side Harlequins, 98
Western Province, xxvi, 1, 21, 49, 98, 134
Western Province Rugby Football Union,
    1, 49
Western Province Rugby Union, xxvi, 1,
    49
Whanganui, 65
Whangārei, 71
Whineray, Wilson, 59
Williams, Abe, 60, 69, 89, 91, 109, 110,
    141
Williams, Avril, 150, 161
Williams, Bryan, 54
Williams, Chester, 150, 161
Williams, Franklin, 108
Williamson, Michigan, 9
Wilson, Stu, 72
Wisconsin, 90, 91, 94, 95, 102
Wisconsin State Journal, 105
Witwatersrand, 157
Wolmarans, Barry, 132
Woods, Donald, 117
World XV, 155

Xhosa, xv

Young, Mike, 118

Zimbabwe, xvi, 155

Zuma, Phumzile, 87
Zwide, Port Elizabeth, xv, xvi

ABOUT THE AUTHOR

Derek Charles Catsam is professor of history and the Kathlyn Cosper Dunagan Professor in the Humanities at the University of Texas–Permian Basin. He is also senior research associate at Rhodes University in Grahamstown, South Africa, where he spent 2016 as the Hugh Le May Fellow in the Humanities. Catsam is the author of *Freedom's Main Line: The Journey of Reconciliation and the Freedom Rides* (2009), *Beyond the Pitch: The Spirit, Culture, and Politics of Brazil's 2014 World Cup* (2014), and *Bleeding Red: A Red Sox Fan's Diary of the 2004 Season* (2005). He has contributed columns and articles on American and African politics and sports to a wide range of publications. Catsam lives with his wife, who is also a historian, his nephew, George, and a menagerie of cats in Odessa, Texas, and maintains his lifelong love for Boston sports teams.

CPSIA information can be obtained
at www.ICGtesting.com
Printed in the USA
BVHW052207130721
611906BV00002B/3